Wars of the Mexican Gulf

Wars of the Mexican Gulf

The Breakaway Republics of Texas and Yucatan, US Mexican War, and Limits of Empire 1835–1850

Benjamin J. Swenson

Pen & Sword
MILITARY

First published in Great Britain in 2024 by
Pen & Sword Military
An imprint of Pen & Sword Books Limited
Yorkshire – Philadelphia

Copyright © Benjamin J. Swenson 2024

ISBN 978 1 39903 370 1

The right of Benjamin J. Swenson to be identified as
Author of this Work has been asserted by him in accordance
with the Copyright, Designs and Patents Act 1988.

A CIP catalogue record for this book is
available from the British Library

All rights reserved. No part of this book may be reproduced or transmitted in any form or by any means, electronic or mechanical including photocopying, recording or by any information storage and retrieval system, without permission from the Publisher in writing.

Typeset by Mac Style
Printed in the UK by CPI Group (UK) Ltd, Croydon, CR0 4YY.

Pen & Sword Books Limited incorporates the imprints of After the Battle, Atlas, Archaeology, Aviation, Discovery, Family History, Fiction, History, Maritime, Military, Military Classics, Politics, Select, Transport, True Crime, Air World, Frontline Publishing, Leo Cooper, Remember When, Seaforth Publishing, The Praetorian Press, Wharncliffe Local History, Wharncliffe Transport, Wharncliffe True Crime and White Owl.

For a complete list of Pen & Sword titles please contact

PEN & SWORD BOOKS LIMITED
47 Church Street, Barnsley, South Yorkshire, S70 2AS, England
E-mail: enquiries@pen-and-sword.co.uk
Website: www.pen-and-sword.co.uk
or
PEN AND SWORD BOOKS
1950 Lawrence Rd, Havertown, PA 19083, USA
E-mail: uspen-and-sword@casematepublishers.com
Website: www.penandswordbooks.com

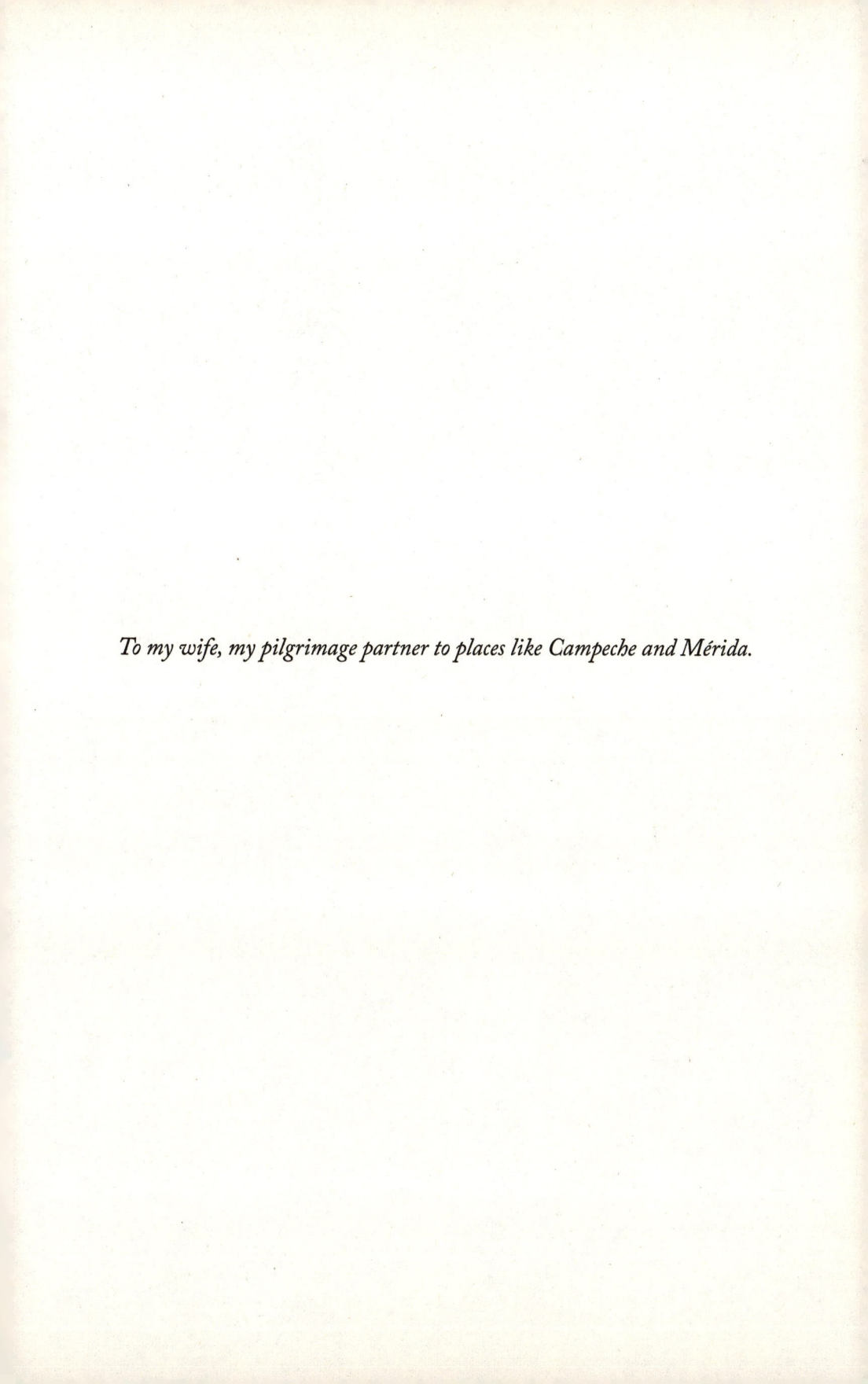

To my wife, my pilgrimage partner to places like Campeche and Mérida.

Contents

Acknowledgements viii
Introduction: The Breakaway Republics x

Chapter 1   'Annexation as War'   1

Chapter 2   'War Exists'   16

Chapter 3   The Caste War   75

Chapter 4   'Savage and exterminating war'   89

Chapter 5   'Eagle and lion watching the same prey'   109

Chapter 6   Limits of Empire   128

Notes 156
Bibliography 176
Index 185

Acknowledgements

I would like to thank the following people for their contributions: Professor William Fowler and his students at the University of St. Andrews for their excellent work in compiling nineteenth-century Mexican pronouncements, the archivists at College Park, Maryland, for their efforts in making available previously unused documents and consular dispatches, Professor Terry L. Rugeley, Emeritus of Mexican and Latin American History at the University of Oklahoma, for his insightful and inspiring scholarship on south-east Mexico, the librarians at the Texas History Trust for digitizing writings and letters of Texan statesmen during the independence years, and veteran US Foreign Service Officer Robert Smith Simpson (1906–2010), whose diary of Justo Sierra O'Reilly this author acquired after his passing. Lastly, I would like to extend my heartfelt appreciation to all my old friends in Central America, from San Cristóbal to San José.

'I have not a doubt, that if the United States had entertained the desire to annex the whole peninsula of Yucatan to our confederacy, there would scarcely have been a dissenting voice, among the inhabitants. Our institutions found worthy representatives in our naval officers; and they became as popular in Yucatan, after an administration of eighteen months, as our people are destined in time to become, over the whole American continent.'

Raphael Semmes, *Service afloat and ashore during the Mexican War*, 1851

Introduction
The Breakaway Republics

On 12 May 1846, Sam Houston, the first and former President of the Republic of Texas, rose in the United States Senate as a senator to address a vote initiating war with Mexico. Houston succinctly stated what his constituents back home believed to be true for more than a decade – that the United States and Mexico were already 'in a state of war'. Houston then explained why many Mexicans believed the same:

> War had existed for ten years between Mexico and Texas; and it had been declared in advance on the part of Mexico, when the question of annexation of Texas to the United States was agitated, that if annexation took place the war would not only be continued against Texas, but would be proclaimed also against the United States ... A state of war now existed as perfect as it could be after a formal declaration or recognition of a state of war by the Congress of the United States.[1]

The Texas Revolution and independence movement, which began in the fall of 1835 and was achieved after defeating General Antonio Lopez de Santa Anna at the Battle of San Jacinto, 21 April 1836, informed other separatist movements such as the Republic of Yucatan, which declared its independence from Mexico in 1840. The Mayan-majority state opposite the Gulf of Mexico, administered and ruled primarily by *criollos*, or people of Spanish descent, even adopted the design of the Texas standard – albeit with Mexican colours: red, white, and green. Although Mexicans used the term 'United Mexican States' (*Estados Unidos Mexicanos*), the main factor aiding the American conquest, aside from US military and naval superiority, was the disunity in that country during the 1830s and 1840s. Like Texas, the existence of an independent rebel republic on Mexico's periphery was a glaring demonstration of the infighting plaguing the neighbour of the nascent North American empire. By the time Texas became an official part of the United States, the question on many people's minds was not whether the war between the US and Mexico could be avoided, but how much territory the nation was willing to absorb. Some wild-eyed expansionists believed no southern limit existed and that the Gulf of Mexico was destined to become an American lake. However, the war and its international implications would prove otherwise.

What many historians of the continental conflict have overlooked is that proponents of it were so aware of Yucatan's position vis-à-vis Mexico's war with the US that annexation of that short-lived peninsular republic became a real possibility informing the larger geostrategic outlook of the United States. Yucatan is often passed over or dismissed outright, but an analysis of its role in the war is essential to understanding the process with which the United States pivoted to empire in relation to other (Latin) American states in the second half of the nineteenth century. In essence, the war was not merely a one-directional aggrandizement of western territory but also demonstrated the limits with which Americans could project power south of its shores. These limitations ultimately forced the United States to seek accommodation with the British in an agreement lasting more than fifty years until the acquisition of the Panama Canal zone in the early twentieth century. Between 1846 and 1848 Americans easily conquered the sparsely settled and contiguous west, but the southern shore of the gulf was an entirely different matter.

Connecting Oceans, Regional War, and Annexation

With a dual-directional perspective in mind, a fuller understanding of the war centralists in Mexico City waged against Yucatan prior to 1846 sheds light on US actions and activities in the gulf during the US-Mexican conflict. Moreover, American interest in Tabasco is illuminated when examining the desire by the Polk administration to secure the Tehuantepec transit route in the Gulf connecting the Atlantic and Pacific oceans. For a generation, Americans believed such a route existed somewhere along the eastern edges of Veracruz and Oaxaca states and in western Tabasco and Chiapas. Reliable maps, including those of northern Mexico, were nonexistent; the best map used by General Zachary Taylor during his campaign in northern Mexico was the one captured from Mexican general Mariano Arista after the Battle of Resaca de la Palma in May of 1846. The most accurate map of the Gulf, the 1847 (John) Disturnell Map printed in New York City, was essentially a copy of the 1825 Henry Schenk Tanner map of North America. Both maps depicted the headwaters of the Tabasco (Grijalva) River – one of the most navigable rivers in interior Mexico – as running near the Cordillera mountains in Chiapas separating the Atlantic and Pacific watersheds. The Disturnell Map, otherwise known as the *Mapa de los Estados Unidos de Méjico*, was considered the 'best' and was the same map used by Nicholas Trist and Mexican commissioners to negotiate the Treaty of Guadalupe Hidalgo ending the war. In other words, even Mexican officials were unaware of its inaccuracies.[2]

In 1842, just a few years prior to the war with the United States, Santa Anna commissioned a survey for the prospects of a Tehuantepec canal and railroad to speculator and promoter José de Garay. Garay's 1844 *Survey of the Isthmus of Tehuantepec* contributed greatly to understanding of the topography of the 200-kilometre isthmus and cited the Coatzacoalcos River, rather than the Tabasco, as the best and closest point on the gulf between oceans. Garay referenced the observations of seventeenth century English explorer and pirate William Dampier:

> Towards the end of the seventeenth century Dampier, speaking of the Coatzacoalcos, said – 'This is one of the principal rivers of this coast; it is not half the breadth of the Tabasco river, but deeper. Its bar is less dangerous than any on this coast …'

As a promoter of the Mexican route, Garay was also keen to give reasons why Tehuantepec was more suitable than its competitors – Panama and Nicaragua:

> It has been lately asserted … that it would be as easy to construct a canal in Panama as it would be in Holland … however, intelligent engineers … point out the great obstacles which the territory presents to an enterprise of this nature.

As for Nicaragua, Garay noted it seemed to 'offer many advantages; but upon a more minute examination there appear many difficulties, and these of an almost insurmountable nature.' Extreme climate and expenses were also cited by Garay as factors inhibiting the construction of canals in Panama and Nicaragua, but the primary selling point for Tehuantepec was distance.

Besides these purely local advantages, the isthmus of Tehuantepec offers over those of Nicaragua and Panama others of a more general nature for navigation, affording to vessels proceeding from Europe or the United States, which from their destination have not to descend to more meridional latitudes, a communication more direct and through a more genial climate.[3]

Therefore, the three most viable prospects for connecting the Atlantic and Pacific; Tehuantepec, Panama, and Nicaragua, were pursued more vigorously in the war era, and the conflict was seen as an opportunity to achieve long-held goals going back to the beginning of the nineteenth century. In 1820, William Davis Robinson, a US merchant and writer sympathetic to the Mexican Revolution against Spain, wrote optimistically that 'The Isthmus of Costa Rica [i.e. Panama] may hereafter become to the New, what the Isthmus of Suez was to the Old World, prior to the discovery of the route to Asia by the Cape of Good Hope.' Americans overwhelmingly supported the Mexican War of Independence against monarchists and generally looked forward to improved relations with their neighbour. The 'Mexican Isthmus,' Robinson wrote, 'or, as it is more properly designated, the Isthmus of Tehuantepec is the section of all others on the American continent, where the communication between the Pacific and Atlantic oceans should be made.'[4]

Robinson was not short of praise for the Oaxacans, who he believed were 'very industrious' and could cut a canal 'with the greatest facility'. He also claimed others living in the region, 'particularly those of Tabasco and Tehuantepec, assert that they pass with their canoes entirely through the Isthmus.' A year later, in 1821, after Mexico officially became independent, Robinson's work was republished in London in a two-volume set with a forward somewhat flattering to the British given their assistance to the revolution. More importantly, it alluded to a future Anglo-American contest over the region. The introduction noted that Robinson 'looks forward with seeming confidence to the day when the fleets of the United States shall protect the entrance to the canal of Tehuantepec.' Nevertheless, the London edition noted that 'whatever may be the future destiny of North America, England is not the power which would reap the smallest benefit from this communication, or which is least interested in promoting it. The future destiny of America opens a wide field for conjecture, into which we cannot now allow ourselves to enter.'[5]

It is no coincidence that while Polk and Secretary of State James Buchanan were discussing transit rights across the isthmus of Tehuantepec following the US invasion of Veracruz in the spring of 1847, an agreement was being reached with the Republic of New Granada (present-day Colombia) to secure neutrality over the isthmus of Panama. In sum, Americans wanted a shorter route to the Pacific through Mexico but were not about to commit to one route or trust an accommodation with the Mexicans could even be reached. Nor were Americans willing to take Garay at his word – as wartime and post-war surveys of the isthmus were conducted.[6] All options were pursued to acquiring any and all Mexican territory facilitating continental hegemony – including invoking the (thereunto) unnamed 1823 'Monroe Doctrine' prohibiting European interference in American affairs as a threat to prevent British intervention in Yucatan's ongoing Caste War. The British, always protective of their commercial enterprises and naval supremacy, followed events in the region closely and were far from passive, but the Americans were particularly obsessed with the unseen movements and perceived designs of their former and formidable colonial masters. Although it has generally been forgotten, the 1848 Yucatan crisis towards the end of the war was the crux at which Americans began employing the Monroe Doctrine as a justification for their own intervention in Latin American affairs. The doctrine, named in 1849 during the discussion over Nicaragua, was not used in the war, but its application as an interventionist mechanism, replacing that of annexation, was debated in the US Senate in the war's final days and ultimately gained traction as a political tool for expansionists in the conflict's aftermath.[7]

It is evident the war was not only a contest between two North American powers, but affected, or was affected by, numerous states in the region of differing size and influence. The Federal Republic of Central America, Republic of Texas, Republic of Yucatan, Tabasco, Chiapas, Oaxaca, Guatemala, British Honduras and Belize, the British protectorate of the Mosquito Kingdom, Nicaragua, Spanish Cuba, even France to a certain extent, were all impacted by events occurring in the Gulf during the period between 1835 and 1850. By looking at the war from a larger perspective, annexation of Texas prompted US military involvement, but the region was already in turmoil by 1845. War narratives that begin in the northern borderlands in 1846 often pass over important events and sequences relevant to the military and political realities affecting the region and outcome of the war.

As noted, one glaring example is Tabasco. A pre-war context helps explain why Americans under the command of Commodore Matthew Perry launched two expeditions to that state during the war and why it played an ancillary role in the 1850 post-war geostrategic Anglo-American Clayton-Bulwer Treaty addressing Central America. Events occurring in the early 1840s shed light on US naval activity in the Gulf after 1846, and omitting crucial events in the early 1840s is the chief reason historians have ignored the potential acquisition of Yucatan in 1848. Moreover, the historiographical narrowing occurring as a result of limiting the war to two years is compounded by an incomplete analysis of the origins and ending of the Mexican-American War. A prime example in this regard is that the US Congress never issued a formal declaration of war against Mexico.

The aftermath of the war was no less dynamic. Officially ending in 1848, important events occurring in Yucatan before the ratification of the Treaty of Guadalupe Hidalgo in Mexico in the spring of that year threatened to frustrate the conflict's peaceful resolution. When cooler heads prevailed, and Mexico acceded to the loss of their northern territory, American filibusterism and military adventurism – often sanctioned by private and state interests – became the modus operandi for expansionist impulses directed towards southern North America. Adding urgency to much of this action were powerful commercial and shipping interests aligned with the new American project to settle and colonize western territories – particularly California. In addition, American interest in acquiring the island of Cuba subsided during the war with Mexico but was renewed when annexation of Yucatan was abandoned and an Anglo-American agreement over Central America reached.

However, in the pre-war era the term 'annexation' was the rallying cry for the American thrust into Mexican territory, and possibly Yucatan. It defined a generation, precipitated the wars of the Gulf, and portended a larger continental conflict that had the potential to involve other neighbouring states and even Great Britain. Doctrines were not discussed but 'annexation' was everywhere. By 1844, annexation mania had 'excited the whole body politic' to the point that coat companies were appealing to their customers by posting large headlines titled 'Annexation of Texas!!!' and asking, 'What is the annexation of Texas compared with annexation of Devlin & Co.'s light summer coats to the body …' It was humorous hyperbole but demonstrated American fixation with Texas in an era of expansion. The *American Star*, the occupation newspaper of US forces in Mexico City, ran an article on the 1848 marriage of Quartermaster Thomas B. Tucker to Señorita Maria de Luz Bravo in Puebla. 'Let many more such annexations as these take place,' the article read, 'and Uncle Sam will find it difficult to get his sons to leave the country inhabited by Anahuac's daughters.'[8] In essence, 'annexation' was a catchword more potent than the late-arriving phrase 'manifest destiny' because it invoked concrete action utilizing a political mechanism viewed by many – as will be seen – as a declaration of war. After Texas, the search for future annexations was afoot. Preceding that continental altering acquisition, however, were the breakaway republics on the Gulf of Mexico and the federalist versus centralist civil war.

Tabasco and Origins of the Texas-Yucatan Alliance

The origins of the two-year alliance between Texas and Yucatan, which served the purpose of frustrating an invasion of the former by Mexican authorities, originated in their initial cooperation and support of an insurrection in Tabasco. Although revolts were not uncommon in early nineteenth-century Mexico, the rebellion that erupted in late 1839 in the small but productive state abutting Yucatan on the southern end of the Gulf tested the authority of a national government still recovering from the humiliating three-month French blockade of Veracruz – an episode known as the Pastry War (1838–1839). Like those of Texas and Yucatan, the Tabascan insurrection was sparked by the ongoing national political civil war between Mexican 'federalists', who advocated states' rights, and 'centralists', who believed a stronger and more consolidated government ruled from Mexico City was needed to cure the country of the ills plaguing it since independence. Americans knew little about the state before the 1830s (often spelling it 'Tobasco') but slowly learned of its commercial potential. One 1832 article in the *Charleston Mercury* described it as a land rich with massive cocoa plantations yielding three crops a year, 'inexhaustible' logwood-swamps ripe for profitable exportation, 'enormous' sugar cane plantations, and vanilla beans that grew 'wild in the woods'. Like many exotic and unexplored locales Americans were just beginning to discover in the tropical regions of the continent, Tabasco held imaginative potential that required a 'dense and industrious population' to transform it into 'the garden of America.'[9]

Like Yucatan, Tabasco's contact with the outside world was dependent upon the sea, as there were no viable roads connecting it to central Mexico until the twentieth century. Due to this geographic isolation, all news and commerce to the 'mainland' passed through Mexico's main port of Veracruz. In addition, roads between the two gulf states were essentially nonexistent – making them veritable islands connected only by large swaths of coastal mangrove and tropical forests dense with cedar, mahogany and palms. The region is hot, can be both extremely dry and extremely wet, and is therefore the perfect site for the seasonal outbreak of yellow fever that killed locals and scores of unacclimatized dough-faced American soldiers from northern states during the US-Mexican war. Tabasco would also play an important but often overlooked role in the conflict due to its location near a potential transit route between the Atlantic and Pacific oceans – a key objective of President James K. Polk's administration that grew in significance when gold was discovered in the hills of California in 1849.

The key figure in the Tabasco Federalist Revolution was Francisco de Sentmanat. The son of a Spanish officer, Sentmanat was born in Cuba in 1802 six years before Napoleon invaded Spain and seeded the notion of independence among Latin Americans. Sentmanat left Cuba after promoting similar heresies and ended up emigrating to Tabasco and making the state his *cause célèbre*. When fighting broke out to oust the appointed centralist governor José Ignacio Gutiérrez, he was joined by like-minded federalists such as Juan Pablo de Anaya. Although Anaya was a Mexican patriot who played no small role in the independence movement from Spain, he had been exiled in New Orleans and saw the revolt as an opportunity to reclaim his federalist bona fides after being misled into thinking the Texas Revolution was merely a political disagreement with centralists over the nature of the Mexican constitution – a document amended in 1836 from its original 1824 form to suit centralists. Moreover, federalist-leaning Yucatan, on the verge of declaring its independence from Mexico City, supported Sentmanat's mission for the same reason.[10]

Texas officials hoped the Tabasco insurrection would succeed and simultaneously improve their military situation by drawing attention away from leaders in Mexico City anxious to reconquer the northern state – which was constantly on edge over concerns of an invasion. Writing to the Secretary of State Abner S. Lipscomb in early February of 1840, peace commissioner Colonel Barnard Elliot Bee, who was among a handful of commissioned agents in Mexico on a futile mission seeking recognition for Texas and a border settlement, informed his superior that soldiers were massing 'and marching to the Rio Grande ... you have no time to lose.' A justifiably paranoid Bee also wrote that 'the enemy are increasing daily and there is no knowing the day when they will cross' the river. Adding to his perception of international intrigue in the capital, Bee believed, 'Mexico must either come under the yoke of a foreign nation or be lost entirely, her external brawls wars and schisms are fast diminishing the last ray of hope.' For the small but influential faction of Mexican monarchists, internal divisions were proof the country was better off being under European leadership.[11]

The following week, national authorities' plans against Texas were further stalled when leaders in Valladolid, Yucatan's third largest city behind Merida and Campeche, issued a proclamation 'in favor of the re-establishment of the federal system' and denounced 'the deportation of the sons of this Peninsula to sustain a ruinous war' in Texas. The proclamation followed in the footsteps of previous diatribes by the recently appointed 'General Commander of the Liberation Army' of Yucatan, Santiago Imán, who ended up on the wrong side of centralist authorities in the late 1830s and spent time in prison for opposing the government's efforts to institute compulsory military service in Yucatan for the Texas campaign. The state had tired of sending sons (and much-needed workers) to arid departments in northern Mexico. A few days later, on 18 February, Valladolid's pronouncement was strengthened when federalists in control of the garrison in the capital of Merida issued their own proclamation supporting Valladolid and vowed to uphold 'a free and independent state' until the 1824 constitution was restored: 'The state of Yucatan declares itself independent from the government of Mexico, as long as it does not return to the order of the federal regime.' There were objections to separation in Yucatan's second city, Campeche, whose merchant class was more reliant on trade with Veracruz. However, by late spring the holdouts there acquiesced to separation.[12]

News of Yucatan's defiance was a godsend to Texan officials. James Treat, another special agent in Mexico City, wrote to President Mirabeau Lamar that Yucatecan separation was 'making serious head-way, and it is feared the whole department may concur in the grito [cry] for federation.' Like Bee, Treat speculated on an impending invasion that did not materialize, but his hunch about Yucatecan independence was correct. On 4 March the congress in Merida issued a more decisive decree indicating the state was 'free and independent, and by virtue of this, it re-establishes its particular constitution, and the general constitution of the republic sanctioned in 1824.' Essentially, the state declared itself in rebellion – so long 'as the Mexican nation is not governed in accordance with federal laws, the state of Yucatan will remain separate from it, its legislature resuming the powers of the general congress and its governor those of the president of the republic.' The Republic of Yucatan was born.[13]

Texas authorities believed Yucatan's situation improved their chances of reaching an accommodation with Mexico, and Vice President David G. Burnet, who sometimes took on the role of Acting Secretary of State, instructed Treat to convey a letter to Richard Pakenham, the British Minister in Mexico City. Pakenham had been in that country since the late 1820s, served in Washington DC occasionally when his able services were required, and knew better than anyone the complicated political situation in Mexico. It was Burnet's hope that British officials might be willing to mediate a solution to the crisis by holding negotiations in London. The problem for Texas, however, was the British had not yet recognized it as an independent republic. When it did in 1842, Pakenham and a team of veteran diplomats worked vigorously to induce the Mexicans to accept the loss of the breakaway state. They did this to not only prevent war, but also because they believed an independent Texas with commercial ties (mainly cotton) to Great Britain complemented their policy of limiting US expansion and slavery in North America. Texas applied for annexation in 1837 after President Andrew Jackson had it recognized in his last days in office, but the new president, Martin Van Buren, opposed annexation to appease anti-slavery elements in northern states as well as to avoid conflict with Mexico. In this regard, the Texans were well-informed of the British position, and Burnet appealed 'to arrest the shedding of blood' by asking Pakenham for 'any aid which your Excellency may afford' to prevent war. By the end of March 1840, when news of the extent of Yucatan's cleaving with the national government became known, Treat enthusiastically informed officials back home that the 'Revolution of Yucatan has gone through the whole peninsula.' In essence, the rebellions in Tabasco and Yucatan saved Texas from invasion.[14]

As Yucatan ramped up the rhetoric against Mexico City, the military situation for the centralist governor in Tabasco was deteriorating. On 31 May Governor Gutierrez issued a pronouncement calling for the 'restoration of order' and lashed out at the unruly citizens of several communities supporting the insurrection: 'Individuals who have helped the enemy with money, food, horses, canoes, servants, weapons, ammunition and any other war equipment … will be reputed and judged as traitors'.

Gutierrez vowed to have his enemies put on trial and rebuked 'notorious' farm and ranch owners for arming their servants. In a desperate attempt to avoid a popular insurgency, the besieged governor offered 'those same servants, and all individuals who accompany them, the safest protection … at the moment they desert and present themselves to the most immediate authority.' Centralist rule in Tabasco was on the verge of collapse.[15]

Throughout the spring and early summer Lone Star officials prepared their underfunded navy to assist the federalist rebellions on the southern end of the gulf. Fortunately for Texas, the Mexican Navy was not very formidable for a country of its size, and the small but effective Texas Navy played a pivotal role in 1836 by keeping Santa Anna's forces from being re-supplied and protecting its principal seas lanes from Mexican depredations. However, Lamar believed the republic needed a more robust fleet if it wanted to eliminate the threat of a coastal invasion. The fact that large and difficult-to-traverse deserts south of the Rio Grande separated Texas from the rest of northern Mexico made the likelihood of an amphibious assault more probable. Because of this, Lamar had already been preparing an expedition for several months, and the rebellions offered the updated navy an opportunity to demonstrate its capabilities. The fleet's flagship was the 600-ton twenty-gun sloop-of-war *Austin*, commanded by Commodore Edwin Ward Moore. Moore was originally from Virginia and served in the US Navy before joining the independence movement in the late 1830s. Other vessels of the small but effective force included the eight-gun steamship *Zavala* and three five-gun schooners, *San Antonio*, *San Bernard* and *San Jacinto*.[16]

Although Moore was eager to engage the Mexicans in battle, Lamar, who had both financial and international concerns, was more protective of his small fleet. Before the expedition set out, the president, who was in the naval port of Galveston, penned a set of instructions to Moore 'to avoid all offensive means, and not shew [sic] yourself before Vera-Cruz or any other Mexican Port' until news of the outcome of Treat's peace mission became known. Lamar articulated this point twice: 'If you should be attacked, you will of course be at liberty to defend yourself … by destroying, or capturing enemy ships', but added, 'It is the object of this Government to avoid all hostilities with the Mexican Govt until Mr. Treat can be heard from.' Lamar also ordered Moore to 'ascertain the condition of the State of Yucatan, and the disposition of those functionaries administering their Government, whether friendly or otherwise to us, any manifestations of friendship from them you will reciprocate.' With the instructions received, Moore set sail for the Bay of Campeche.[17]

By August of 1840 Juan Pablo de Anaya had made his way to Yucatan to recruit soldiers to aid Sentmanat's revolution. Shortly thereafter, Commodore Moore arrived to carry Anaya from that state to Tabasco and (as ordered) get a sense of how the Yucatecans felt about Texas. Moore reported that the Yucatecan governor 'was anxious that the most friendly relations should be established at an early period', and even stated that 'the ports of the State of Yucatan were open to any Texian vessel.' This ad hoc cooperation was essentially the genesis of the short-lived Texas-Yucatan alliance. A widely reprinted article from the *New Orleans Bulletin* explained the compact by citing 'St. Anna's paper' *El Censor*, an estimated need for 12,000 soldiers and ten ships to conquer Texas, and its relation to Texan support for the Tabasco rebellion. Included in the general belief among Mexican leaders 'that the government at Washington is opposed to the Mexican' centralist agenda, Santa Anna's mouthpiece disavowed the notion 'that Yucatan and Texas are provinces of the United States' while proclaiming 'that Yucatan has been revolutionized by New Orleans, and that Anaya was sent thence to operate against Tabasco.'[18]

That fall, after Treat's efforts in Mexico City were rejected, the combined forces of Anaya and Sentmanat seized Tabasco's capital city San Juan Bautista (Villahermosa). The last remaining centralists surrendered at the end of November. In Veracruz, Bee reported rumours that an assault on Texas had 'been postponed, some say until January, others … say that the sixty thousand men are to be raised to defend the various Mexican ports and not to invade Texas.' No one knew exactly what was being planned, but what was certain was the breakaway republic would be forced to remain on edge for another year. Back in the United States, people began paying serious attention to events in the gulf. Most Americans learned of the rebellion based in reports from New Orleans newspapers promoting the Texas cause. One report from the *New Orleans Bulletin* noted the victory in Tabasco was achieved with the active support of the Texas Navy and Yucatecan forces. 'The States of Texas, Yucatan, and Tobasco [*sic*], have now a common interest and feeling, and, it is believed, are ready to unite in the common cause against the common enemy of the three States.'[19]

The Americans were not the only outside observers discussing Gulf affairs. The British were keeping an eye on French activity in the region amid rumours they were interested in recognizing an independent federalist republic of Yucatan. 'The suspicion has existed for a long time past of the determination of the French Government,' *The Times* of London reported, 'to acquire, if possible, a permanent footing in Spanish America.' Reports from New Orleans on the pending invasion of Texas were also of interest, and it was generally believed the Mexican government were becoming 'more unpopular, and a *rumpus* is expected soon from some quarter or another.' Indeed, the wars of the Gulf were just beginning.[20]

British Recognition and 'Balance of Power'

William Kennedy was born in Ireland in 1799 and spent time in London before travelling to Canada in 1838. While there, the recently born Republic of Texas piqued his interest and Kennedy traversed half the continent to begin writing a book he published in 1841 under the title *Texas: The Rise, Progress, and Prospects of the Republic of Texas*. Kennedy admitted that at the time the British knew very little about the breakaway state or its history, but his work was so well received he was commissioned as a special agent by Foreign Secretary Lord Aberdeen and tasked with providing some insight into the ongoing war between Mexico and Texas and what the potential annexation of that republic to the United States meant to British interests. Although initially Great Britain did not recognize Texas independence because of their objection to slavery and desire to maintain good relations with Mexico, those objections were eventually cast aside in 1842 because the British believed an independent Texas limited the potential expansion of the United States, which as a growing power threatened British interests in Canada and the Caribbean. This strategy, which in the early 1840s became known as the 'balance-of-power' policy, was so widely resented among American expansionists that it exacerbated an already existing Anglophobia and strengthened the US relationship with Texas.[21]

There were many reasons to believe another Anglo-American war was possible. In 1837 former Toronto mayor William Lyon Mackenzie organized an insurrection among the farmers of Ontario in an attempt to wrest political control over Canada from the colonial authorities. The rebellion received substantial sympathy and support from Americans living in the border region – particularly around the city of Buffalo, which used a local American ship the SS *Caroline* to ferry weapons and supplies over the Niagara River. When Mackenzie's forces were defeated by loyalist soldiers and volunteers in early December 1837, they fled to Navy Island and aboard the *Caroline* declared the Republic of Canada. To British authorities, this movement declaring an independent republic alarmingly mimicked that of Texas. On 29 December, a royal Canadian unit seized the *Caroline* while she was moored on the US side of the river (at Schlosser's Landing), killing American Amos Durfee and wounding several others. They then set fire to the ship and sent her over Niagara Falls.

Americans were outraged. New York governor and future US Secretary of War William Marcy sent a message to the state legislature proclaiming that the 'territory of this state has been invaded, and some of our citizens murdered, by an armed force, from the province of Upper Canada.' The New York *Daily Herald* concluded that 'War with England seems almost now to be unavoidable.'[22] Americans from Detroit to Buffalo began organizing and coordinating with the rebels to invade Canada. On 5 January President Martin Van Buren issued a statement 'to prevent any unlawful interference' by US citizens in the conflict, and urged 'insurgents' organized on US soil supporting the rebellion to respect neutrality laws and 'return peaceably to their respective homes.' To help enforce Van Buren's policy and prevent the escalation of cross-border violence, General Winfield Scott, who later commanded the campaign to seize the Mexican capital in 1847, was ordered to the Niagara region.[23] London newspapers closely followed the news to gauge American sentiment: 'People, in expectation of a battle, had assembled … The excitement here is great. Curses, not loud, but deep, greet you on every side. Men do not huzza – they grit their teeth, and talk of vengeance!'[24]

Despite US authorities' efforts to curtail violence, several incidents occurred in 1838. In addition, secret organizations supporting the rebels called 'Hunters' Lodges' were established along the undelineated border stretching from Vermont to Michigan in places such as Rochester, Buffalo, Cleveland and Detroit. According to the historian Andrew Bonthius, the 'bi-national Patriot movement' required considerable cooperation between the British and American governments to avoid war: 'Patriot filibustering posed the question of war between the US and Britain, ultimately compelling the two nations to coordinate diplomatic and military efforts to suppress the movement.'[25] Border raids continued, and prisoners were taken after numerous engagements. Several rebel leaders were hanged. In 1839, seventy-nine Canadian men were 'convicted of treasonable practices', put aboard HMS *Buffalo* and sent to Hobart, Tasmania, where they would be less of a problem for British authorities. Others followed.[26] Fighting also broke out in northern Maine along the border with New Brunswick – prompting officials to push for a demarcation of the long border. Mackenzie was briefly jailed in New York but, due to widespread support from the American public, was pardoned by Van Buren in 1840 and became a US citizen. In 1842 the Webster-Ashburton Treaty delineated the vast US-Canadian border (until Minnesota/Ontario) and settled the *Caroline* issue. Americans had other concerns about the Oregon Territory as well, and bellicose language from expansionist Democrats threatening invasion of British Columbia was heard in the presidential election of 1844.

With that in mind, Kennedy noted in his book that 'war between England and the United States would be one of the greatest calamities that could befal [sic] either.' Due to previous border controversies, and because Americans sympathized with the Texans, it was a delicate matter. Furthermore, the British knew less about the Texians (white Texans) than they did about Canadians and required the services of experts like Kennedy. Kennedy noted in his introduction that he was curious as to how a small group of settlers 'chiefly of Anglo-American origin ... were enabled to repel the armies of Mexico and to found a Republic of their own.' He overlooked the thousands of Tejanos – ethnically Mexican Texans – who fought for independence alongside whites in the revolution, but his observations concerning the effectiveness of the Texian way of war – honed after years of fighting native tribes – resulted in a formidable martial spirit:

> [I]n the frontier States, the mounted riflemen, composed of the robust yoemanry [sic] and officered by the ablest and most popular planters and professional men, many of whom have, perhaps, had a military education at West Point, form a description of force not to be surpassed in partisan warfare. The necessities of the State, or Federal Government frequently call them to the field, and occasionally keep them embodied for months, during which they acquire habits of discipline and subordination. Living in rustic independence, and inured to the hunter's life, they regard war

as a superior kind of excitement, and are always ready for action at the summons of their country; while, to the younger men, ambition, or adventure, is a sufficient stimulus to arm and march.[27]

Kennedy also expounded on the initial effort by Texas to become a part of the United States – citing an 1837 letter from the Texan minister to the US, General Memucan Hunt, to US Secretary of State John Forsyth, requesting annexation. In 1837 the outcome of the revolution was far from certain, and Hunt wanted Forsyth to know annexation would 'ensure to the United States the complete command of the Gulf of Mexico.' Hunt noted that the 'admirably suited' port of Galveston, where the Texas Navy was based, was flush with oak to build ships and strategically located to 'protect on the shores of the Gulf of Mexico, the concentrated trade of the west, at New Orleans, of Alabama, at Mobile, and of the Florida cities.' Hunt did not mention the Yucatan peninsula but he did reiterate that owning Texas entailed American 'supremacy over the waters of the gulf ... even the possession of Cuba would bring with it those facilities of controlling and keeping in check the pretension of a rival power, which would accrue from the extension of the limits of the United States to the line of the Rio del Norte.' Forsyth likely concurred with Hunt's outline, but the proposal was rejected, because Texas was officially at war with Mexico and the US wanted to maintain cordial relations. 'The United States might justly be suspected of a disregard of the friendly purposes of the compact,' Forsyth replied, 'if the overture of General Hunt were to be even reserved for future consideration, as this would imply a disposition on our part to espouse the quarrel of Texas with Mexico.'[28]

Before leaving for his assignment, Kennedy proffered his opinions to Aberdeen about how the breakaway republic fitted into the larger geopolitical picture facing the British in North America. He commented that the Hunters' Lodges in the northern states were established 'for the purpose of overthrowing British rule and influence in North America', and that American expansionists were eager to extend the borders 'from Hudson's Bay to the Rio Grande and the Gulf of California with the Island of Cuba as an insular appendage'. As a result, Kennedy believed British leaders required 'awakening attention to the subject of American encroachment' in the western borderlands, which was the genesis of the British 'balance of power' approach to US affairs in North America hinging on Texas: '[U]nless

English influence be employed in raising up a stable independent power on the South-Western and North Western frontiers of the Union,' he wrote in 1841, 'a very few years will suffice to place the whole of the territory they covet under the sovereignty of the United States. There lies the danger to the maritime and commercial supremacy of Great Britain.'[29]

Crisis and Confederacy

Although the British had obvious geostrategic concerns about US expansion, the Mexicans were facing an existential crisis that could ultimately lead to the dissolution of their country. Mexico's main governmental organ in the capital, *Diario del Gobierno de la Republica Mexicana*, noted in early 1841 that military expenditures for maintaining an army to deal with the rebellions in 'Texas, Yucatan and Tabasco' were increasing 'debts in the public treasury'. Mexican leaders were also following Texas' foreign relations and their efforts to obtain recognition from various states, particularly Great Britain, and highlighted a speech by President Lamar blaming 'Mexican influence' for delaying British 'recognition of our independence'. Despite setbacks, optimism for a peaceful solution still existed to 'bring back to their bosom the lost departments of Yucatan, Tabasco and Texas!' On 5 February *Diario* printed an excerpt from Xalapa's *Conciliador*, in Santa Anna's home state of Veracruz, calling on the 'Congress of the Nation ... to try to decide the fate of the Republic.' The Xalapa newspaper warned of the 'dangerous path' into which the breakaway republics 'have thrown themselves blindly,' and argued 'neither Yucatán nor Tabasco have improved their condition in any way, martyred in the clutches of the discord of which they are prey: struggling with misery and with the demands of the parties, and of those who, usurping the title of liberators are their true tyrants.' There was a plea to 'get serious about agreeing on defense measures for the entire border; and to provide resources for the Texas campaign to become effective.' In essence, *Diario*'s editorial outlined a crisis much larger than that of breakaway states:

> When speaking of Texas, it occurs to us ... that England has recognized the independence to which the colonists who lord over that part of the republic have aspired, and this declaration, whatever the conditions with which they have won it, perhaps it will encourage them to extend their usurpations to the banks of the Rio Grande ... while the commissioners

of Mexico and the United States are arranging in Washington the limits of both republics, the Anglo-Saxon race crosses those that it itself imposed at the beginning.[30]

By spring, vitriol against the breakaway republics increased as did impatience with national political leaders. In addition to national strife, factional fighting between federalists, centralists and native tribes in the northern state of Sonora worsened, and the support of one of that state's newspapers for Yucatan made *Diaro*'s columns – as incensed centralist leaders increasingly focused on traitorous conduct: '*Cosmopolita* and the other opposition newspapers, which with incredible impudence support and sustain the rebellion in Yucatan, with such boldness as could the Texas papers.' The 1838/9 Pastry War with France and the infighting during that episode was also examined. 'The most ungrateful Mexican to his country would blush to blame his government for the end of the war with France,' the *Diario* stated. 'Is this how one has the courage to remember the war against the French? Are these the patriots, the liberals of our soil?' More consequential, however, was an admission reflecting a growing desire for change in the national leadership:

> The government is blamed for the affairs of Texas, and these gentlemen, instead of fighting the adventurers who threaten our independence, insert in their newspaper the commendations of Anaya, the vilest and most prostituted traitor that Mexico has had since Independence. Those pages of ignominy, which the pen of Yucatecan immorality consecrates to the history of its ruinous peninsula ... What audacity! What a shame![31]

Meanwhile, in Tabasco, Sentmanat was still solidifying his hold on that state after a rival federalist faction under the leadership of cocoa baron Nicolas Maldonado splintered the revolution. Adding to the upheaval was the ongoing collapse of the Federal Republic of Central America (1823–1840), which was ruled from Guatemala City for most of the period but began to unravel in 1838 when Nicaragua announced its separation. The resulting regional political vacuum led to widespread civil strife, and violence spilled over into neighbouring Chiapas – whose territory skirted parts of Guatemala and southern Tabasco. On the defensive, Maldonado took refuge in centralist Chiapas and began conducting raids on the northern city of Comitán. In response, Sentmanat issued a pronouncement in May vowing to 'look for the enemy in their own positions to avenge the blood that they have shed of our compatriots.' Violence against civilians was common at this point – as Sentmanat invoked the deaths of 'defenseless citizens, who on their knees implored in vain the victor's clemency.' The filibustering Cuban held out an olive branch to 'pacific centralists' but condemned those who violated 'the principles recognized by civilized peoples in the way of waging war' and vowed 'no consideration' would be extended to the 'assassins … in the unfortunate action of Comitán'.[32]

According to the historian Terry Rugeley, that June Sentmanat launched his offensive and achieved a major victory against Maldonado despite having his horse shot from under him. There was also speculation about 'post-facto executions' of surrendered soldiers, but the cocoa *caudillo* was spared and sent to Campeche to be confined for several months, before fleeing to Veracruz to plead his case to national officials. Anaya, for his part, attempted to keep up the momentum on the side of federalists by launching an ill-fated expedition further into Chiapas to remove that state's centralist leadership, but the death of nearly two hundred of his soldiers marked his unspectacular exit from the Tabasco scene. Former governor Gutierrez similarly tried to re-seize San Juan Bautista after recouping his forces near the Veracruz-Tabasco frontier but ended up as a prisoner in the capital. Rugeley notes that national leaders in Mexico City, who received most of their reports from the isolated Veracruzan town of Acayucan, 'had virtually no leverage over this anarchy.'[33]

Around the same time that Sentmanat was allegedly executing prisoners, James Webb, Secretary of State of Texas, informed President Lamar about his failed mission to Mexico City to establish diplomatic relations. Mexican leaders were not interested in talking and blamed the Texans for starting the fire which led to multiple revolts. Even being open to discussion was viewed as traitorous capitulation – inviting ridicule at the very least and suspicion among most. Despite all the failed attempts by Texas commissioners to talk peace, news from Yucatan and Tabasco increased their confidence. 'I now conscientiously believe that we can renew the war,' Webb wrote. 'Yucatan and Tobasco [*sic*], two of the most important states of Mexico, as you are aware, have already seceded, and declared themselves independent of the existing government.' Webb believed Yucatan and perhaps even Tabasco were ready to formalize an alliance. 'Let Texas enter into arrangements at once, with Yucatan and Tobasco, and each party mutually recognize the independence of the other,' he wrote, 'and then let them conjointly renew and prosecute the war until the central government shall be forced into terms, or put down beyond the hope of resuscitation.' Webb believed if the three breakaway states worked in tandem, putting down the rebellion would be impossible. 'In renewing the war conjointly with Yucatan and Tobasco, Texas would only be expected to furnish her navy – the whole of the land operations to be carried on by the Federalists.' In his opinion, the lack of available means for federalists to deploy soldiers to that part of the Gulf constituted both a liability and advantage:

> The Federalists of Yucatan and Tobasco have now everything that is necessary to carry on the war successfully, but a navy, and they want no assistance from us but such as the navy would afford. Without a navy they can make no effectual impression upon the sea ports, and that is the most essential object to be obtained ... Hence the great anxiety of the Federalists to make terms with us, because they believe with our assistance in taking their ports, they can immediately bring the central party down.[34]

Webb's instincts were correct. In July, Lamar wrote to Yucatecan Governor Miguel Barbachano to express his friendship and 'earnest desire to establish with the States of Yucatan, Tobasco and such others as may throw off the yoke of central despotism in Mexico'. He indicated that Yucatecan merchants would be received 'upon the same terms as we extend to the most favored nations', namely the United States, and inquired if the Yucatecan congress was interested in a 'more permanent' agreement to secure 'a full and complete acknowledgment of the respective rights of both countries from those who are now our enemies'. Barbachano replied, noting Commodore Moore's recent 'distinctions' and the 'greatest satisfaction' with Lamar's proposal 'to strengthen his relations with the people of Texas, and unite with them to support the cause of freedom that they have proclaimed against the oppressive government of Mexico.' Barbachano also told Lamar that his letter would be printed in the newspapers and reciprocated their mutual sentiment by concluding that the centralists of Mexico were 'now our enemies'.[35]

Soon afterwards an 'alliance' was formalized. Yucatan agreed to pay $8,000 a month for the Texas Navy's support. American archaeologist and explorer John L. Stephens, who arrived in Yucatan that September, noted in his work, *Incidents of Travel in Yucatan*, that he was in Merida when the Texan schooner *San Antonio* docked at the port of Sisal bringing the proposition. According to him it 'was accepted immediately' – the worst-case scenario for the centralists had come to fruition. 'Yucatan was widening the breach,' he wrote, 'and committing an offence which Mexico could never forgive, by an alliance with a people whom that government ... regarded as the worst of rebels, and ... was bent upon exerting the whole power of the country in an effort to reconquer.'[36]

Eligio Ancono, a nineteenth-century Yucatecan governor and secretary to the Mexican Supreme Court, wrote a popular history of Yucatan published in 1879 after his tenure as governor. It was his belief that the close relationship between Texas and Yucatan was designed to 'defend themselves against the dictatorship' in Mexico City but claimed that – although the Yucatecans sent an envoy to Texas to discuss a formal alliance – it never became official because 'the Texan government imposed a condition on ours that it proclaim its absolute independence from that of Mexico.' Ancono admitted that the envoy, Colonel Martin Francisco Peraza, 'limited himself to contracting three vessels,' for which Yucatan would pay Texas, but iterated that 'the projected alliance could not be carried out.' For the most part, neither side believed their agreement constituted a formal military alliance but was rather a temporary partnership forged out of strategic necessity.[37]

Regardless of the details, for authorities in Mexico City, news of extended cooperation between the two the states flanking their principal port caused concern. Moreover, if Yucatan and Tabasco decided to unite against the centralist government, the entire peninsular region south of the isthmus of Tehuantepec could be permanently lost and some other entity could arise to reconstitute a northern-led Federal Republic of Central America, which was probably what Anaya had in mind when he sent his forces into Chiapas. Rugeley notes that Justo Sierra O'Reilly, son-in-law of Santiago Méndez Ibarra – a prominent *campechano* merchant who alternated the governorship with Barbachano on numerous occasions – visited Sentmanat in 1842 'to promote the creation of a southwest federation' composed of Chiapas, Tabasco, and Yucatan. This three-state republic was not merely based on geography, but the fact that they at one time constituted 'a single circuit court in the early republic.' O'Reilly's mission was unsuccessful, but it would not be the last time his father requested him to seek allies; he was later sent to the United States in 1847 when the outcome of the wider war was far from certain. Nevertheless, shifting borders and rumours of alliances alarmed centralist leaders.[38]

Coup, Common Enemy and Accommodation

The crisis in Mexico had reached a tipping point, and influential leaders felt drastic measures needed to be taken to prevent the country's dissolution. In the early autumn of 1841, Mariano Paredes, a conservative and monarchist, met with Santa Anna west of the capital in a place called Tacubaya and formed a junta to overthrow the government. In many ways the two men made an unlikely team given that Santa Anna was a republican, but the cunning general from Veracruz ultimately used the opportunity not only to depose a government he believed was incapable of addressing the existential crisis caused by the breakaway republics, but also to have Paredes pushed aside. To make this manoeuvre palatable to the scheming classes in Mexico City, Santa Anna formally adopted the tenets of centralism and seized power with the help of more articulate and like-minded 'santanistas' such as José Tornel. According to Santa Anna's biographer Will Fowler, the Veracruzan had long believed in the principles of federalism, but 'the major tasks of reconquering Texas and bringing an end to the secessionist revolt in Yucatán' took priority over political philosophy. Another factor Santa Anna had to keep in mind 'was the growing threat posed by the United States', which was beginning to take a more active and ominous interest in Mexican affairs vis-à-vis Texas. In May 1842 Mexicans even attempted to address the flow of men and munitions into Texas from the United States with a protest indicating the latter could be in violation of treaty terms, but these concerns were dismissed. If Mexico could not unite and a larger war against the United States broke out, victory would be difficult to achieve.[39]

While Santa Anna's political views and positions often changed depending upon circumstances, he was first and foremost a military officer who made pragmatic decisions irrespective of the intransigent centralist-federalist ideologies that inhibited cooperation. When viewed through a military lens, it is apparent Santa Anna attempted to overcome the disastrous political infighting preventing Mexico from reintegrating the breakaway states. Santanistas, many of whom were Veracruzanos such as Tornel, believed the same. As Minister of War, Tornel supported Santa Anna's 1835/36 campaign in Texas and believed a heavy hand was required to subdue the rebels.

At an important October meeting of the Mexican Congress, Tornel made the case that direct rule in Mexico was required to meet the demands of the moment. He cited the various issues facing Napoleon Bonaparte in France and Fernando II in Spain – both of whom ruled over powerful nations made up of regions holding 'dissimilar customs' and traditions. He noted it was 'necessary to be frank' about the 'very disastrous' constitution of 1836, and that others considered 'the era of centralism a great crime, that for its establishment Texas was lost and the department of Yucatan was separated.' He harangued the aristocracy as men who 'hang on to their family tree', and praised the 'clergy who distinguished themselves so gloriously in the struggle for independence, who produced the best of the generals of the time.' He also argued that what 'seems to be ignored' among Mexicans was that the Texas revolution was not about 'the change of the federal system' or the constitution, but rather about independence. 'When speaking of Texas, ... that country [has been] the object of the aspirations of the United States for half a century ... whose aim is separating it at the first opportunity and appropriating it.' Indeed, there was plenty of evidence, going back decades, that American leadership coveted Texas. The first major attempt in 1812, culminating in the defeat of a combined American and Tejano force at the hands of royalists at the Battle of Medina on 13 August 1813, was due in part to their numerical inferiority in an era before white colonization. By the 1830s, that equation had changed considerably:

> The distant ones proclaimed their independence, because reviewing their resources, they already considered themselves strong, and because in addition to counting on the sympathies of the citizens of the United States, they relied on the promises and open protection of the Washington cabinet. The fall of the federal system served merely as a pretext, because the Mexican nation, having admitted them into its bosom, could not exempt them from running their own fate.[40]

The two republics appeared similar, but there were differences. Tornel dispelled the idea 'that the Yucatecan separation proceeds from the same cause or motives' as those of Texas. According to him, the 'true design' of Yucatan was not only separation, 'but a war cry,' and that that state had been 'offered more, perhaps, than could be offered, and nothing else has been demanded of him except that he put on uniforms in the agreement

Introduction   xxxiii

with the other departments.' Tornel lamented that 'the catastrophes in Texas and Yucatan attributed to the fall of the federation,' complimented the efforts by the 'meritorious General Paredes' for taking a bold step towards the 'regeneration' of Mexico, and with an eye perhaps on the United States, closed by invoking the unity needed to meet the occasion with a defence of Santa Anna's previous tenure as a benevolent ruler and defender of Mexico:

> I will not tire of recommending to Congress that it not avert its vigilant gaze from the dangers that may even threaten our independence: union is necessary for it to be saved, and for a long time it will also be for our governments to be strong for foreign defense ... To our glory, there has been a Mexican who, invested with all the power of a dictatorship, has not committed such possible and almost natural abuses in similar circumstances: the dictatorship in the hands of General Santa-Anna has been a hollow reed that has not weighed on the heads of the people.[41]

Another statesman rising to prominence during the period was the young Guadalajaran Mariano Otero. Appointed to the junta's council to represent his home state of Jalisco, Otero became only one of four deputies opposing the Treaty of Guadalupe Hidalgo ending the US-Mexican War. Although as a staunch federalist he disagreed with Tornel and Santa Anna on many issues, one thing they all believed was that the US cast a covetous eye on that 'precious portion of the beautiful country that providence entrusted' to Mexico, and that the northern region was 'in imminent danger of being invaded by that formidable race of the United States, who regard it with envy, who regard it as their prey, and who seek to seize it by abusing our weakness, and taking advantage of the proximity of its population and the advantages of its political situation.' Drawing distinctions between Mexicans and white Europeans to create solidarity among disparate social classes was a common rhetorical device of the era, and Otero was no different. In fact, racial arguments were common among Mexicans, Texians and Americans, and later, when ethnic war erupted in Yucatan in 1847, *criollos* and Mayans:

> But in addition to this question that complicates the state of our foreign relations, of this question produced by the constant clash of the races

of the North and the South, and in which Mexico is the custodian not only of their honor and their rights, but from the fate of the southern races of the new world, who must one day exert such an astonishing influence on the future destinies of humanity, the deeply concealed, selfish and Machiavellian politics of Europe, also deserves our attention.[42]

That most of the leadership of Texas was white made it easier for Mexicans to use racial rhetoric. However, Yucatan was ruled by people who would have been indistinguishable among the junta formed to deal with the breakaway republics. When Santa Anna assumed administrative powers in October of 1841, one of his first actions was to send emissaries to Tabasco and Yucatan to see if violence could be avoided. The two emissaries commissioned by Santa Anna to meet with Sentmanat reached Veracruz and outsourced their mission to the military commander there, Francisco Marín, who returned in early November after making a little headway. This diplomatic activity caught the attention of prying eyes in the Gulf, and it was reported in the New Orleans *Picayune* that Sentmanat was willing to meet and affairs were 'unfavorable' – as reopened trade between Tabasco and Veracruz signalled a *rapprochement*. True to his nebulous character, Sentmanat was playing both sides.[43]

Since Tabasco was ruled by one man, bringing it back into the union meant placating Sentmanat by appealing to his oversized ego. The skilful Santa Anna knew exactly how to do that, and succeeded by bestowing upon the Cuban the title of 'General Commander of Tabasco' – despite the caudillo's previous pronouncements against centralism. Political abstractions meant little compared to the primary mission of bringing the breakaway states back into the national fold. The threat of invasion was likely also a factor in Sentmanat's sudden change of heart. At any rate, unlike Anaya, Sentmanat was obviously more committed to his own survival than the federalist cause and would be dealt with later. Yucatan, on the other hand, with a strong and unified legislative branch, required a skilful negotiator.

For that mission Santa Anna sent Andrés Quintana Roo, a well-respected hero of the Mexican Revolution. Quintana Roo was ushered to Campeche in an English brig (most likely to evade Texan scrutiny) and from there made his way along the 'royal road' to the capital of Merida. On 4 December he presented his credentials to Governor Santiago Méndez, and the proposals were read before the Yucatecan Chamber of Deputies. Substitute Governor

Miguel Barbachano and councillor Juan de Dios Cosgaya began negotiations with the commissioner on 17 December. Quintana Roo argued that Yucatan was not capable of becoming a sovereign state able to protect itself and that its natural and historical allegiances were to Mexico. Terms included accepting military appointments from the central junta and allowing a battalion of soldiers to be stationed in Yucatan on a permanent basis for the preservation of peace. These proposals were rejected by Barbachano and Cosgaya.[44]

A few days later, a compromise seemed more unlikely after Quintana Roo denounced the Texas-Yucatan alliance as an 'insult' to the junta in Mexico City and declared that to reach a deal the alliance needed to be dissolved. Quintana Roo also added that the 'disagreements between brothers were concealable; but that the league with treasonous, ungrateful colonists and enemies of the republic, would always be seen as an unforgivable crime.' Ancono noted the 'Yucatecan commissioners responded to this charge by claiming the supposed alliance with the Texas government did not strictly exist,' and their presence in Yucatan was predicated on the fact that Yucatan was constantly 'threatened by the Mexican government ... which in time could become its natural ally.'[45]

Neither side appeared willing to compromise until the impasse was broken in late December. Quintana Roo agreed to allow Yucatan to retain a number of important provincial rights, including the authority of the governor over the military forces assigned to the state. For their part, Yucatecan officials promised to sever ties with Texas if the treaty was ratified by the junta. By the time Quintana Roo set out to return to Mexico City in early 1842, publicity surrounding the negotiations had reached Texas, and some ships from its squadron had landed at Sisal. Quintana Roo was unhappy about their presence and chartered a New Orleans vessel named *Luisa* for his return voyage to Veracruz. After the envoy embarked from Sisal, Moore seized the ship in clear violation of international norms. Quintana Roo later wrote that the Texians 'threw themselves like bandits on board the *Luisa*, and propagating with wild shouts ... told us that if within a quarter of an hour we did not allow ourselves to be taken prisoners aboard their war corvette *Austin*, which was within sight, they would fire on the boat.' Quintana Roo later recalled the event in a pamphlet published that year in Mexico City:

> The captain of this ship protested against the insult made to the flag of his nation. For my part, I made present my inviolable character as envoy of a recognized government and friend of the United States, under whose flag I was protected with all those who accompanied; but those pirates, prevailing with force and trampling on the principles most sacred among all nations, violently threw us into their boat and took us to the *Austin*, as prisoners...[46]

Moore allowed an aide appointed by Yucatecan authorities to return to Sisal to inform Governor Méndez. The governor was predictably outraged at Moore's actions, and before having Quintana Roo abruptly released, ordered forces be sent to Sisal to placate the anger and assuage the honour of the respected envoy. Quintana Roo continued on to Mexico City, while Yucatecan officials sent word to Texas about Moore's 'scandalous attack ... that has provoked public indignation, and for which he has made a serious direct offense against the Government of this State, under whose guarantees the imprisoned individuals were found, almost all of them Yucatecans.' In April, Yucatan formally requested that Texas 'withdraw the squadron of that Republic from the service of this government for the impulsive causes', citing improved relations with Mexico and the false assumption that the junta 'are not thinking of invading us for now.' They were seriously wrong about that assumption.[47]

Mexico Invades Yucatan

On 31 May the Quintana Roo treaty terms to which Yucatan agreed were rejected by the junta and plans were made for an invasion. John L. Stephens, who was passing through Merida on the last leg of a journey through the region, was in the Yucatecan Chamber of Deputies when Santa Anna's 'ultimatum' was read. 'A smile of derision flitted over the faces of senators, and it was manifest that the terms would not be accepted ... The Indians were all quiet, and, though doomed to fight the battles, knew nothing of the questions involved.' On 5 July, the Yucatecans realized the central government's hostile intentions when one of the peninsula's warships, anchored in the waters off Campeche, was stormed in the early hours and its crew taken prisoner. Soon after, Yucatecan authorities put the government on a war footing and Miguel Barbachano issued a call to arms. On 22 August four Mexican warships and three transport ships carrying 1,500 men appeared in front of the island city of Ciudad del Carmen south of Campeche. The war against the breakaway Republic of Yucatan had begun.[48]

News of the immediate capitulation by leaders in Carmen spread like wildfire throughout Yucatan, and people began looking for centralist collaborators and internal enemies deemed to be working with the junta. Soon after, the head of the Yucatecan squadron capitulated, giving up three vessels to the enemy. Cries of treason rang out amidst accusations that Yucatecan centralists were working with Santa Anna. Passions were inflamed, the populace armed itself, and newspapers compared the coming struggle to 'the ancient and modern peoples who had fought against tyranny, and the Yucatecans were encouraged to imitate the heroism of the Spaniards, when their homeland was invaded by the hosts of Napoleon.' Adding to the animus directed at the central government was the ever-present belief that if Yucatecans did not make a stand 'they would once again be uprooted from their homes to go to die in a foreign land.' Towns set up defensive garrisons, and some 6,000 soldiers were enlisted among an agitated populace.[49]

The immediate campaign objective for the invaders was Campeche, and centralist leaders established a beachhead some 50km south of the city at Champoton and waited for reinforcements to arrive. By the end of October, 4,000 troops arrived from Veracruz under the expedition's main commander, General Vicente Miñón. The garrison at Campeche was undermanned, but the formidable walls of the coastal city offered a defensive advantage. Yucatecan forces under the command of Lieutenant Colonel Pastor Gamboa attempted to slow Miñón's march outside the city at Lerma but were forced to retreat. Shortly thereafter, centralist forces easily positioned themselves on the heights overlooking the walled section of the city – giving credence to suspicions that traitors among the Yucatecan army were assisting the invaders.[50]

Despite the setbacks, and bombardment from the entrenched positions of the centralists, Yucatecans were determined to defend the city. Colonel Sebastian López de Llergo and roughly 1,000 men attempted to expel Miñón's cannons from the heights but failed after much bloodshed. This led him to harass centralists from flanking positions to mitigate the assault, which contributed to prolonging the siege. Food and arms were reaching the besieged, and the *Picayune* reported the city was 'well supplied with provisions and munitions of war, foreign vessels evading the blockade with the greatest ease'. By early January the two sides were at a stalemate, but a factor favouring the defenders was the outbreak of disease among the invaders. Furthermore, the longer the siege extended, the more difficult it became for the Mexicans to get supplies – particularly since the surrounding population either fled or opposed them. These factors combined to make life difficult for both sides, but centralist forces suffered from low morale and desertion. Miñón's solution to this predicament was to send roughly 800 men to occupy the nearby village of China, which was surrounded by several productive haciendas capable of providing both meat and maize for his hungry soldiers. Centralist positions in China thereafter came under sporadic attack by small parties of Yucatecans, but dislodging their entrenchments came at too high a price. By mid-February, even the Campechans were beginning to tire, and a massacre on the 13th of prisoners accused of being traitors punctuated their exasperation.[51]

After more than five months with little progress, centralists were becoming increasingly frustrated, and reports indicated Santa Anna was offering extra pay to those who enlisted. He also announced that 'the war against Yucatan is a national affair, and that it is to be prosecuted with the same spirit as that against the "perfidous Texians".' As a result, Mexico City officials decided to take a different approach by attempting to initiate a coup in the capital of Merida. It was believed that if a change of leadership could be effected, opposition would collapse. Yucatecan forces under Colonel Llergo observed three Mexican vessels moving off the coast and with 1,600 soldiers followed the ships as they sailed north to ostensibly land near Merida. When Llergo's forces arrived in that city – convinced centralists were landing somewhere in the vicinity of Telchac, west of Sisal – arrangements were made with acting governor Barbachano to enlist guerrilla units in the vicinity to confront the enemy's approach to the capital. Yucatan, with its difficult roads, dense vegetation, and tribal territory controlled by local *batabs* (Mayan chieftains) with authority over thousands of men, made insurgent warfare quite effective – particularly since the defenders knew the terrain. Two and a half thousand centralist soldiers disembarked and engaged Llergo's forces in several heated skirmishes over a period of days before Barbachano requested Llergo to withdraw to Merida to fortify the city. On the morning of the 16th a representative of the centralist forces approached an outpost on the edge of the capital with a white parley flag. Soon after, General Pedro Ampudia, who was appointed by Santa Anna, arrived in Campeche – effectively nullifying the northern commanders' desires to end the conflict. Partisan attacks continued, and it was clear to everyone that Ampudia's presence could not prevent the inevitable centralist capitulation.[52]

A week of renewed attacks in the north, along with reinforcements of guerrillas led by Colonel Gamboa, took their toll. Soon after, Mexicans found themselves encircled on three sides near Tixkokob, and surrender became unavoidable. Terms were finalized on 24 April. The northern forces were required to submit a request to Ampudia for ships and to evacuate their forces to the Gulf port of Tampico. If centralist forces were still in Yucatecan territory after ten days, partisans were allowed to resume their attacks and new terms would be required. When Ampudia's ships failed to appear off the coast, their departure date was extended. To guarantee their departure, hostages were left with Yucatecan authorities. By mid-May all of the forces sent to force a coup in Merida had withdrawn from the peninsula. Meanwhile, in Campeche the siege continued, but Ampudia was forced to reluctantly seek terms and saved face by renewing the original negotiations for Yucatecan reincorporation into Mexico. Yucatecan authorities agreed to send commissioners to Mexico City if centralist forces were completely withdrawn from the peninsula.[53]

Ampudia agreed to the terms, but instead of sending his soldiers back to Veracruz, used the opportunity to deal Sentmanat a blow by sending his forces directly to Tabasco. That summer, Ampudia entered San Juan Bautista with nearly 3,000 men hungry for victory, and after two hours of fighting, the Cuban *caudillo* was forced to flee. The *Picayune* reported that Sentmanat was 'betrayed by some of his officers' and hastened to Merida to 'organize a new force'. When he found few there interested in renewing hostilities, he went to Havana and from there to New Orleans – the favorite sanctuary for exiles ousted from Mexico.[54] Although Sentmanat fell out of favour with Santa Anna and the centralists in Mexico City, the Yucatecans were content with their hard-won victory – a victory shared with the Texas Navy off the coast of Campeche.

Last Battle of the Beginning of the War

On 18 April, while anchored at the old French fort of La Balize, near the mouth of the Mississippi River, Commodore Moore received information from the American schooner *Rosario*, which arrived after sailing for three days from Campeche. The captain of the *Rosario* informed Moore that Mexican forces outside of Merida had capitulated and the Mexican steam-powered frigate *Montezuma* was anchored somewhere off the coast at Telchac. Soon after, the flagship *Austin*, along with the 16-gun brig *Wharton*, sailed directly to Yucatan, facing headwinds, and arrived one day after the *Montezuma* left. After learning from the Yucatecans at Sisal that the *Montezuma* had passed the port, Moore continued along the coast until he arrived near Lerma on April 29. The following morning, as the first rays of sun appeared, the Texans rose to find Mexican vessels heading in their direction. At 7.35 the first shots were fired. Cannon fire killed two men aboard the *Wharton* and more than a dozen Mexican sailors aboard their heavily manned vessels – including the iron-hulled frigate *Guadalupe*. Also present near Campeche were a handful of Yucatecan gunships.[55]

Over the course of several days the two sides kept their distance, with Moore stationed in and around Campeche and the Mexican ships at Lerma. At Campeche it was learned that the confrontation on 30 April had prevented the centralists and federalists from completing an armistice because the Mexicans demanded the Texans withdraw as a precondition for talks. Apparently this did not bother the Yucatecan authorities, because Moore left port after being offered two long 18-pound cannons for the *Austin* and a long 12-pound cannon for the *Wharton*. These additions were welcomed, since both Mexican steamers, the *Guadalupe* and *Montezuma*, mounted two massive 68-pound Paixhans guns. On 16 May the two squadrons faced off again at mid-morning for a few hours, resulting in damage to both the *Montezuma* and *Guadalupe*, and the Mexicans suffering serious casualties. The *Austin* also received considerable cannon fire and took on water, but casualties were limited to three men dead and nearly three dozen wounded. Although Moore had apparently defied the odds, the Texan victory was attributed to an astute use of long-range firing, with perhaps an amount of luck in avoiding a direct hit from a Paixhan. Seven dead sailors on the Texan side and some thirty on the Mexican side meant Moore could return to Galveston a victor.[56]

US newspapers hailed the 'gallant little Texan navy' and proclaimed the 'lustre of the Lone Star has been rendered more brilliant as a result.' The *New York Herald* cited a report from New Orleans that the 'walls and churches in Campeachy were crowded ... and thousands of brunettes waved their snow white handkerchiefs a los bravos Texanos.' Although Moore was welcomed as a hero in Texas, President Houston was incensed with the commodore's actions in disobeying clear orders on several occasions to return home before the battle. Writing to the former Secretary of War, George W. Hockley, Houston commented that Moore's deeds 'proved him always a pirate upon the national treasury. His last acts of assumption, mutiny and piracy outdo all his former delinquencies [*sic*] and crimes.' Houston had tough words regarding Santa Anna as well, but also believed Texas was not ready for a full-scale conflict and it was 'foolery ... to make war without means.'[57]

When the *Austin* arrived in Galveston amidst cheering audiences and cannon salutes, Moore was suspended from command on Houston's orders and underwent a tribunal to determine if his insubordination was justified. Multiple charges, including piracy, were brought. In early 1845, after a five-month trial, the former commodore was acquitted on eighteen of twenty-two charges against him, but in the public mind he remained a hero of the republic.[58] How then, does one reconcile the seemingly contradictory views of Houston who believed in the spring of 1846 that 'War had existed for ten years between Mexico and Texas' yet was so willing to prosecute a man considered a hero for making allies in the Gulf and battling forces that could be used to invade and subdue the Lone Star republic?

Houston had numerous concerns, but his immediate dilemma was posed by the Texas prisoners of war held in Mexico. In September 1842 Texans and Mexicans engaged in a series of skirmishes near San Antonio resulting in the deaths of three dozen Texans. In response, that November, without official authorization, Texans organized a retaliatory expedition of several hundred soldiers and pushed through Laredo towards Ciudad Mier – located on the Mexican side of the Rio Grande. In late December, when more than three hundred Texans led by Colonel William S. Fisher crossed the river and entered the town, they realized it was garrisoned by a sizeable force commanded by General Ampudia. Thomas J. Green, captured in Mier on Christmas Day after a deadly firefight, chronicled the capitulation and forced march into the heart of Mexico. Before the prisoners set out mid-January, Green and Fisher penned a note to their comrades lamenting their 'lot to become captives to the nation with which we are at war'.[59]

On 11 February, while halting at a hacienda in the northern Mexican state of Tamaulipas, 181 prisoners overwhelmed their guards and escaped into the desolate desert country. However, as soon as their food and water ran out, the group was quickly sapped of morale and strength, and all but five of the escapees were either recaptured or willingly returned to Mexican authorities.[60] When an incensed Santa Anna, who was already dealing with frustrations surrounding the Yucatan campaign, was informed of the escape attempt, he sent word to the commander to shoot *all* of the prisoners – an order that was rejected by General Francisco Mejia but replaced with *decimation* – Latin for a 'removal of a tenth'. Green explained that the Mexicans first placed 159 white beans on the bottom of the clay jar, then added seventeen black ones to the top of the pile in the hopes of killing as many officers as possible – since they would draw their beans before the rest. Green wrote that they 'drew their beans with manly dignity and firmness … Some of lighter temper jested over the bloody tragedy.'[61]

Despite official protests from the British and US governments about the unsanctioned expedition into Mexican territory, Houston appealed to agents of those governments to use their good offices to have the Texans released. This was Houston's immediate concern in May just prior to Moore's second naval engagement with Mexicans in the waters off Campeche, and he expressed those sentiments to Captain Charles Elliot, the British Chargé d'affaires in Texas: 'I fear the sailing of the fleet will have a baleful influence upon the fate of our prisoners who have claimed so much sympathy of the newspapers.'[62]

The upcoming 1844 US presidential election was also a factor in Houston's thinking. In the years after 1836, Texas had unsuccessfully applied for statehood in the American Union, and that unofficial referendum came up again in the form of the presidential election of 1844. If the Democrats won, and their expansionist pro-annexation platform was therefore sanctioned, Texas would be able to fight its former master with the full force of the US federal government at its disposal – backed by popular consensus. That was the outcome that Houston desired. If the Whigs won, and annexation became less likely, Texas needed to secure diplomatic recognition from Mexico with the help of the British to avoid a prolonged war; this kept the situation in a constant state of tension. Elliot outlined this assessment to the British Undersecretary of Foreign Affairs in late 1842, writing that the 'people of Texas are gasping for peace, and the best bidder.' For that reason, Elliot argued

> that the only safe solution would be a formal offer upon the part of Her Majesty's Government to Texas … of real independence … there

is no choice between this, and the virtual, early, and permanent lapse of Texas within the sphere of United States influence, and policy; and I cannot help adding here, that I do not believe that the government and people of the United States have just or moderate purposes with respect to Mexico. To put Texas between them … would put an end to all combination of that kind, and be a very helpful weight in the preservation of peace, and a just balance of power on this continent.[63]

However, the British arrived too late at the conclusion that an independent Texas, recognized by Mexico, would contribute to a proper balance of power in North America. For many, the larger war had already started, and Texas' annexation to the United States was already a foregone conclusion that no last-minute diplomatic effort could prevent. The breakaway republics, at war for years, had not tested their foes but the minds of those disinterested Americans who could easily be persuaded that Mexico had always been their enemy and that Texas needed protection. Ultimately, the question of war or peace was decided by the American people.

Chapter 1

'Annexation as War'

I do not make annexation dependent upon this assent. It is to be sought, and obtained, if practicable; but Mexico may refuse to give it. She may still keep up a desultory war, and affect to reclaim her revolted province ... if the solution to the question brings war, we shall at least have the consolation to know that it comes constitutionally! ... Mexico cannot conquer Texas. Another invasion will be more disastrous than the former; and the signal for its commencement will be the signal for the commotion of all the vast territory of the Mississippi. Proclamations, and laws of neutrality, can have no force against passions. The news for a battle would be the summons for a joyous rendezvous to all the young and fiery spirits of the Great West.[1]

Senator Thomas Hart Benton, 10 June 1844

The US presidential election held in late autumn of 1844 was not merely a contest over which party would administer the executive branch of the federal government; it was a referendum on whether the nation would go to war with Mexico. The margin of victory was razor-thin, but the ascendancy of James K. Polk to the post of Commander-in-Chief meant a plurality of voting Americans believed the United States should annex the breakaway state and accept the consequences: that incorporation of the Lone Star Republic meant inheriting an ongoing war with Mexico.

From the time Texas submitted its first application for annexation in 1837 the belief that incorporation entailed war was common among Americans and Mexicans and became widespread as 1844 approached. In addition, northern anti-slavery activists believed southern expansionists advocated annexation to extend slavery into that territory and simultaneously overwhelm northern representation in the federal government. Quaker abolitionist and writer Benjamin Lundy subscribed to this conspiracy in his 1837 compilation, *The War in Texas*, and quoted former US President John Quincy Adams' 1835 speech claiming Texas 'insurrectionists' were essentially Americans 'revolutionizing the country; and that they are dependent upon this nation, for both the physical and pecuniary means, to carry the design into effect.' Similarly to Mexican rhetoric overlooking Tejano contribution to Texan independence, Adams' belief was that the looming conflict represented a larger racial conflagration pitting 'soldiers of fortune' such as Santa Anna against white settlers. In his dire prognostications, Adams believed such a war would become 'a war of races ... the Anglo-Saxon American pitted against the Moorish-Spanish-Mexican American, a war between the Northern and Southern halves of North America, from Passamaquoddy to Panama.'[2]

While Lundy represented a growing northern dissatisfaction with the persistence of slavery, moderate politicians who believed adding Texas to the American Union was a provocation were more reluctant to make public claims due to the fear of backlash from vocal southerners. One expansionist who put Adams in his crosshairs was Henry Stuart Foote. Foote was one of a handful of key Polk allies in the Senate during the war and played a prominent role in the effort to annex all of Mexico and later Yucatan at a critical period in late 1847 and early 1848. In 1841 Foote published *Texas and the Texans*, in which he was flourishingly critical of Adams' efforts to keep the breakaway republic out of American hands. Foote labelled the former president one of 'the enemies of Texas and the Texans' and a 'Goliath-of-Gath Ex-President of a great Republic ... and mischievous peddler of interested Politico-Fanaticism, who ever attempted to shuffle off his false haberdashery upon honest and confiding men and women.' Foote argued that the initial rejection of annexation made Texas 'at once a great Empire – leaving her resources under her own control, and placing her in a position much better than that of the States of the Union.' According to Foote, the source of this power was in the abundance of fertile land 'destined to be covered with the cotton-plant and sugar-cane, and offering the attractions rarely combined of an exuberant soil ... to tempt the adventurous industry of our people.' Foote believed that rather than move directly west, Anglo-Saxon migration and settlement was bound to encircle the Gulf, thus replacing the population along the coast who had been there since time immemorial:

> My impression, too, is that as there lies on the east of the Rocky Mountains an immense region where the cultivation of the soil is very difficult and unproductive, the stream of population, instead of going directly across those mountains, will turn to the South of them – and that the great route to the Pacific, the only resting-place of our people,

will be along the Gulf of Mexico, through the lower south-western states and Texas.[3]

Like most nineteenth-century statesmen, Foote subscribed to commonly-held racist beliefs, but to his credit included the 'amiable and accomplished' Lorenzo de Zavala's crucial role in the Texan Revolution. Foote had few good words for native tribes either in his book or later as a senator from Mississippi – adhering to the assumption that they would eventually be replaced by more productive Anglo-Saxons and Spanish Americans sympathetic to US institutions, including slavery. The only obstacle to unleashing that potential, in his mind, was annexation.[4]

Mexicans also followed sectional divisions in the United States but used the terms 'acquire' (*adquiriendo*), 'aggregation' (*agregación*) and 'admission' (*admisión*) when addressing the subject. During the years after Texan independence, *Diario*'s editors in Mexico City printed excerpts from US antislavery groups' petitions to the federal government opposing annexation as if those groups were articulating the official Mexican position, and believed those pleas carried more weight in the larger debate than they did. In essence, many naively hoped anti-slavery sentiment in the north and New England was stronger than the impulse to push the boundaries of the United States. Ultimately, when the issue arose again in the 1844 presidential election, the Mexicans were caught off guard because Polk was relatively obscure, but the popularity of the Democrat party platform brought victory. In sum, they overestimated the power of anti-slavery feeling among Americans vis-à-vis the desire for territory; and when the invasion commenced in 1846, they discovered that among the soldiers fighting side-by-side with southerners were indifferent northerners from every state who were more concerned with adventure and glory in their nation's first foreign war than with the plight of the slave. This assumption was a strategic and costly gamble on the part of the Mexicans – who might have been better served engaging with the British to reach an accommodation rather than futilely seeking to regain militarily what was lost. Nevertheless, it was extremely difficult for moderate Mexican statesmen to even consider talking with the Texans, given the militaristic rhetoric emanating from the junta prior to the war.[5]

In 1883 the conservative historian and poet José María Roa Bárcena articulated the Mexican position concerning annexation in his work *Memories of the North American Invasion*. Roa Bárcena noted that in 1843, Jose Maria

Bocanegra, the Minister of Foreign Relations who worked with US officials to have prisoners of the Santa Fe Expedition released, was concerned over 'the spirit and tone of the North American press in favour of the admission of Texas to the Union', and informed US Minister to Mexico Waddy Thompson that Thompson was 'obliged to prevent an unprecedented aggression in the annals of the world from being consumed ... at the expense of the disasters of war.' In addition to proclamations in 1843 directed at foreign invaders in Texas, Juan Almonte, the Mexican Minister in Washington, issued his own ultimatums equating annexation with military aggression – forcing the US Secretary of State Abel Upshur to respond: 'As to the threat of war made in advance, in the name and by the express order of the Mexican Government, the undersigned reminds General Almonte that it is neither the first nor the second time that Mexico has given the same warning to the United States, under similar circumstances.' Relations further deteriorated in 1844 when Secretary of State John C. Calhoun and Texas commissioners effected a treaty of annexation in Washington for consideration in the Senate. Bocanegra's reaction, which had become official policy, was that 'Mexico would have to consider the ratification of the treaty as a declaration of war.'[6]

Americans understood as much from press reports, noting how the issue 'united all parties' in Mexico, and how the Mexican government 'would listen to no propositions' regarding Texas because the government – regardless of party affiliation – 'repeated its former declarations that it would consider annexation as a declaration of war.' Although Calhoun's treaty was rejected by annexationist senators like Thomas Hart Benton because they believed annexation required full congressional approval (i.e. both the House and Senate), it nevertheless demonstrated to Mexican officials that events were moving headlong in the direction of annexation and the upcoming presidential election was the deciding factor. Adding to the war chorus was increasingly belligerent language from the Democrat party towards Great Britain, which tied the entire expansionist platform together to create one grand geostrategic project justifying continental ambitions. Philadelphia's *Public Ledger* encapsulated the platform: 'They want California, they want Texas, they want Oregon; and possessing the whole, they would drive us out of the Pacific, and annoy seriously in the Gulf of Mexico.'[7]

Although James K. Polk was a national figure among the informed political class, Whig presidential candidate and Kentucky senator Henry Clay had long been a household name. Because Polk represented the Democratic platform calling for the 'whole of the Territory of Oregon ... and the re-annexation of Texas at the earliest practicable period', it was incumbent on Clay to articulate his position on Texas, but he avoided doing so as long as possible to preserve fragile sectional alliances within the Whig party. On 13 April 1844 Clay visited Raleigh, North Carolina, at the behest of party members holding a rally, and spoke for two hours before fireworks closed the celebrations. A few days later, Clay penned a letter and had his friend Senator John Crittenden forward it to the editors of the *National Intelligencer* – the main Whig organ in the US capital. In the letter, Clay expressed his position that 'if the government of the United States were to acquire Texas, it would acquire it along with all the incumbrance which Texas is under, and among them the actual or suspended war between Mexico and Texas.' Clay's words were clear enough, but he added, 'Of that consequence there cannot be a doubt, annexation and war with Mexico are identical!' Clay's letter was published on the 27th and that same day, former president Martin Van Buren's opinion appeared in the *Washington Globe* outlining his belief 'that Mexico and Texas are now at war – that immediate annexation would therefore involve us in a war with Mexico.' That summer, Clay stood his ground again by adding that Mexico had 'repeatedly and solemnly declared, that she would consider annexation as war with her.' Thus, the positions were crystallized for voters. One Democrat newspaper in Ohio succinctly summed up the contest:

> The great issue between the Whig and self-styled Democratic parties at this time is Henry Clay and peace – or James K. Polk and war. Do not be alarmed, for this is really the great issue. Let us see what the facts are – Henry Clay is opposed to annexation – James K. Polk is in favor of immediate annexation, Mexico has declared that if the United States should annex Texas they should consider it a declaration of war against Mexico. Then to vote for James K. Polk, who goes in for immediate annexation, is to vote for this Government going into war with Mexico – is it not?[8]

Informing political developments during the election season were reports of military activity in the Gulf region. The Louisville *Morning Courier*, in Clay's home state of Kentucky, reported that President John Tyler, who was becoming more bellicose in his rhetoric against Mexico, 'ordered a military force to repair to the frontier of Texas' in the Fort Jesup area 'to open communications with the president of that republic, and act as circumstances might require.' Tyler apparently also 'ordered a naval force to Vera Cruz, to remain off that port, and prevent any naval expedition of Mexico' to Texas. A few weeks later, after news reached Austin that the Senate had rejected the annexation treaty, Mexican general Adrien Woll, whose headquarters were at Mier, informed Sam Houston that 'hostilities are reopened', citing violations of the armistice agreement by Texans. 'Notwithstanding my regret in thinking that blood is once more about to flow,' Woll wrote, 'the fortune of war cannot but be favorable to those who fight for their country against usurpers.'[9]

Woll's threat was serious, and in September of 1842 he captured San Antonio de Bexar – the westernmost outpost of the Republic of Texas. Joseph Milton Nance, an historian who wrote about the Frenchman turned Mexican general in the twentieth century, noted Texans generally 'respected' Woll for his 'gentlemanly conduct' if not his military abilities, and he was commander of the Army of the North when an armistice was signed on 15 February 1844. Writing to his negotiators before that agreement was reached, Houston asked them to present 'my salutations to General Woll, and assure him of my high appreciation of him as a soldier, and a gentleman; and express a desire on my part that our relations may never be less courteous than when we dined together at Col. Milton's in New Orleans.' Woll was also a loyal *Santanista* and knew the territory, and for that reason, Texan authorities and especially Houston were relieved when informed of potential US assistance given their disappointment after the senate rejection.[10]

'A poor passport to favor'

While the question of war and peace was being decided in the United States, Sentmanat was in New Orleans organizing an expedition consisting of a few dozen men to reclaim the kingdom of Tabasco stolen from him by General Ampudia. According to Terry Rugeley, Sentmanat recruited his young and inexperienced mercenaries in the wharf area of the port city by claiming he was working for the Mexican government to create a 'Texas style' colony of white settlers. At the moment of their departure, the *Picayune* reported the ship's decks 'were crowded with men of all nations, but principally Spaniards, and they were busy cleaning their muskets and other arms.' The article noted there were 'a few Americans among his men' and they were obviously not emigrants headed to Honduras – which was their cover story. The *Picayune* closed by saying, 'We shall soon learn the success of this bold enterprise.' Although the *Picayune* was sympathetic to Sentmanat's mission – as he had numerous friends in New Orleans – their informant and reporting was so diligent the information was in Santa Anna's hands before the expedition landed in Tabasco.[11]

After a few days at sea the filibusterers were forced to make a hasty landing near the coastal town of Chiltepec when fired on by a Mexican brig patrolling the coast. The *New York Herald* reported that the men 'jumped overboard on the beach' while their ship, the *William A. Turner* of New Orleans, was racked with grapeshot until it sank. As a result, Sentmanat and his mostly Spanish fighters 'brought away nothing but what they stood in.' A few days later, General Ampudia, who had remained there as governor after the failed invasion of Yucatan, met and crushed the small force at Jalpa on 10 June. A handful of the expedition's men were captured, but Sentmanat escaped into the forest, eluding Ampudia for two days before being caught. On 12 June he was lined up with the remainder of his men and shot. The US Consul in Campeche, John F. McGregor, was one of the first to be notified of the expedition's failure and forwarded to Washington a flyer he had received deploring the treatment of Sentmanat. The authors did not lament the death of Sentmanat, who they asserted had no 'prestige among us' and who 'did not profess any principles' – they protested, instead, the fact that Sentmanat's body was strapped to a horse, taken to San Juan Bautista, 'exposed to public scrutiny for three days, his head cut off by the hand of a criminal and fried in oil' and then displayed atop a pole in the Plaza de Armas. Such 'savage' treatment was a violation of all accepted norms. The anonymous authors conceded that Sentmanat had to be executed, but the mutilation of his body stained their image as Mexicans:

> That the barbarians of the Middle Ages: that the Hottentots and Caribs had proceeded in this way ... but some Mexicans offer us in the year 1844 such a frightful scene ... Who are the filthy executioners who have thus dishonored the Mexican name? Wretched! Undoubtedly they were not born in Mexico nor have they been nourished with the substance that a magnanimous and generous nation produces ... do not confuse patriotism with ferocity, nor men with beasts.[12]

Santa Anna would probably have condoned Ampudia's decision to have Sentmanat shot, but what was done to his corpse caused a stir. Predictably there were denials, until the *Picayune* confirmed that indeed 'his head was severed from his body and boiled in oil.' The Spanish and French consuls in Tabasco filed protests, and Ampudia – who apparently expressed 'surprise at the remonstrances' – was summoned back to Veracruz. 'Boiling men's heads in oil would be a poor passport to favor at any other court than Santa's Anna's,' the *Picayune* morbidly jested, but noted Santa Anna 'utterly disavows the act' and had had Sentmanat's remains sent back to New Orleans for a proper burial. The Louisville *Morning Courier* took a more neutral stance against the 'impudent, foolhardy, wild, and unwarranted expedition' and Sentmanat's fate: 'Whilst we protest against the laborious cruelty practiced by the Mexicans, we are of necessity compelled to look at the circumstances ... Thus ends one of the wildest, most hair-brained [*sic*] adventures of modern times.'[13]

While Sentmanat's execution did not affect the outcome of the presidential election, it did nothing to improve the image Americans had of Mexicans going into the remaining months of the presidential contest. According to the *Evening Post*, Mexican sailors were being treated so poorly in the port of New York that the Mexican consul general there, Juan de la Granja, filed a complaint. 'We fear from his statement,' the *Post*'s report read, 'that the behavior of some of our countrymen towards them has been grossly and shamefully violent.' This behaviour was partly inspired by numerous articles appearing in New York newspapers in June prior to the arrival of the Mexican war steamers *Guadalupe* and *Montezuma*, both of which took part in the battle with the Texas Navy at Campeche and were built by the British for the Yucatan campaign. Below one report on their arrival appeared a short article: 'Rats. – If they are troublesome sprinkle unslaked lime in their holes and about where they congregate, and they will depart without fail.' The *Buffalo Daily Gazette* was less subtle about the visit: 'So, Mexico, with whom we are on the verge of war, is sending her vessels to New York, to be repaired and armed and equipped, so as to be more efficient against us!' The pro-Polk newspaper argued that the visit 'overthrows all the blustering of the opponents of annexation about plunging the nation into a war,' and claimed that repairing them was treasonous.[14]

'Equally menacing to all'

On 3 December, with the election of Polk confirmed, President John Tyler sent a message to Congress outlining affairs between Texas and Mexico and grievances causing 'injury to the United States'. Tyler accused Mexico of attempting to 'renew the war' and asserted that such a conflict would involve the United States. 'The war would thus be endless,' he wrote, adding that the 'great popular election which has just terminated afforded the best opportunity of ascertaining the will of the states and people upon it.' A week later, a joint resolution for annexation was introduced to Congress, and on 18 December Tyler submitted another message warning Mexico not to interfere in US affairs by provoking war and '[regressing] to a period of barbarism … of which the late inhuman massacre at Tabasco was but a precursor.' Tyler also cited the 1836 execution of James Walker Fannin and 400 other Texans at Goliad after his surrender to Mexicans and further absolved the US of the consequences of annexation. If Mexico 'shall aggravate the injustice of her conduct by a declaration of war against them,' he wrote, 'upon her head will rest all the responsibility.'[15]

Sabre-rattling by the US president obviously portended conflict, but the situation was further exacerbated by domestic turmoil in Mexico. In the summer of 1844 Santa Anna's wife died, and a power vacuum developed in the capital when he temporarily stepped down to settle personal affairs. Jose Joaquin de Herrera assumed the presidency for a period of less than two weeks before Valentin Canalizo, a former supporter of the ousted president Bustamante and friend of Santa Anna, became interim president. Adding to the chaos, at the end of October, Mariano Paredes, who was still fuming after being pushed aside by Santa Anna in the 1841/2 coup installing the junta, launched a revolt in the city of Guadalajara prompting Santa Anna's return. Santa Anna suppressed the rebellion, but by November the political repercussions of the revolt had spread to the capital and Canalizo attempted to control events by suspending Congress. When the public turned against him, Canalizo negotiated a settlement with Herrera and a handful of deputies in exchange for leniency. On 6 December Herrera reassumed the presidency. Historian Will Fowler writes that during this chaotic episode Santa Anna was more than happy to allow Canalizo to take the fall, since the memory of the 1842 coup was still on the minds of most Mexicans. Nor would it be the last time a coup effected a change in leadership, as Herrera was ousted on the eve of the war with the US after rumours surfaced that he was negotiating with the Americans to resolve the Texas crisis.[16]

In early 1845 Mexico officially severed diplomatic relations with the United States. Most observers viewed the move as a prelude to wider hostilities, but the British were still advocating Texan independence and Mexican recognition. Lord Aberdeen wrote to Charles Elliot, the British chargé d'affaires in Texas, 'that the continuance of Texas as an independent power, under its own laws and institutions, must conduce to a more even, and therefore a more permanent, balance of interests in the North American continent.' Aberdeen's admission concerning Texan 'institutions' demonstrated the British willingness to turn a blind eye to slavery if it meant checking the expansionist ambitions of the incoming administration. The concession came too late, however. By the end of March, the annexation resolution had passed, and incensed Mexican authorities, responding also to public anxiety over the loss of their northern department, were obligated to send troops north. Luis Gonzaga Cuevas, the Minister of Foreign Relations who also negotiated the treaty ending the war, submitted a *Memoria* to the Mexican assembly indicating that even though 'the independence of Texas perhaps would not make necessary a war with the American republic; from its annexation, this must inevitably result.'[17]

A last-minute effort by the British and French to prevent annexation also proved futile, despite the hope that an accommodation could be reached. If Texas could be persuaded to remain independent – contingent upon official recognition of independence from Mexico – then annexation, and thus a wider war, could be avoided. This was the strategy British diplomats employed in April and May of 1845, cautioned by Aberdeen to not rupture Anglo-American relations in the process. Writing in 1910, the historian Ephraim Douglas Adams noted that Aberdeen instructed Elliot to 'act with the greatest care, always remembering that friendly relations with the United States were to be maintained at any cost.' When Elliot believed he had secured certain conditions from the Texan government to delay annexation if Mexico agreed to peace, he set out for Mexico to attempt to convince Cuevas. His means of getting there, however, aroused suspicion. Elliot left Texas on HMS *Electra* destined for Charleston, and then, once offshore, transferred to HMS *Eurydice* headed for Veracruz, from where he travelled to Mexico City. French ministers in Texas and Mexico were also supportive of the plan.[18]

Mexican officials received Elliot and considered his proposal, and Cuevas tentatively affirmed the agreement. However, due to heated opposition from Mexican leadership, more than two weeks passed before an official signature was attached to the document that Elliot needed to secretly convey back to Texas. On 23 May Elliot left Mexico City, but by that time, rumours of the nature of his mission were known to the public. Adams wrote: 'When the report of the Mexican mission appeared in the public press of the United States it aroused the greatest indignation, as might have been expected.' Moreover, Elliot's mission, and the manner in which he carried it out, confirmed the suspicions of expansionists who had constantly asserted the existence of British designs to interfere in annexation. 'Here was a capital opportunity to charge Great Britain with "secret" designs, it being known that Elliot had had a "secret" part in it'. According to Adams, Aberdeen 'resented the secrecy and mystery that clothed' Elliot's mission to Mexico, because it contravened British tradition of conducting diplomatic affairs in a transparent manner. Nevertheless, the damage to relations had been done as annexation became a foregone conclusion and Texas opinion shifted decidedly towards incorporation.[19]

Americans now had reason to be agitated. 'There is little or no room to doubt that the English minister has performed the part of the go-between in the transaction,' the *Picayune* reported in late May. Although he knew of the mission, Texas President Anson Jones denied initiating it – the result being that American ire was directed at the British. The *Niles' National Register* quoted the *Picayune*'s summation of Elliot's anticipated arrival in Galveston, taunting them by claiming 'they little dream of their reception at Galveston.' For expansionists, war was on the horizon, and there were few obstacles left to prevent it. 'These people ... think that the acknowledgment of Texas independence will prevent annexation,' the article proffered, 'and thereby they will get clear of declaring war, as they had threatened. They swear, however, that if Texas prefers annexation to acknowledgement, they will declare war.'[20]

Washington's *Daily Union*, an Anglophobic Democrat publication and the incoming administration's mouthpiece in the capital, responded to commentary from *The Times* regarding their characterization of annexation as being akin to 'the crown robbers who affected the partition of Poland.' Included with a history lesson chiding 'John Bull' for interfering with annexation, the *Union* conjured plausible but imagined schemes regarding

British intentions and praised Texas for avoiding the 'meshes of the great British net'. Texas, the Democrats proclaimed, was finally where it belonged, and 'her hope and her destiny were here with us – and now she is ours.' With the acquisition secured, expansionists were free to focus elsewhere. 'It is a sad mishap to England ... Strange, indeed, that the 'Times' should charge us with the desire of acquiring California, when the eager eye of England herself is even now anxiously fixed upon the same country.' The *Union* echoed the belief held by Americans that the British, who already possessed territory on the Pacific coast, and even attempted to annex Hawaii in 1843, were looking to acquire California. 'No wonder that the "leading journal" seeks to rouse up Great Britain to participate in this hypothetical war with Mexico,' they lectured their readers confidently, 'or to anticipate us in the occupation of the goodly ports of the Pacific ... we have the means of taking California, in case of war, without sending our troops around Cape Horn.'[21]

The British were not the only recipients of Democrat contempt and conspiratorial projection. The French were long accused of being co-accomplices in the Anglo-French *entente cordiale* – whose perceived goals (from an American perspective) included limiting US expansion vis-à-vis Texas and preventing war with Mexico. As the most vocal proponent of the 'balance of power' strategy, French Foreign Minister François Guizot was particularly resented by Democrats incapable of restraining themselves from gloating over their victory:

> Our unparalleled growth, our vast maritime strength, and, above all, our extension of the great principles of free government, render us obnoxious to every sovereign, every minister in Europe – whether the limited monarchy of England, the military system of France, or the relentless despotism of Russia: our success is equally menacing to all. Here are daily growing and spreading the doctrines that must ultimately prove fatal to the oligarchs of the Old World.[22]

Given their capabilities and the geographic proximity of their empire to US interests, the British caused American expansionists much more anxiety than the French. In that regard, the Democrats were eager to perceive European machinations and monarchical revanchism in events surrounding the war. Some of this paranoia, however, was not totally unfounded, given ties between Mexican monarchists and Europeans, and later, as the war progressed, the arrival of Spanish Carlist guerrillas from France who attacked General Winfield Scott's logistics line between Veracruz and Mexico City. The actions appeared coordinated and were proof enough to cast suspicion on European agents who expansionists believed were aiming to control the outcome of the war. For that reason, one of the most effective and persuasive arguments was that if the United States did not seize whatever territory it could, then surely Great Britain or France would. This argument played an important role in American deliberations regarding Yucatan in 1848, which was embroiled in a major crisis caused by the opening of the Caste War. Next to the editorial haranguing of the French appeared another piece entitled 'Territorial Aggrandizement'. The editorial cited John Louis O'Sullivan's New York *Democratic Review* claiming that 'at no distant day the rebellion, revolution, and independence of provinces of Mexico' such as 'Chihuahua, New Mexico, California, and Yucatan' would 'doubtless follow the example of Texas, and ask for admission into our union.'[23]

In his 1966 work, *The Monroe Doctrine and American Expansionism*, the historian Frederick Merk noted that expansionist sentiment, coupled with similar protests against British and French efforts in Texas, was articulated in Polk's inaugural address to Congress in early December 1845, when he referred to the 'magic phrase "balance of power"' three separate times in his message. 'We may rejoice that the tranquil and pervading influence of the American principle of self-government was sufficient to defeat the purposes of British and French interference,' Polk stated, reiterating the common theme that 'our rising greatness as a nation, [is] attracting the attention of the powers of Europe; and lately the doctrine has been broached in some of them, of a "balance of power" on this continent, to check our advancement.' In essence, the threat of European meddling was a more powerful and persuasive slogan demanding prompt action than the ambiguous and belated phrase 'manifest destiny'.[24]

Yucatecan Independence and *casus belli*

On 1 January 1846, roughly four months before the war began, the Yucatan Assembly issued a decree proclaiming their independence from the central government. 'Yucatan will not, under any title, recognize the government established in Mexico or to be established hereafter, whatever principle it proclaims or the denomination attributed to it.' More importantly, the pronouncements stated, 'Yucatán finds itself to request the protection of a foreign nation ... stipulating with the government of the United States the most perfect neutrality in the war that must arise between Mexico and that nation for the annexation of Texas.' Essentially, Yucatecans believed the war was inevitable, would not participate, and were positioning themselves to benefit from whatever outcome ensued. Observers in the US eagerly labelled the pronouncement 'another revolution' and hailed the peninsula as 'a separate republic.' Just as O'Sullivan's *Democratic Review* had predicted, it appeared that Yucatan was following in the footsteps of Texas.[25]

Later on, when the war was nearly at an end, Senator Sam Houston, who was arguing to send American soldiers to Yucatan and possibly annex it, repeated what he had believed to be true at the beginning of the conflict, that 'annexation did bring about the war. In fact, by the annexation, the United States adopted the war.' That was an opinion both Mexicans and Texans could agree upon. 'I had, however, hoped and believed that no Senator,' he said, 'upon reflection, and who had carefully examined the facts, could doubt that annexation was the cause, and the sole cause, of the war with Mexico.' According to Houston, annexation 'was declared by the Mexican functionaries that it would be considered a cause of war.' Moreover, the Mexicans had already become agitated after the US recognized Texan independence, and when the annexation treaty reached Congress, 'the Mexican minister declared, that if the treaty should be signed, he would regard it as a cause of war, and take his passports to leave the United States.' That event also occurred, Houston noted, as all events and actions pointed towards an inevitable collision and annexation 'regarded as a *casus belli*, and war would result. War has resulted.' Furthermore, the armistice agreed upon by Texas and Mexico was broken when discussions of incorporation were hastened, and when Mexican soldiers 'passed the boundary of Texas, and attacked the troops of the United States, thus continuing the war which had existed with Texas, and incorporated by annexation into the national affairs of the United States.' For that reason, there was no official declaration of war by Congress. Houston argued, 'In this case [a declaration of war] was useless. War had never ceased between Texas and Mexico, and Texas had then become a part of the United States, so that the war existing with one State of the Union, must, of necessity, involve the whole Union.' In essence, annexation was tantamount to initiating war with Mexico.[26]

Manifest Decision

The phrase 'manifest destiny' first appeared in the 1845 July-August issue of John L. O'Sullivan's *Democrat Review*, and its second and more prominent unveiling came on 27 December 1845, when it appeared in the New York *Morning News* in an article concerning Great Britain and issues relating to the Oregon Territory. By that time the presidential election had long been decided and the issue of annexation effectively settled pending formalities. In other words, the phrase played no role in either the election or the dispute the US inherited between Mexico and Texas. The term was not in existence when Texas and Yucatan broke away from Mexico, nor on the lips of sailors firing cannons at Mexican frigates in the Bay of Campeche in 1843. Sullivan's term held no significance to the men of the ill-fated expeditions that set out to Santa Fe, Mier or even Tabasco. The two words were not scrawled into the walls of prisons holding captured Texans, sung by adventurers who rushed to Texas when fighting began in 1835, nor whispered in the last breaths of Texians, Tejanos and Americans who died defending the Alamo. 'Manifest destiny' did not prompt the war but was rather a message that amplified previous statements by people such as Henry Foote, who as early as 1841 were claiming a 'glorious destiny' for Texas. The phrase cannot be professed to have helped launch the war because those decisions had already been made, and the war was already in existence. On 17 August 1845, about the same time that 'manifest destiny' first appeared in print, Colonel Henry Stanton, Assistant Quartermaster General, wrote a letter to Major Charles Thomas in Philadelphia. 'Your letter of yesterday,' he wrote, 'advising me of the shipment for New Orleans of the wagons and harness which you were requested to have made on the 16th ultimo, came to hand this morning. Whether Mexico has declared war or not, we may want more wagons in Texas.' Indeed, vote or no vote, a collision was already underway.[27]

Chapter 2

'War Exists'

Rumors foreshadowing war with Mexico now came thick and fast. They told of disputes on the frontier, of activity at arsenals and navy-yards, of movements of ships and troops toward the Southwest, of the massing of Mexican forces under General Ampudia. Stories of hostile encounters were circulated one day, to be contradicted the next. It was reported that ten thousand Mexicans were marching to the Rio Grande, that Americans were volunteering in New Orleans to meet them, and that regular troops were landing in Texas.[1]

William H. Seward, *An Autobiography*, 1877

There is little disagreement among historians on the controversial start of the war in the disputed borderlands in April of 1846, but what is generally misunderstood is that no constitutional declaration of war by Congress was invoked. Rather, on May 11 a vote was held in the House of Representatives and the following day in the Senate, in which those bodies essentially accepted Polk's assertions that 'war exists, and, notwithstanding all our efforts to avoid it, exists by the act of Mexico herself.' Included within that message was a reference to John Slidell's failure to secure a 'peace adjustment' by purchasing the disputed territory and a reiteration by Polk that he 'had ordered an efficient military force to meet a threatened invasion of Texas by Mexican forces, for which extensive military preparations have been made.' That force, under the command of General Zachary Taylor, was sent to Corpus Christi and stationed at the mouth of the Nueces River – in contested territory on the north and south banks. There was no mention of a pre-war clandestine mission to California or the naval build-up in preparation to control Mexican ports and the Gulf.[2]

By the time annexation took place in the spring of 1845 the US Navy's Home Squadron had already been patrolling the Gulf for several months, and the US Pacific Squadron, which required at least six months to round Cape Horn, was on its way at the end of March. In March 1846, on the eve of the war, US Navy Secretary George Bancroft could claim 'a great naval force' in the Pacific and that 'every port from San Francisco to Acapulco lies open to our ships.' Less than one month before fighting broke out in Texas, Bancroft wrote that in 'the Gulf of Mexico we have a still larger force; and our little army of occupation is advancing to the [Rio Bravo] Del Norte.' Indeed, despite all the talk of avoiding conflict and last-minute diplomatic efforts, the administration had prepared for war.[3]

Considering the threat of Mexican aggression against the recently annexed state of Texas, Polk's concrete steps in mobilizing US forces prior to the official start of the war have been interpreted differently. Some historians have defended the president, claiming his actions were prudent in the face of a potential invasion, while others have believed his motives were more Machiavellian and designed to provoke conflict. The third, overlooked, perspective is that Polk's pre-war decisions to bolster US forces at land and sea were simply the result of a belief that *de facto* war was in existence after annexation but that the political and constitutional process – which at the literal level meant an official declaration of war from Congress, and at the very minimum congressional approval (which is what occurred) – were required to legitimize the necessary major military campaigns and the funding required for them. In essence, the presidential victory by expansionists in late 1844 meant that many politicians were behind the times, and that indeed war existed. This is one reason it was so popular in its initial phase and why it was extremely difficult for Whig representatives from the anti-war north – particularly New England – to object to allocating resources for it. Eager volunteers from both the North and South enlisted for duty. Very few politicians, except for South Carolina's senator John C. Calhoun, took principled positions against the war claiming there was not enough information that 'war existed' and it was the constitutional duty of Congress to issue a declaration. However, for the former Texas president and senator of that new state, Sam Houston, the US had simply inherited an ongoing conflict of 'ten years' and war 'existed as perfect as it could be after a formal declaration or recognition of a state of war by the Congress of the United States.'[4]

On 17 September 1845, roughly six months before Congress gave its approval to launch an invasion, Polk called a 'special meeting' of cabinet members to discuss John Slidell's proposed peace mission and the steps Mexicans were apparently taking to prepare for conflict. In his diary, Polk noted that reports from New Orleans indicated that in late summer President

José Joaquin de Herrera 'had issued a circular to the army, through his Secretary of War, breathing a war spirit,' and the recent appointment of General Anastasio Bustamante to the position of commander of the Mexican Army. The following month, and *before* Polk sent instructions to envoy John Slidell to 'settle the pending difficulties between the two countries', the president 'held a confidential conversation' with Lieutenant Archibald H. Gillespie 'on the subject of a secret mission on which he was about to go to California'. In sum, Polk did not wait for Slidell to return before making other war preparations.[5]

In 1939 the historian Allan Nevins published a biography of American explorer and officer John C. Frémont, who was sent to California by Polk to conduct an exploratory expedition under the auspices of the War Department and to protect US interests in the event that California declared its independence. Nevins defended Frémont's pre-war actions, claiming that they resulted in the US acquiring California, and argued they were inspired partly by public threats emanating from Mexican officials, the severing of diplomatic relations, notifications to Mexican ministers in Paris and London and indications the Mexicans were mobilizing for war. He wrote that Mexican reaction to annexation in July 1845 caused 'a burst of passion [that] shook the higher circles of the republic. "Union or war!" was the watchword enunciated by various newspapers.' Mexican reports were widely distributed in US newspapers. With war hysteria in the public sphere, Frémont's efforts to wrest California from Mexican hands, which Frémont later defended, were ostensibly sanctioned by US authorities whose chief concern was British and French designs on the territory. Nevins added that new 'guns were mounted at Vera Cruz and the fortress prepared for an attack; munitions and provisions were accumulated at Matamoras on the northern border; from many points came news of the mustering of troops.' Even anti-annexationists like William H. Seward were inclined to believe war inevitable and wrote to Thurlow Weed, a prominent New York publisher, that 'The papers seem to foreshadow war with Mexico … The people had war with Mexico before them, in the election last fall. We thought best to avoid it, but they are supreme; and the battle must be fought with all our energies.' Frémont was court-martialled for his conduct – which absolved administration officials of wrongdoing – but his dishonourable discharge was commuted by Polk because his actions resulted in California falling into American hands – exactly the outcome that Polk desired.[6]

Although obtaining California was a key administration objective, it was a minor theatre of war compared to what was required in the Gulf of Mexico. Fortunately for war planners, in the early 1840s American authorities saw a need to expand and update the capabilities of the US Navy – particularly after the British attempted to annex the Hawaiian Islands in 1843. In Congress, former president John Quincy Adams advocated the creation of a naval base at Pensacola in the 1820s and worked with Virginian Abel P. Upshur, Secretary of the Navy from 1841 until his tragic death in 1844 on the Potomac during a firing demonstration aboard the USS *Princeton*. Upshur reorganized and streamlined the service, wanted to enlarge the fleet to at least 50 per cent of the Royal Navy, and made several other notable changes such as creating various bureaus dealing with naval yards, docks, equipment, and repairs. Therefore improvements made on the eve of the Mexican-American War took on added significance when Polk put the service on a war footing – turning what was essentially the legacy service of the War of 1812 into something more modern.[7]

Pre-war reforms ensured a robust capability during the war, but arguably their most important consequence was the ability to man the numerous vessels procured for the squadron after 1846 with educated and competent naval officers. This need arose from the obvious fact the United States Navy needed to be reinforced to complete its Gulf operations – particularly the large joint-force amphibious landing at Veracruz in 1847. At the beginning of the war in 1846 the Home Squadron consisted of seven gunboats and three steamers – a total of ten vessels – but by 1847 that number had risen to sixteen: six gunboats, five steamers and five bomb-vessels fitted with mortars to bombard fortifications on land. Many of the ships added to the fleet were purchased in New York City.[8]

Coinciding with an updated and expanded navy was a re-evaluation of traditional offensive strategies. Generally known for his role as commanding general during the Civil War, a younger Henry Halleck was sent to Europe in 1844 by Winfield Scott to study Napoleon's war in Spain and returned believing a smaller and more disciplined force would offset the logistical requirements of a larger army. Scott concurred, and when the enemy refused to acquiesce after Taylor's 1846 victories in northern Mexico at Palo Alto and Monterrey, it was decided an amphibious assault on Veracruz and capture of the capital was the best approach to victory.

An amphibious assault not only afforded the invaders an element of strategic 'surprise' (which will be discussed), but allowed the US Army to avoid moving men and material through one of the most arid regions of Mexico. Halleck outlined this expeditionary strategy in his 1846 *Military Art and Science*: 'The proper duty of our navy is not coast or river defense; it has a more glorious sphere – that of the offensive.' A formidable Mexican navy did not exist, and thus US logistics – albeit stretched to a certain extent – would not have to deal with the interruptions that plagued Napoleon's forces in Spain when his supply lines extended from the extreme north to the coastal stronghold of Cadiz. Moreover, if the campaign succeeded, others, such as the British, would be forced to consider coastal invasions as a threat. Essentially this was the same reason the British were feared by their enemies, and Halleck understood that because the work he had completed preceding *Military Art and Science* was devoted to coastal defence. In 1846, he outlined his vision with a retrospective analysis of the US Navy's role in the War of 1812. 'In our last war, instead of lying in harbor ... they scattered themselves over the wide surface of the ocean, penetrated the most remote seas.' In his opinion, offensive operations 'rendered benefits a thousand-fold greater, to say nothing of the glory they acquired for the nation, and the character they imparted to it, than any that would have resulted from a state of passiveness within the harbors.' Therefore, going forward, the US Navy, which had become a permanent federal institution supported by the national government, had a new role to play:

> Confident that this is the true policy as regards to employment of the navy proper, we doubt not that it will in the future be acted on, as it has been in the past; and that the results, as regards both honor and advantage, will be expanded commensurately with its own enlargement. In order, however, that the navy may always assume and maintain that active and energetic deportment, in offensive operations. [9]

Blockade, Belligerence and Blank Certificates

A year of US naval operations in the Gulf preceded Winfield Scott's landing at Veracruz. The principal objective of those operations was the blockade of Mexican ports, some of which were seized early in the war. The operation was commanded by Commodore David Conner, who established the Home

Squadron's naval base directly south of Veracruz at Anton Lizardo on 14 May 1846 – two days after Congress officially sanctioned the war. Twenty kilometres from Veracruz and separated from Mexico's main port by the Rio Jamapa, Anton Lizardo was a good location to intercept ships leaving Veracruz, which was protected by the sixteenth-century island castle of San Juan de Ulúa. During the Pastry War the French captured the fort after considerable bombardment but did not hold it long due to supply problems, disease and cannon fire emanating from the massive walls of Veracruz. For that reason, US war planners decided to avoid similar mistakes by using Anton Lizardo as a base to control Mexico's main port.

Raphael Semmes, a naval officer who later made life extremely difficult for the Union Navy in the Civil War due to his successful raiding, spent much of his time at Anton Lizardo in 1846 and chronicled his experience in his 1851 work, *Service afloat and ashore during the Mexican War*. Although Semmes may have agreed with Halleck on expanding the Navy's role in offensive operations, the 'glorious sphere' of his service did not materialize until several months into the conflict. Much of 1846 was viewed by sailors and observers back home as lacking the anticipated romantic grandeur of past conflicts – particularly those of the Napoleonic Wars. Semmes commented that 'our belligerent fellow-citizens, many of whom supposed a ship to be little other than a high-pressure western steamboat, expected us to lay waste the whole of the enemy's coast, by fire and sword.' He also explained that lethargic sailors eager for the din of battle were 'annoyed' by impatient newspapers 'which ought to have been capable of appreciating the true state of things ... and were disposed to pass censure upon us.' Furthermore, 'natural obstacles' in Gulf geography prevented direct engagement – as dozens of coastal Mexican towns 'were more effectually defended by reefs, sand-bars, and shallows, than were his inland towns by redoubts and intrenchments.' At any rate, most of the fighting in 1846 occurred in the northern theatre where Taylor was in command, but the American press – which romanticized the conflict in several ways – wanted cannon fire and beaches stormed to accompany America's first foreign war. Unsurprisingly, Scott also received criticism for the lack of bloodshed when the US Army laid siege to Veracruz in 1847. Despite the criticism, Semmes wrote that the navy 'continued to perform its arduous and thankless duties.'[10]

Particularly relevant to Semmes's assessment was a demand the US Navy 'adopt a much more enlarged and liberal policy' to prosecute the war.

Comparisons with the British and French navies were commonly drawn, but what may have annoyed American sailors was the comment from critics that the effort amounted to a 'paper blockade' – a critique put forth by *The Sun* of Baltimore: 'Our navy is not at all commensurate to the interests, dignity and character of the nation,' *The Sun* opined, 'and it is inadequate even to the Mexican war. Were it not so, there is good reason to believe that the war might have ended by this time.' The term 'paper blockade' was cited among the war's Whig detractors who were re-debating the War of 1812 and haranguing the navy for not reaching the level of the British – especially along the extensive western coast of the continent. 'Paper blockades are obsolete; they belong to another time,' the *Richmond Daily Whig* chided. 'Does he intend still farther to imitate the British policy ... ? Or is this proclamation mere *brutum fulmen*?'[11]

Another issue arising from the blockade was the question of privateers. Since the Mexican Navy could not oppose US forces directly they attempted to mount a maritime resistance by issuing 'letters of marque' – a legal form of wartime piracy dating back hundreds of years. Semmes commented that when President Mariano Salas succeeded Paredes he made 'strenuous efforts to get afloat a number of privateers, which should prey upon our commerce'. He also added that such a 'system of predatory warfare, more than any other, equalizes the strength of nations on the water. Fleets and heavy-armed ships are of no avail against the lighter heels and more erratic wanderings of this description of force.' Semmes understood the advantages lighter and faster vessels had over larger ones, and during the Civil War he raided US commerce aboard the converted mail ship and merchant steamer CSS *Sumter*. That ship breached Union blockades, took more than a dozen merchant ships in the Caribbean and Atlantic and constantly outran her pursuers. In 1851 he noted this 'incalculable injury' was prevented in the Gulf because Mexico was not a maritime country. Nevertheless, Salas attempted to circumvent that problem by creating a 'monstrous doctrine' of issuing 'blank certificates of naturalization to the Mexican consuls at Havana and other places, with directions to those officers to fill them up with the names of any adventurers that might offer.'[12]

Cuba was at the centre of the maritime region connecting the Gulf of Mexico to the Atlantic and was one of those places where young men landed looking for work and opportunity. It was part of the Spanish empire, wealthy, active and in constant connection with the other principal Gulf ports – as demonstrated by Sentmanat's failed filibuster from New Orleans. Havana was already a capital of intrigue before the war, but the blockade made it especially so. In June 1846 the *Picayune* reported the famed *Guadalupe* and *Montezuma* had sailed to Havana from Alvarado 'under the English flag.' The newspaper cited rumours, based on reports appearing in Veracruz newspapers the previous month, that Mexican officials were urging the issue of 'letters of marque against our commerce'. It further suggested that 'the present Mexican vessels of war may far better be engaged in privateering than in any other service, or than in lying idle, liable to constant attack.'[13]

The US diplomat in Havana was Robert Blair Campbell. A South Carolinian who served in the War of 1812, Campbell held office as a state senator and representative in the US Congress before being appointed to Havana in 1842 after Nicholas Trist was recalled. On 3 June Campbell informed Buchanan that the 'steamers formerly Mexican' were indeed in Havana 'under the English flag as private property ... and could not leave this port under their former character.' The Mexicans had evidently made arrangements with someone from Great Britain to prevent the seizure (or sinking) of their two best vessels. As to the letters of marque, on 10 November Campbell wrote to Buchanan that he had received a package of material from an informant based in Veracruz. Campbell explained that the informant was normally in communication with Commodore Conner but 'suspicions attaching to him' forced him to relay through Havana the information confirming the existence of Salas's citizenship and privateering initiative. In addition to providing a translation of the 'form of the act of naturalization of a foreigner in Mexico' dated 10 September, Campbell attached another translation of a 'passport of navigation' form outlining 'the provision of the regulations for privateers, issued September 24, 1846.' Despite these developments, Campbell was confident the Spanish would not assist the Mexicans in their efforts to contest US naval supremacy in the Gulf, concluding that 'no privateer will sail out of the port of Havana and I do not believe there will be one from any port on this island.' Ultimately, although the Mexican effort to enlist privateers in the Gulf failed to coalesce, Polk publicly mentioned Campbell's report in his message to Congress on 8 December. He also stated that his initial concern over privateering extended beyond Cuba, and included Puerto Rico, but that he had 'received assurances' from the Spanish that they would prevent 'any attempts to fit out privateers in those islands against the United States.'[14]

First Battle of Tabasco, Yucatecan Factions, and Fandangos

While Veracruz and Havana remained under watchful eyes, Tabasco became the focus of attention. After Taylor's major victory against Ampudia at the three-day Battle of Monterrey ending on 24 September 1846, many sailors and Marines, concerned the war would end prematurely, were eager for heroics. In addition, the aborted naval action against the coastal town of Alvarado near Veracruz on 16 October intensified the thirst to establish a wartime legacy. Tabasco held little importance in the larger military situation facing the US Army in the north, and Americans were hoping it would remain neutral, but if it decided to separate itself from Mexico (like Yucatan), the resulting border, ostensibly along the Isthmus of Tehuantepec separating Mexico from the south-east, would produce a new dynamic. The Mexicans understood this problem in their ongoing effort to 'Mexicanize' independent-minded provinces before and during the war, which is why Ampudia left the state in the able hands of *Santanista* and Yucatecan Colonel Juan Bautista Traconis. Like Santa Anna, Traconis was a military officer and nationalist uninterested in the niceties of political ideology. He participated in Santa Anna's invasion of Texas in 1835, battled the French in 1838, fought fellow Yucatecans in the early 1840s campaign and even managed to hasten to assist Santa Anna's defence of Chapultepec Castle in September of 1847 before the US Army seized Mexico City. Always willing to fight, Traconis was an excellent substitute for Ampudia.[15]

The officer who tested Traconis in Tabasco was Commodore Matthew C. Perry. Better known for his expeditions to Japan in the 1850s, Perry was anxious to get into the war and was later slated to replace Commodore Conner. One of his early biographers, William E. Griffis, wrote that in February of 1846 Perry 'received information from Mexico which satisfied him that war was inevitable, and that he would soon be in the land of the cactus, the eagle, and the serpent.' He applied for duty, received orders to command the recently built steamers *Vixen* and *Spitfire*, and was ordered to Veracruz. Incidentally, both vessels had been constructed in New York for the Mexican Navy, but were purchased by the government when hostilities commenced. In addition, Griffis stated, 'the Gulf or Home squadron was divided' at the time due to criticism of Conner's inability to overcome the coastal environment making it difficult for sailing vessels to launch attacks against Mexican ports. Although Perry and Conner were of similar age,

Perry represented a new generation of naval officers educated at the Sandy Hook School of Gunnery in New Jersey – which produced the US Navy's first corps of engineers. Griffis wrote that those officers 'were eager to serve under their former instructor' and knew the steamers were of lighter draught than the sails and more likely to see action in places such as Tabasco. For that reason, when Perry arrived in the Gulf in late September, Conner was in 'charge of the sail, and Perry of the steam vessels.'[16]

In the nineteenth century, Americans familiar with Tabasco referred to the river winding more than 70 kilometres to the capital as the 'Tabasco River.' To Mexicans it was known and remains the Grijalva – named after Juan de Grijalva, one of the first conquistadors to explore the Mexican coastline in the early sixteenth century. Today the geography is essentially the same, apart from dredging and added irrigation canals feeding Tabasco's rich agricultural land. Albeit on a vastly smaller scale, the river system in many ways resembles the Amazon, is prone to flooding and is fed by numerous tributaries that snake in and out of hundreds of lagoons of various sizes. At the entrance to this riverine labyrinth lies the near-coastal town of Frontera, which is where the US Consul was located due to passing commerce destined for or leaving the capital. On 30 June, after news of the war's outbreak reached Tabasco, Mexican officials closed the US office in Frontera. Despite the closure, on 12 July the consul there by the name of E. Porter sent a dispatch informing US officials that a local steamship named *Petrita* had taken about 150 men from San Juan Bautista until they reached 'a place called Pueblo Nuevo', after which 'they were to march about forty-five miles into the interior to suppress an insurrection which … is general through the whole southern part of the Republic.'[17]

The information would have been useful to Buchanan and Perry. US authorities were extremely interested in obtaining transit rights over the isthmus – this was, among other things, a *sine qua non* in negotiation of the treaty ending the war. An insurrection there had the potential to upset the delicate political equation in southern Mexico. How did E. Porter manage to obtain so much information from the *Petrita*'s captain? According to the Mexican War and naval historian Karl Jack Bauer, the *Petrita* and another ship called the *Tabasqueño* were owned by Luis S. Hargous, a wealthy merchant who 'held a monopoly of steam navigation on the Grijalva'. In 1842 Hargous was appointed Mexican consul for the port of New York – a fact only relevant in understanding how the *Petrita*'s captain, a Mr. Hinckley of

New York, managed to feed Americans essential information about Mexico at least as early as 1843 while running routes to various Gulf ports. The fast screw steamer was trusted with official envoys from Mexico, carried news to the *Picayune* via Veracruz and Tabasco, provided vital reconnaissance before the siege of Veracruz and, as will be discussed, stowed a handful of escaped Texan prisoners of war from Veracruz to New Orleans in 1844. In essence, for years Captain Hinckley assisted US and Texan interests in the Gulf. With that in mind, it is no surprise the *Petrita* was enlisted by Perry to help navigate the maze-like waterway between Frontera and San Juan Bautista in a confrontation known as the First Battle of Tabasco. Bauer notes the *Petrita* was 'seized' when Perry landed a garrison at Frontera, but that action was likely a ruse to protect the captain given his willingness to help the Americans, and the fact that, of all places, the ship was conveniently docked there when Perry's seven-vessel fleet arrived on 23 October. Griffis wrote: 'Two river steamers, which plied between the city and port, Tabasco and Frontera, were lying at the wharf ... One had steam up and the supper-table spread. After these had been captured by cutting out parties, the captors enjoyed the hot supper.' One can imagine which vessel provided the 'hot supper'.[18]

Word of Perry's arrival spread quickly. The following day, just as the Americans appeared downstream from San Juan Bautista, Traconis issued a defiant pronouncement declaring the city to be 'in a state of siege.' Civilians were encouraged to take up arms to repel the invaders who were 'heading to this capital with the purpose of harassing it' and warned that anyone 'who directly or indirectly provides assistance to the enemy ... will be judged as a traitor.' Writing in the early twentieth century, Mexican War historian Justin H. Smith believed Perry 'blundered' by prematurely asking for the town's surrender – a gesture abruptly refused by Traconis, who played 'the fearless patriot'. Soon after, Perry's cannons concentrated their fire on the Mexican flag atop the city's fort. When the flag fell, it was mistakenly believed Traconis had surrendered. Griffis wrote that Perry used his soldiers 'while their war-blood was hot' and ordered Captain French Forrest and two hundred men, including a few dozen Marines, to seize the fort; but they were unaware that Traconis had positioned his forces outside the centre of the city to shoot at the Americans 'from the chapparal' as they approached. At that point, Perry realized he was undermanned, had underestimated the resolve of the Tabascans and Traconis 'and the risk too great for the prize.' As evening fell, he prudently returned to Frontera with a handful of vessels seized from San Juan Bautista. Despite the skirmishing, only two Americans and five Mexicans were killed. Traconis took the opportunity to declare a righteous victory against the invaders who 'came to the gates of this capital' and fled 'in terror due to your perseverance and the heroic courage that you have manifested.' The gloating, however, may have played a role in Perry's 1847 return with a larger force.[19]

The assault on Tabasco was inglorious but it did open a fissure between the state and the government in Mexico City. Just as Yucatecan leaders in Merida were thinking about returning to the central government, the Traconis regime was issuing statements outlining their disgust at national officials and President Salas, who 'abandoned the state and its garrison' before Perry's arrival. As a result of 'having refused' to provide assistance, Tabascan officials proclaimed 'the separation of this state from the obedience of the Mexican government.' In reality, there was little federal forces could do, given that their main priority was defeating the larger army threatening northern Mexico and San Luis Potosi, the lucrative mining state south of Monterrey. For that reason, when Santa Anna returned to Mexico from exile in Cuba vowing to rescue the country from becoming 'the prey of Anglo-American ambition', Yucatan issued a pronouncement supporting Santa Anna's 'vigorous patriotism, and … strong feelings in favor of Yucatán' – believing the 1843 agreement with Quintana Roo would be realized.[20]

Yucatan was attempting to placate both sides. One example of this occurred in a message from Pedro Manuel de Regil Estrada, a wealthy merchant in Merida, to US Secretary of State Buchanan. On 25 October, when news of Perry's arrival in Tabasco reached Merida, Regil Estrada sent Buchanan a letter stating he 'had a conference' with Governor Barbachano and came away from it concluding Yucatan was in a 'perfectly neutral position with respect to the unfortunate conflict between Mexico and the United States'. Regil Estrada, whose business was stalled due to the blockade, also informed Buchanan of the difficult 'political position' of Yucatan. However, what was translated into English at the US Consulate in the port of Sisal was worded entirely different, said nothing nuanced about Yucatecan neutrality and specifically indicated 'the Mexican government has recognized the stipulations signed in Mexico on the 14th December 1843.' Moreover, the dubious translation claimed, 'Yucatan is bound to reannex herself to the Mexican Republic' – another statement added entirely at the translator's discretion. The US State Department likely did not notice the discrepancy given that the administration believed Yucatan had indeed forgone its neutrality and returned to the side of the enemy, but it provides evidence of the difficult position facing Yucatecan officials and was one of the main reasons why Yucatan split into two separate factions – one led from Merida and the other from Campeche.[21]

Another reason for the split between Yucatan's two main cities was the US Navy's seizure of the nearby port of Carmen. Located nearly equidistant from San Juan Bautista and Campeche, Ciudad de Carmen – often referred to as 'Laguna' del Carmen due to its location on an island fronting the large Laguna de Términos – was one of the most hospitable places in the gulf for US sailors. Many histories cite late December of 1846 as the point at which Perry seized Laguna, but Semmes, whose work appeared in 1851, claimed Perry 'was dispatched' to the port shortly following his arrival – an episode that appears chronologically in his work before the expedition to Tabasco. The reality is more complicated and partly illuminated by wartime reports from the US Consul there, Eneas McFaul Jr., whose office remained open during the war. While in New York in May, and before returning to his post, McFaul reiterated to Buchanan 'the importance of the Carmen Island' and how the Yucatecans were 'earnest in throwing off the yoke of the central government and are determined to invoke the aid of the United States'. When Eneas returned to Laguna in September he informed US officials that the USS *Somers*, captained by Commander Duncan N. Ingraham, visited the port in July, and that in early September the USS *Porpoise*, captained by Lieutenant William Hunt, 'came inside the bar to town demonstrating the safety of the harbor, which will, I trust induce other vessels to visit this place frequently.' Their reason for visiting was to purchase 'supplies' and 'fresh provisions for the squadron'. Semmes later wrote of Laguna:

> This being the first maritime town captured on the gulf, its possession was of considerable importance to us, as it enabled us to draw hence, for the use of the squadron, beef-cattle, fruits, vegetables, and other anti-scorbutics, of which we had long felt the want. Everything was paid for at its full value, and Laguna, in a short time, became more flourishing, under our rule, than it had ever been before.[22]

In his 1896 work, *The Home squadron under Commodore Conner*, Philip Syng Physick Conner, the son of Commodore Conner, interested in protecting his father's wartime legacy, specifically pointed out Semmes' apparent 'errors' in his work regarding his claim that Laguna was the first maritime town captured by arguing the 'expedition to Laguna [was] made to appear as having preceded those to Tabasco and Tampico' and that 'Tampico was occupied in advance' when Conner took that port on 14 November 1846. However, given the statement made by McFaul about the visits by the *Somers* and *Porpoise* in July and September, respectively, it appears that Semmes' assertion was not entirely inaccurate. While Laguna may not have been officially under US occupation at the time, the Navy had obviously developed an amicable working relationship with the port prior to Conner's seizure of Tampico. The fact that officials at Laguna left the US office open is evidence enough of their feelings regarding Americans.[23]

Mexican historian María Cecilia Zuleta Miranda believes American interest in Laguna 'is explained not only for military-defensive reasons, but also strategic and commercial' realities. This assertion is based on the port's 'access gates to the Isthmus of Tehuantepec' and its use as a centre for smuggling. In essence, the US Navy purchased what it needed and in exchange turned a blind eye to Yucatecan activities circumventing the blockade. Conner's assessment of the goodwill that developed between Yucatecans and Americans as a result of US efforts to avoid 'wanton destruction of property and acts of mere rapacity' was accurate, and 'proof of this is the case of Yucatan, which affords the remarkable instance of a conquered country requesting the continuance of its conquest.' In addition, it was Perry, more so than Conner, who wanted to stymie the illicit trade. On 16 November he informed the new Secretary of Navy John Y. Mason that 'many cargoes of cotton from New Orleans had been landed' in Mexico and a 'considerable illicit trade is doubtless carried on with the United States, all this can & should effectually be put a stop to.' Perry also believed some of the 'military munitions' ending up in Mexican hands via Yucatan were coming from the Europeans.[24]

Regardless of the timing of the official occupation, Laguna, like Mexico City for the US Army, was a joyful place for sailors looking for wartime diversion. Semmes wrote that '[so] many were the attractions of this neutral port, clean shirts included, that it became a sort of privilege for us rough blockaders to be stationed there.' When Perry officially took the port 'without opposition' he appointed a handful of military governors such as Abraham Bigelow, who 'became so popular … he might have … set up an independent state for himself!' Semmes added that Bigelow, who served as administrator until the end of the war, was also liked among 'the women, as with the men, through the medium of sundry balls and parties; which were gotten up in fine taste, and always crushingly attended.' Perry's early biographer, William E. Griffis, concurred with Semmes, noting that 'Laguna flourished and commerce increased.' He also stated that US officers 'were very popular not only with the dark-eyed senoritas, but also with the solid male citizens and men of business. Social life throve, and balls were frequent.' Understandably, American officers thought highly of themselves and their mission, which was reflected in the recollections of their time spent there.[25]

Commander Benjamin Franklin Sands, the first officer to govern the supply hub, also penned a memoir recalling an evening in Laguna when several crew members were kept ashore for duties and 'were persuaded to join a party gathered at the English consul's house to attend a fandango ... with the natives of the place.' Sands wrote that when the sailors made their way into the consul's main entertainment room they found themselves 'in the midst of men in shirt-sleeves, with scarfs around their waists, hats on, etc., – and women ... their whole costumes being the chemise and petticoat, with now and then a bandana handkerchief thrown over the shoulders.' Sands recalled later how he 'often laughed at my being an actor in such a ludicrous scene', but it demonstrated that Laguna was indeed a place American sailors could forget about the monotony of blockade duty and cruising for Mexican vessels:

> Three or four couples were engaged [in] dancing, snapping their fingers in lieu of castanets, the men cutting all sorts of antics, whilst the women, with eyes modestly cast down, shuffled around in a parrot-toed fashion to the monotonous music of flute, fiddles and guitars. They made the music a little more lively on our entrance, and began a waltz to it, and I picked out the least ugly girl I could see, and at it we went; the thermometer over 100, and with the perspiration pouring down we whirled about, regardless of keeping time, and altogether most ungracefully. It was a most disagreeable piece of exercise.[26]

The second year of the war, however, brought considerable challenges to the armed forces of the United States. When the Mexicans refused to submit after their defeat at the Battle of Monterrey in late September of 1846, it was decided the US would take the fight to the heart of Mexico. Semmes wrote that Veracruz was 'the only seaport of any importance on the Mexican Gulf', which was true enough for those doing business with Mexico City or, in the case of the US Army, who wanted to capture the capital. George Meade, who participated in the battlefield victories of Taylor, pondered Perry's assault on Tabasco in his war diary:

> I have not seen the official account, but it appears to be the impression that they did not do as much as they might have done. If they cannot take a town with only three hundred soldiers in it, and no artillery, what are they going to do against San Juan de Ulloa?

That was a good question. The answer was the largest amphibious assault and Joint Forces operation in US history to date.[27]

Scott's 'new line of operations' and Tampico

After the Battle of Monterrey Taylor concluded a two-month armistice that required Ampudia's forces to move south, and Scott submitted a proposal to open a 'new line of operations' to capture the Mexican capital by way of Veracruz. To do this, he required a force large enough to oppose the Mexican Army but agile and small enough to supply and to move relatively quickly if needed. The ideal number, in Scott's estimation, was around 15,000 men, and thus word was sent to Taylor that many of his best officers and soldiers required for the new campaign were ordered to proceed to their new base and staging area at Tampico – the northern Mexican coastal town captured easily by Conner on 14 November. Officers leading these battle-tested units included General John A. Quitman and Scott's longtime friend and War of 1812 veteran General William J. Worth. Around 12,000 soldiers arrived, short of the mark, but a blessing given that Taylor was not aware that Santa Anna was heading north from San Luis Potosi pining for glory with 20,000 soldiers to confront a drastically reduced force of less than 5,000 men. John Reese Kenly, a volunteer from Baltimore who chronicled his time in Mexico, wrote that Scott 'overlooked' the fact 'that Taylor was to act on the defensive after Worth and his best troops were withdrawn, with an uncertain reinforcement of new regiments to replace them.' However, the young captain, who went on to become a general in the Civil War, offered his gracious perspective on 'the game of cross purposes' among both Mexican and US generals. In his 1872 memoirs dedicated to Taylor, he wrote:

> If Scott were ignorant of the strength of the army at San Luis, he is less blameable [*sic*] than Santa Anna; if the latter had reason to believe his government could protect its Capital, he is less obnoxious to censure than Scott; the whole truth is, however, that they were alike indifferent as to the other's purposes or means of accomplishing results, violating a maxim of war which tyros in the military art are familiar with.[28]

While it is difficult in hindsight to judge the grand strategy, given that Taylor brilliantly defended his forces at Buena Vista in February and went on to become the US President, an overview of the war shows that Mexicans under Santa Anna were moving north to confront the Americans while the Americans were readying a force at Tampico to hop along the coast by sea and take the city with the shortest and best route leading to the capital. Had Taylor been crushed at Buena Vista, historians would likely not have looked upon Scott's endeavour so favourably. However, one important factor is that Santa Anna's forces were quite exhausted after marching hundreds of kilometres through the desert, and only 15,000 arrived out of the 20,000 who left San Luis Potosi. Nevertheless, Scott's strategy could be considered a gamble, and what made it more so was that he needed his army to be in the Mexican highlands west of Veracruz before summer, when the dreaded tropical sickness known as *vomito*, or yellow fever, was most likely to afflict the army. It was a seasonal scourge best avoided by a small force with limited means of re-supply and reinforcement.

On 12 December, after three months of camping in the woods near Monterrey, Captain Kenly and the rest of the Baltimore Battalion began their march to the coast – a distance of 500km through the states of Nuevo Leon and Tamaulipas. Two weeks later and more than halfway to the Gulf, the unit entered Ciudad Victoria without opposition. It was a gruelling march through difficult and diverse terrain that included dry deserts, canyons, forests and wet lowlands. Kenly noted how the soldiers from Baltimore reacted when they neared the coastal plain of Tampico, and 'the roar made by the breakers tumbling in from the ocean' elevated 'the spirits of the men to the highest pitch, and liquors flowed from unknown sources through the swarming hive of the division.' He also described how the men were starved of urban diversions after months of camping in the wilds of Mexico. 'A town or city is to a marching soldier the fountain of life,' Kenly wrote, 'so long and so fruitlessly sought by Ponce de Leon. To our battalion, the image presented was more attractive than that held up before the followers of Mohammed as their paradise of repose.' While the men had seen the din of battle and survived, they were not the frontier-forged soldiers of the Texas borderlands:

> A man raised in a city, a genuine cockney, is nowhere at home except in a crowd of people, traversing thoroughfares lighted up with shop windows, and with resting places for the idle and thirsty, in drink-shops and billiard-saloons. Our men were good soldiers, but they were all city-men, and their absence for nearly eight months from the United States had made them picture exaggerated pleasures from a visit to Tampico, which the sutler had told them was overflowing with attractions from New Orleans. They were sadly disappointed in the realization of their fancies.[29]

On 25 January, following a 'sultry march' through an oak forest and 'dense thicket of chaparral', the battalion stopped at the edge of a lagoon and made camp. The coastal area of Tampico was pitted with lagoons and thickets harbouring creatures nonexistent in the drier country they came from. To the northern soldiers everything seemed exotic, new and potentially dangerous. The decision to halt despite being close to Tampico caused 'vexation' and was akin to being 'ordered to march back to Monterey.' The men were less than 20km from their destination yet forced once again to endure the elements. Kenly recalled the wet ground, thorn-ridden underbrush and 'hot steam' emanating from the earth when the sun rose the next day: 'It was a horrid, low, swampy place ... the men were just getting their coffee, when this huge lizard, several feet in length, heated by the fire, ran from the hollow log which was being used to cook with, and the men scattered and ran for some distance before they rallied and captured it.' Later that day, the unit surgeon informed Quitman that the site was unhealthy. The assessment was not only based on the suffocating humidity, but as well as the mosquitoes 'and the usual insects we have been tormented with, we had for companions last night several varieties of pinching-bugs, large spiders, and what the men seemed to dread more than anything else – scorpions.' Kenly wrote that when one man's leg was bitten by a scorpion, 'a whitish swelling the size of a hickory nut' appeared before the surgeon managed to treat the wound with hartshorn.[30]

On 28 January, after traversing lime and lemon orchards, the battalion approached the hills a few kilometres from their 'El Dorado' – Tampico. Located north of the Panuco River separating Tamaulipas and Veracruz states, the name 'Tampico' is derived from the pre-Columbian Huastec term 'place for otters' (literally 'water dogs'). In the early sixteenth century Franciscan monks founded a mission and monastery nearby that stood for more than a hundred years before the site was abandoned and mostly forgotten. Kenly wrote, 'It was a famed locality in the days of the Montezumas; and Viejo Tampico, on the opposite side of the river, was a bishop's see when Panuco was a department of Mexico, in the days of the Viceroys.' In 1823, two years after Mexico gained its independence from Spain, a port was re-established at the city's current location to serve commercial interests attached to the export of silver from the mines of San Luis Potosi – a trade coveted by Europeans and Americans looking to exploit that wealth. Like many of Mexico's coastal towns, however, the sand bar at the Panuco's mouth made navigation difficult for heavy draught vessels. Shortly after Conner seized the city, Captain Alvin Edson, who took part in the First Battle of Tabasco the previous month, went upstream with the steamer *Spitfire* and schooner *Petrel*, landed a small party of Marines at the town of Panuco and blew up some ammunition they found there, before returning to Tampico. A week later, 500 soldiers arrived by sea and the Marines were relieved of duty.[31]

However, the Americans were not interested in navigating upstream but instead wanted Tampico as a staging area for their amphibious attack on Veracruz. While Kenly and other units from the northern theatre made their way to the Gulf from the Texas borderlands, English immigrant George Ballentine, who had been waiting anxiously in Tampa Bay, Florida, since October, was finally issued orders in December to prepare for deployment. 'So desirous were we of escaping from the dull monotony of this place, of which we were exceedingly tired, that I believe many heard the orders to prepare for leaving it with much satisfaction.' Ballentine recalled that before leaving, the state needed to raise volunteers to protect the wives and children of the married men and officers – as the Seminole tribe, unsubdued by the US Army, was known to be in the area. One woman, 'the wife of our Lieutenant', Ballentine wrote, 'who had four small children, she cried for a whole day, it was said, when the order came. Poor woman!' According to him, that same officer ended up dying roughly nine months later at the Battle of Churubusco outside Mexico City after being 'pierced in the body with three musket-balls.' Two weeks after receiving orders, a merchant ship named *John Potter* arrived from Charleston to take the soldiers to Tampico. On 2 January the men aboard the brig lost sight of the Floridian coast.[32]

The 300-ton *John Potter* carried almost 200 men across the Gulf. Some men, former sailors, passed the time assisting the captain, while another man, whom Ballentine described as recently discharged from a medical facility and 'partially insane' was given nonessential work. This man apparently believed 'the ship swarmed with a crew of horrible-looking old witches, numbers of whom he saw perched upon the rigging, and who he constantly affirmed would lead the vessel into difficulty.' Ballentine wrote that his madness 'was of a mild form, and he was perfectly quiet,' but that he could not abandon the disturbing idea that their ship 'would never leave the gulf; and though he sometimes took a turn at the wheel, steering as well as the others, yet he always kept eyeing the rigging with a troubled and suspicious glance.' Another man from Northern Ireland named Hogg, who joined the unit at Tampa Bay, also became mentally unstable after enlisting, was hospitalized for a period, but eventually deemed competent because the doctor believed the young man simply regretted his decision and was attempting to secure a discharge. After boarding the *John Potter*, Hogg was put on sentry duty. One day, he crawled out to the ship's forechains, stripped off and threw himself into the sea. Ballentine wrote that they tried to get a boat lowered, but Hogg 'had gone nearly a mile astern, and had he not been a very good swimmer, he must have drowned.' Adding to the belief that Hogg was a goner was the fact that 'sharks were numerous in those seas, and as there had been one reported alongside several times since we sailed, few questioned the fact of the poor fellow's insanity after that occurrence.'[33]

After ten days at sea the men aboard the *John Potter* sighted the coast of Mexico and the mountains of the Sierra Madre Oriental behind it. Premature jubilation presaged their arrival in port, and Ballentine wrote that 'the voyage ended, we were congratulating each other upon the short and withal pleasant trip we had made.' The first mate, whom Ballentine considered an 'excellent sailor', was eager to make port that evening but the captain, hearing suggestions from other officers who wanted to disembark in daylight, decided to wait until the following day. It was a bad decision, as 'northers' – extremely strong winds that ply the Gulf from September to April – were in peak season. The next morning, as they came within a couple of kilometres of the shore, 'a heavy, dark-looking cloud which had been gathering ahead of us for the previous ten minutes, began to sprinkle the deck with a few large drops.' The veteran sailors of the Gulf knew exactly what was about to hit them, and what had started out benignly soon turned to 'whistling and hissing sounds, amongst the running gear and shrouds', then, soon after, 'changing finally into the wild roar of the hurricane, as the vessel careened over nearly on her beam ends, showed that there was no time to be lost; the gale was on us, and our only chance was to "cut and run", as the sailors term it.' Ballentine believed the ship was saved because the experienced sailors noticed the approaching storm and hauled down a handful of sails before the gale hit. 'Indeed but for the extraordinary exertions of the officers and sailors composing the crew, I believe we should have been driven on the sands; and some days afterwards, when the gale had moderated, the captain confessed that we had a very narrow escape.'[34]

For three days the cold norther battered the *John Potter*. One 'old tar' commented to Ballentine that the insane man who had seen witches in the rigging had brought 'ill luck on the vessel, it must be him they follow, for no one else sees them but him ... if I was the skipper, the first day I went into port, would be the last day the unlucky beggar would ever put a foot on the *John Potter*'s deck.' The winds were intense and waves crashed against the ship's sides. Ballentine believed he had 'never seen a gale last so long with such continuous and unmitigated fury.' Most of the men stayed below deck, coming up every now and then to take stock of the weather and the condition of the ship. On 20 January the passengers were re-supplied with food by an American steamer carrying information to General Scott at Brazos Santiago, but she could not afford the time to tow them. A few days later, as the ship neared the mouth of the Panuco River, a vessel manned by Mexicans 'jabbering and laughing to one another in their own language' presented itself to escort the *John Potter* to the port of Tampico. After crossing the bar at the mouth of the river, the anchor was dropped because the tide was too low to proceed upriver. As soon as it hit the water, Mexican merchants appeared. 'Our vessel was now immediately surrounded by a whole fleet of canoes,' Ballentine recalled, 'with fruits and vegetables for sale, which they sold exceedingly cheap; and finding plenty of eager purchasers ... oranges, pineapples, plantains, bananas, etc., was speedily disposed of.' Tobacco and alcohol – 'a poisonous description of liquor, under the denomination of brandy' – were also available in town, at a mark-up price sold by contractors accompanying the US Army. The next day, after they finally disembarked, Mexican ladies took their clothes for washing.[35]

After a week of drilling and marching at camp, Ballentine observed the arrival of 'a strong reinforcement' of soldiers from the northern theatre; Kenly's Baltimore unit from Monterrey was probably part of it. The Englishman-turned-American was particularly impressed with a regiment of cavalry from Tennessee, who were a 'set of stout fellows, well clothed, armed, and mounted, at least for volunteers; and they were said to have behaved very well in action.' Their enlistment periods were also expected to expire in the coming months, and according to Ballentine they were not about to re-enlist despite pleas from the regular officers to do so, because 'the poor fellows had "seen the elephant", and were perfectly satisfied with the exhibition.'[36]

In his seminal 1985 work demonstrating how the Mexican War captured the imaginations of Americans, Robert Johannsen explains the phrase 'to see the elephant.' At its onset, the war was popular among a new generation looking to emulate the patriots who fought the revolution, and pro-war writers and advocates were keen to romanticize the invasion against Mexico as a noble crusade spreading liberty and enlightenment over a continent. To 'see the elephant' thus meant to be disenchanted of such notions after experiencing the actual toil and hardship that accompanies the lives of soldiers. Johannsen quotes 'Jake' Jacob Oswandel of the First Pennsylvania Volunteer Regiment, who kept a diary during his experience in Mexico and at the siege of Veracruz. Writing to his parents from near Mexico City, Oswandel thanked God he was 'still in the land of the living, and in as good, if not better health than the day I left Mifflin county, Pa.' However, despite having 'seen the elephant' and being unsure when the war would end, Oswandel promised that 'we will put our shoulders to the wheel and push until the work is thoroughly completed.' In another account of the Mexican War, Albert Gallatin Brackett, who served in Scott's campaign as a volunteer from Indiana, wrote about how, on 1 January 1848, as he was heading home across the Gulf after leaving Veracruz, sighted 'the low swamps with wild and rank grass growing among the many islands' that led to New Orleans. After the waters were turned dark by the muddy freshwater of the Mississippi River, their boat passed a grand estate along the river, where three young girls 'came running toward us at full speed.' Brackett recalled in his work, written a few years after the war and before the Civil War, that the oldest among them 'was one of the most beautiful women I ever saw', and she 'waved her handkerchief toward us, and gave us three cheers.' To a soldier who had gone from Veracruz to the Mexican capital and survived the ordeal,

> the cheering was more musical than the warbling of birds, and God knows I shall never forget it. Our men returned the cheers with a zest and feeling which I had never heard before. They seemed perfectly carried away with excitement, and as long as the ladies were in sight, they kept it up. This, thought I, is a pretty fair reception on our return to our native shores, and if it holds out, it will pay pretty well for 'seeing the elephant'.[37]

Despite the threat of disease and occasional starvation, life in the US Army in occupied Mexico was not entirely without its distractions. Every evening in occupied Tampico, band music played by Americans could be heard in the main plaza, and the numerous houses of entertainment, which accompanied large forces wherever they went, opened to provide opportunities to unburden recently paid soldiers of their hard-earned cash. Ballentine called the proprietors of establishments selling liquor and *aguardiente* and offering gambling games 'human vultures' – as Mexicans 'were prohibited from selling spirits to the soldiers ... but these camp followers were winked at by some means or other, and the scoundrels had a complete monopoly of the sale of liquor, and were permitted to poison and plunder the soldiers with impunity.'[38]

On 19 February, three days before Taylor's astonishing victory over Santa Anna at Buena Vista (near Saltillo), Winfield Scott arrived in Tampico. Kenly noted the men were already in good spirits due to being paid 'all arrearages due' and supplied with new uniforms and shoes, and acted like 'boys home for the Christmas holidays, and it is a pleasure to see them so happy.' Thus, Scott's arrival was a bonus to a good week, and the sound of cannon salutes preceded the commanding general's arrival in town. Even the locals came out sharply dressed to witness the spectacle of troops marching and drums beating. 'The ladies crowded the streets,' Kenly wrote, 'dressed in a style which astonished me. I never saw anywhere more fashionably dressed women, European in everything, except where Parisian modes fail; the head, adorned with their beautiful black hair.' The town was occupied by a foreign invader, yet the seeming disinterestedness of the locals – particularly many of the women whose 'curiosity to see General Scott subdued their repugnance to the *Llanquies*' – was emblematic of the war on many levels. Much as in Laguna, many citizens were indifferent to being occupied and felt sparing loyalty towards the political and military authorities at war with each other and the Americans. Provincial Mexico and far-flung towns of the Gulf often harboured little connection to the leaders in Mexico City who were desperately attempting to foster a nationalist spirit necessary to repel the invaders.[39]

Tampico, like Mexico City after it was conquered, offered a stunning example of how an occupying army was capable of building goodwill when its mission was not predicated on forced requisitions or absolute subjugation, but accommodation and equal treatment under the law. In that regard, the same disconnect that existed between Mexico's rulers and common people, many of whom were *mestizo* or of indigenous background, was similar to that which existed between US privates on the ground and leadership in Washington formulating and effecting visions of continental empire. Although the local citizens no doubt viewed the celebratory spectacle and returned to their homes wondering about their futures, Friday, 19 February 1847 in Tampico was, paradoxically, a scene of glee for US forces:

> In the centre of the plaza, the fine band of one of the artillery regiments was playing, surrounded by a dense mass of soldiers of all arms, and sailors from the men-of-war in port. The adjacent coffee-houses were filled with officers, and rumor, her tongue now again free, filled Tampico with the buzz of her joy. Everybody talked, everybody knew what was just told him, everybody was delighted, and everybody made a night of it, except the town-guard, and it had a night of it, for there was the sound of revelry on the banks of the Panuco. Drunken soldiers and drunken sailors fraternized, and the long bitter oath of the western volunteer and teamster drowned the caramba of the Mexican ... Everything was overflowing with enthusiasm and life on the eve of the descent upon Vera Cruz.[40]

While Scott's strict martial law prescriptions imposed on soldiers resulted in a comparatively benign occupation, it was not without its incidents. The northern theatre of war witnessed numerous excesses against civilians –

many of which were committed by Texans. The urban action during the Battle of Monterrey, which resulted in the storming of residential areas of the city, afforded an outlet for revenge, and northern anti-war newspapers were eager to highlight such actions, justifying their opposition to the war. The *Liberator* of Boston, a staunchly anti-war publication, was a veritable amalgamation of newspaper excerpts pointing out the violence. One article republished from the *Charleston Mercury* entitled 'Outrages of the American Soldiers' reported that generals were unable to 'restrain the passions of the volunteers' after the battle. 'As at Matamoros, murder, robbery, and rape were committed' by undisciplined soldiers. 'It is thought more than one hundred inhabitants were murdered in cold blood, and one Mexican soldier, with Gen. Worth's passport in his pocket, was shot dead at noon day in the main street of the city, by a ruffian from Texas.' Another post cited the 'Austin (Texas) Democrat' reporting on an incident involving the murder of a Texas volunteer named David Horseley and the retribution exacted on the locals by the regiment under the command of Texas Ranger and Colonel John Coffee Hays. The *Liberator* added box brackets to provide context:

> The news spread like wildfire among Hays's men. [Hays' regiment had been disbanded for disorderly conduct.] They determined to take ample vengeance. Woe to the Mexican falling in their way! ... Infuriated by the cowardly meanness of the murder of their fellow-soldier, and remembrance of the many foul and blood butcheries upon them in former times [in Texas,] they spared not a man. It is thought eighty or one hundred Mexicans fell to avenge the death of Horseley!! Terrible retribution! Gen. Taylor was inclined to order all disbanded troops, such was the excitement, to leave Monterey in 48 hours.[41]

Despite the violence – many incidents of which were romanticized using Napoleonic parallels – most Americans lauded the battlefield victories that ultimately propelled Taylor into the White House in 1848. The Virginian general was not known to be overtly political or disciplinary, which appealed to both his soldiers and admirers, and apart from resting on his laurels, there were numerous reasons to not attempt an invasion of San Luis Potosi. Among them was logistically prioritizing Scott's Mexico City campaign and a desire to keep Texans from further entering Mexican territory beyond the Rio Grande. In Taylor's words, this was done to prevent further 'extensive depredation and outrages upon the peaceful inhabitants'. In June 1847, he wrote that 'scarcely a form of crime that has not been reported to me as committed by them ... the mounted men from Texas have scarcely made one expedition without unwarrantedly killing a Mexican.' It was a prudent decision based on a 'constant recurrence of such atrocities, which I have been reluctant to report to the department, [and] is my motive for requesting that no more troops may be sent to this column from the State of Texas.'[42]

Excesses and unwarranted violence against Mexican civilians contributed to Taylor's decision not to press further into Mexico once the ranks of his army were reinforced. Many of the Texas 'volunteers' – including those later sent to central Mexico by Polk to assist in getting rid of guerrillas along the logistics line between Mexico City and Veracruz – joined the war officially as militia, which was legally problematic for Scott's population-centric counter-insurgency initiatives, given that militia operated under a more liberal set of laws of war and if tried by court martial for wrongdoings were granted a jury of their peers (fellow militiamen) and not regular soldiers. For the most part, however, American soldiers, sailors and Marines under the command of West Point- and US Navy-educated officers in the Gulf treated civilians amicably when compliance was forthcoming and paid for goods at market rates, which Mexicans of various classes appreciated.[43]

Lobos and Logistics

Once Scott implemented martial law after arriving in Tampico he wasted little time in preparing for the main objective. For more than three months the complicated process of coordinating with Quartermaster General Thomas S. Jesup in New Orleans had been ongoing, and it was decided the secondary staging area for launching the attack on Veracruz was the small island of Lobos, located just off the coast roughly 120km south-east of Tampico and 200km north of Veracruz. Situated near Red Cape (Cabo Rojo) north of the town of Tuxpan, Lobos was first seen by early sixteenth-century Spanish explorers Francisco Hernández de Córdoba and Juan de Grijalva and later became known as a haven for pirates preying on Spanish ships. In 1829, a few years after Mexico achieved independence, Spain unsuccessfully attempted to reconquer the breakaway republic by sending a 4,000-man force from Havana led by General Isidro Barradas, who used Lobos as a rendezvous point with the goal of seizing Tampico. The force was formidable at sea but on land they succumbed to the difficult terrain, disease and attrition at the hands of a smaller Mexican force led by Santa Anna – which ironically may have factored into his decision to relegate coastal defences in the war with the Americans.[44]

Whether or not Scott knew of the small island's storied past is speculation, but its use as a base for unofficial activities was known among the mariners in New Orleans. Jesup wrote to Marcy in December of 1846 that Englishmen 'used this anchorage in their smuggling operations more than a century' and that 'every seaman' was aware of the ridges to avoid when approaching the coral formations surrounding the island. This statement was confirmed by Conner's assessment to Scott in January that 'Blunt's Coast Pilot' – the essential guide for mariners written and compiled by Edmund M. Blunt in the early nineteenth century and reprinted extensively during the era – contained 'full and exact directions for the entrance' to the bay west of the island providing protection from the northers. Scott confirmed in February the protection the harbour provided from a two-day gale that 'brought down all the vessels' from Tampico and was 'even better than ... anticipated'. The 1847 fifteenth edition of Blunt's *American Coast Pilot* featured a letter written by Perry aboard the USS *Mississippi* – at the time his flagship vessel that took part in the Veracruz operation and later capture of Tabasco. In it, Perry noted 'the clearness of the atmosphere' often preceding the high winds allowed mariners a view of the Mexican highlands and Mount Orizaba. Published immediately after the capture of Veracruz, Blunt's newest edition also commented on the port, the castle, and its relation to the northers: 'N. 27° W., at about 4 leagues distant from Point Anton Lizardo', Perry wrote, 'is the castle of San Juan de Ulua, which forms the Harbor or Port of Vera Cruz, which is more known and frequented than all the others in the Mexican Gulf and likewise the most dangerous to take, particularly during northerly gales.' Perry also described the port as 'an open roadstead' not dissimilar to Castle Harbor in Bermuda, which was also protected by fortifications. Veracruz was 'not a commodious harbor ... covered with several islands, on one of which the fortress of St. Juan de Ulua is erected.'[45]

Despite the benefits Lobos provided as a secondary staging area south of the island of Brazos Santiago (Matamoros) and Tampico, there were still a number of problems historians frequently overlook in their eagerness to arrive at Veracruz. For those more interested in battles, Lobos is seemingly unimportant, but when examining the logistics of the war, its location, and the problems associated with readying the large amphibious force, are worth examining. Scott knew he could obtain various supplies inland after seizing Veracruz, but most of the essentials of waging war including men, weapons, equipment, horses and draught animals for hauling goods and cannons, needed to be brought to Mexico. Bauer, whose seminal twentieth-century work focused on naval operations during the war and the contributions of the Marines, understood Scott's various dilemmas in organizing the expedition – noting that the general felt 'the pinch of the transport shortage' while moving US forces from the north to Veracruz. It was indeed a monumental task, and Jesup admitted as much in December when he requested from Marcy four additional quartermasters from the army and ten assistants to be sent to New Orleans. 'The quartermaster's department is far from being efficient: the officers are efficient, individually,' he wrote, 'but they are not sufficiently numerous' to handle the massive logistics required to carry out the project.[46]

The Mexican War was not the first campaign testing US ability to project military power. Jesup, who had been Quartermaster General since 1818, had a personal history with Scott in his unsuccessful effort to subdue the Seminoles of Florida in the second phase of a long-term war in the unconquered state purchased from Spain in 1819. As in Yucatan, the difficult terrain and wet environment made cavalry-centric warfare nearly impossible. Potter Woodburne, an officer who served for a few months in the Second Seminole War (1835–1842), chronicled some of the 'difficulties' that existed 'for many years' between Scott and Jesup as a result of the ordeal. 'The great disadvantages under which Gen. Scott laboured on taking the command in Florida,' Woodburne wrote in 1836, 'necessarily delayed his movements until a very late period. He found the Quartermaster's department extremely deficient, and therefore encountered much difficulty in transporting his supplies.' However, Woodburne did not put all the blame on Jesup because the war was being waged by generals using Napoleonic tactics in an environment inimical to that style of warfare:

> To penetrate a country like that of Florida, necessarily requires much preparation and great labour; there being no chain of posts or settlements through it, the army are compelled to carry an enormous load with them, and one who has ever been in the service knows the tardiness with which an army moves when encumbered with a heavy baggage train. To increase the evil, large quantities of rain fell about the first of

March, and subsequently, which made the roads almost impassable for heavy teams, and broke down the horses very much.[47]

Myer M. Cohen, another officer who served under Scott during the Seminole War, was critical of tactics, political leadership in Washington and inefficient logistics in an era where the US Army relied heavily upon private contractors to ensure the timely arrival of essential supplies. The questions he posed were rhetorical: 'Whence arose the awful deficiencies of transportation and supplies? Why were not rations conveyed ... in steamboats? Why were depots selected, injudicious, because distant from the scene of operations?' Cohen's work, highlighting insurgent warfare and Scott's difficulties in seeking out the enemy and ensuring his soldiers were supplied and fed, read like a prelude to what both Jesup and Scott were attempting to avoid in the larger, more expansive and more distant war with Mexico: 'Why not an adequate force of US regulars and volunteers sent, at once, to Gen. Clinch, an old and able Indian fighter, instead of waiting [until] Scott could come into the field from Washington, and gather, on the way, large masses of men, too cumbrous for rapid movements?' Cohen's litany of complaints echoed those of Scott, who was determined not to repeat the same mistakes in Mexico:

> Why were not hard bread and bacon (which require not equal delay and difficulty in cooking) furnished instead of flour and pork? Why were poultry-wagons and old, broken down, horses, sent into a country requiring the best appointed trains and teams? If the departments cannot shift from themselves the responsibility involved in the answers to these questions, they must be content to stand out, as melancholy monuments of governmental dilatoriness, and indifference to the sorrows and the sufferings of bleeding or butchered individuals.[48]

In actuality, both generals carried baggage from the previous war. Scott was often too conceited to admit to error but smart enough to learn from mistakes – albeit without acknowledging it. 'Perhaps no expedition was ever so unaccountably delayed – by no want of foresight, arrangement, or energy on my part,' he wrote to Marcy aboard the USS *Massachusetts* at Lobos. The reality is that, while logistics and the complications of supplying the amphibious operation fell short of expectations, their mutual dependency and history in Florida likely resulted in more planning and energy devoted to the operation. Correcting previous mistakes was critical to success in America's first foreign conflict, and both generals understood victory in Mexico would define their legacy – eclipsing the importance of the Floridian conflict on the opposite side of the Gulf.[49]

As noted, the other source of pressure was the timeline Scott set for himself and others because of the seasonal sickness. 'Indeed, the season has already so far advanced,' he informed Marcy in late February, 'in reference to the usual return of the yellow fever on the coast, that I can now only wait a day or two longer.' Scott was anxious to commence the invasion but was waiting on General Worth from Tampico and the brigades under Generals Quitman, Gideon J. Pillow and James Shields. Those soldiers, Scott wrote, were battled-tested and 'quite efficient from tactical instruction and habits of subordination'. There were also two cases of smallpox among the 2nd Pennsylvania Regiment on Lobos, and thus Scott's letter to Marcy was probably intended to apply pressure on Jesup. He repeated that urgency was 'most critical to this entire army' and that everyone involved in the operation 'knew from the first … that it would be fatal to us to attempt military operations on the coast after, probably, the first week in April, and here we are at the end of February.' Scott's letter was sent too late to have an effect on Jesup, but it does highlight the logistics issues and frustrations he faced.[50]

Landing and Siege of Veracruz

Worth and Pillow did arrive. On 2 March Scott and several staff officers boarded the *Massachusetts* and with a norther blowing behind them headed in the direction of Veracruz. Three days later, they passed the port, arriving at Anton Lizardo around noon. They then boarded the *Petrita* (renamed the *Champion*) with Conner and set out towards Veracruz to do some last-minute reconnaissance of the location the commodore chose for disembarking – a beach named Collado south of the city and outside cannon range. After examining the beach, they steamed towards the island castle of San Juan de Ulúa. In his memoirs, Inspector General Colonel Ethan Allen Hitchcock wrote that as the group passed one of the smaller islands, at a distance from the castle, one of the colonels aboard the *Petrita* noticed the Mexicans were readying their batteries. Another said, 'They are using their sponges: we shall have a shot presently. Sure enough! A small white cloud told us that we had become an object of interest to them.' Hitchcock wrote that the first two shells 'fell short' and the third exploded above them, scattering shrapnel. 'The fourth passed directly over us and fell in the water a hundred yards beyond. We were in a ridiculous position.' The *Petrita* quickly steamed back to Anton Lizardo. Had the Mexicans hit their mark, the entire campaign would have been jeopardized.[51]

According to Scott, after the Pastry War the Mexicans rebuilt much of the castle and 'doubled' its armaments. As a result, Santa Anna believed it to be so formidable that the city of 15,000 people was only lightly garrisoned. 'When we approached, in 1847,' Scott wrote, 'the castle had the capacity to sink the entire American navy.' Santa Anna's decision proved to be a serious miscalculation, because the Americans developed a different strategy, undermining the importance of the castle by taking the city first. Scott explained that by seizing the city, the lifeline to the garrison manning the large batteries on the island fortress protecting the harbour was essentially severed. For that reason, Mexicans relying upon San Juan de Ulúa's 'impregnable strength had neglected to lay in a supply of fresh water and provisions – as these could be sent over daily from the city. The capture of the latter, therefore, placed the castle entirely at our mercy.' In essence, Scott did not attack the castle, but the supplies of the men manning it. Semmes concurred with this decision, as 'it would have been a great piece of folly in the government to have assaulted Vera Cruz, and its castle, by sea. It would have been attended with great destruction of property – perhaps the sinking of some half-a-dozen ships.' Avoiding a direct assault where the Mexicans expected it made it much easier to take the city.[52]

Fortune also played no small role in the success of the operation. On 9 March – a perfectly sunny afternoon free of northers – Scott watched beyond the range of Mexican cannon as roughly 5,500 men filled more than sixty specially designed surfboats holding seventy to eighty men each and landed at Collado beach 'without the loss of a boat or a man, and, to the astonishment of all, without opposition.' Some of the soldiers included in the first wave were Marines led by Captain Edson. To compensate for the surfboats that did not arrive in time for the operation, the Navy's smaller vessels conducted ship-to-shore escorts, eventually landing more than 12,000 men in all. This task was made exponentially easier by not being under fire. Accompanying the landing was a diversionary attack at sea by the *Spitfire* under Commander Josiah Tattnal, which acted as a target for fortress and city cannons. A handful of the *Spitfire*'s shells landed in the city, while the steamer, like the *Petrita*, avoided being hit. Tattnal's biographer wrote: 'The eyes of the navy and of the army were upon him during this gallant engagement; and Commander Tattnall by his perseverance and courage won the admiration of them both.' The action also helped the siege by informing the US forces of the exact locations of the Mexican guns within the city.[53]

Oswandel was among those rowed to shore in the surfboats. After landing, the tired soldiers stacked their muskets, unloaded their knapsacks, gobbled a piece of fat pork with a side of biscuit and went to sleep in the sandhills skirting the beach. Sporadic fire from Mexican soldiers beyond the hills punctuated their sleep during the night. In the morning, shots from the castle in the harbour were aimed at their camp but fell short of their mark, and the men breakfasted on mouldy crackers and more fat pork before falling into line to circle the city. Oswandel wrote that 'it was one of the marches the volunteers will never forget.' As the line snaked its way, men fell out of formation due to fatigue and thirst, and one 'could hardly walk ten steps without seeing some poor soldier, whose tongue was thirsty for water, laying on the wayside and begging for a drop of water.' Oswandel also witnessed the desperate condition of one lieutenant in their company, Casper M. Berry, who was suffering from too much sun. 'It looked as if you could almost see his brain gushing out of his forehead. He is not expected to live.' The men trudged on through cactus and thicket, distracted every now and then by Mexican fire from their left flank. Some skirmishing resulted, but generally there was little resistance apart from the occasional desperate shell from San Juan de Ulúa 'whistling, cracking and snapping through the chaparrals like lightning.' More blood was shed by the thorns in the sandhills of Veracruz than by Mexican resistance to the army surrounding their prized port.[54]

The soldiers of the 1st Regiment Pennsylvania Volunteers set their sights on one of the large sandhills with a commanding view of the city, climbed its thorn-strewn sides, charged and dispersed a small company of Mexican soldiers guarding it and planted their state flag atop the small summit that would soon be used to help bombard Veracruz. 'From here can be seen a fine view of the city,' Oswandel recorded in his diary, 'and from appearances it looks like a fair city, with plenty of domes ... splendid country seats, mansions, gardens, lawns, flowers, shrubbery, trees, cultivated fields.' The contrast between the beauty of Veracruz and the barren landscape surrounding it made Oswandel – who was in the midst of 'seeing the elephant' – wonder how exactly Mexicans eked out living from a landscape so different to the green valleys of his central Pennsylvanian county. Unlike 'where we came from,' he wrote, 'it is a barren wilderness, mostly covered with wild, ragged, small knotty trees, gnarled and twisted, with wild chaparral, with thorns from one to five inches long.' His amazement was shot through by privation, noting that the landscape offered no opportunities for forage. 'Nothing grows here but sand hills and wild chaparral. Snakes would even starve to death. Even drinking water is not to be found in this miserable section of country.' The next day, they began digging entrenchments, and trying not to get buried 'in the floating drifts of sand' created by the northers sweeping the coast.[55]

While the positions and trenches were being readied, the cannons and artillery were hauled into place. An account of some of the methods the Americans used to get their equipment and animals ashore was written in 1847 by passed midshipman William G. Temple, but was not published until Conner included it in his 1896 work the *Home Squadron*. The only publication of the era that mentions Temple's work is that of novelist and historian James Fenimore Cooper, who published a history of the US Navy in 1853. Known for his romantic masterpiece, *Last of the Mohicans*, Cooper's various works promoted expansion and advocated a strong US Navy to compete with the British. Cooper quoted what he believed was the 'substance' of Temple's short '*Memoir of the Landing of United States Troops at Vera Cruz in 1847* compiled from original sources' but left out some of the finer logistical details. In Conner's book, Temple describes how the *Petrita* ferried nearly 500 draught animals from the larger vessels closer to shore that were then 'made to swim ashore in tow of the surfboats'. Field artillery was carried on small, reinforced boats, and when they reached the shore, gangway planks with side battens were extended so the guns could roll over the surf without getting wet. According to Temple, this was done 'with such rapidity that not a cartridge was wet in the ammunition boxes.' The three larger and much heavier 8-inch Paixhans and three 32-pounders were brought to shore in a similar manner with their 'vents and muzzles tightly stopped with putty' because they were rolled into the surf with slings attached and then transported on massive timber wheels. These were hauled by teams of sailors and soldiers 'with very great labor, through the sand to the position assigned to them, a distance of about one mile.'[56]

By 13 March the investment of the city was complete. A week later, American trenches were within 550 metres of the walls of Veracruz – within satisfactory range of their target, made possible by the meticulous efforts of Captain Robert E. Lee and other engineers who ensured digging parties were provided ample cover from the constant shelling coming from the city and castle. Hitchcock chronicled in his diary how the soldiers were eager to begin the assault given they had been laying trenches for 'thirteen days before the city without firing a gun upon it'. Sporadic skirmishing occurred on the outskirts of Veracruz against small units attempting to thwart their progress, but for the most part US forces owned the essential geography surrounding the port. Despite three days of 'continual discharges of heavy mortars and paixhans' from the Mexicans, Hitchcock wrote, 'they have not touched a single man in the trenches.' The work was completed in less than ten days. Scott later praised chief engineer Colonel Joseph G. Totten 'and his accomplished assistants' for their efficient siege preparation – obviating the need to storm the city in a bloody man-to-man confrontation that would have inevitably cost more civilian casualties.[57]

On 22 March, after the city's refusal to surrender, Scott opened up his batteries on Veracruz. 'For four days and nights shot and shell were poured into the city,' Kenley wrote, 'and the fire rapidly returned by the guns of the city and castle. The suffering and loss of life in the city were great, and each hour that passed added strength and effect to the fire of the besieging force.' It was at this time that Perry officially replaced an exhausted and ailing Conner as commander of the Home Squadron. Writing of the Mexican conflict in the post-Civil War era, Griffis explained that the Mexican War 'was a school of artillery practice and marked a distinct era of progress.' One of these areas centred around the innovations of West Point graduate Major Samuel Ringgold. Ringgold was killed at the Battle of Palo Alto in 1846, but prior to the war developed the concept of 'flying artillery', or lighter guns mounted on easily manoeuvrable carriages. 'The flying artillery of Ringgold, in the field, and Perry's siege guns, in the naval battery at Vera Cruz, were revelations to Europe of the great advance made by Americans in this branch of the science of destruction.' Ringgold's innovation not only contributed to Taylor's victories in the north but was perfectly suited to the small and disciplined force under Scott's command that later seized Mexico City. On the afternoon of 25 March, the city of Veracruz ceased firing and officially surrendered. By 29 March, after terms were agreed, the American flag was raised over both the city and the castle of San Juan de Ulúa.[58]

Despite a few setbacks, Scott had plenty to boast about. In his Civil War-era memoirs he compared the amphibious assault to the 1830 French invasion of Algiers, which he described as 'the most complete armament, in every respect, that ever left' European soil. Moreover, the 34,000-soldier expedition, carried out under the leadership of Napoleonic War veterans Admiral Guy-Victor Duperré and Marshal Louis Bourmont, faced considerable opposition from Algerians while landing their soldiers, which Scott dismissed in his effort to bolster his achievement. He also measured the two assaults against each other, arguing that French disembarkation was carried out 'in a wide bay, which was more favorable than an open beach directly on the ocean' – which is what the Americans did at Collado. To establish a beachhead, the French landed 9,000 soldiers on the first day of the operation, and 'thirty to forty lives were lost by accidents, or upsetting of boats; whereas, on the present occasion, twelve thousand men were landed in one day, without ... the slightest accident, or the loss of a single life.'[59]

Another less appreciated measure was the notable lack of civilian deaths. During the siege Scott and his officers contemplated storming the walls of the city, but it was decided that such an assault would inevitably cost the lives of hundreds of soldiers and civilians. He contrasted his relatively 'scientific' siege against the more traditional desire for heroic appearance. 'I entered fully into the question of storming parties and regular siege approaches. A death-bed discussion could hardly have been more solemn.' Epitomizing a changing outlook on warfare during the era, Scott decided against such 'slaughter' – opting for capitulation even though the press back home desired a 'butcher's bill' to accompany sensational headlines. Scott may have been referring to any number of newspapers, such as the New Orleans *Delta*, which invoked his War of 1812 history when making predictions – that of either 'starving the poor VeraCruzanos into terms, or ... cast the hazard of his die upon the bloody arbitrament of a storm, and revive the glories of Chippewa and Lundy's Lane under the heavy fire of San Juan d'Ulua.'[60]

Counterintuitively, the *Delta*'s editors believed avoiding the *vomito* season by storming the city would 'be the most glorious, and we think the least destructive and dangerous to our troops.' Conversely, others defended Scott's decisions against foreign and domestic critics who claimed the action was excessively violent, thus demonstrating there was nothing to be done to appease the expectations of distant observers. One editorial in Washington's *Daily Union* was particularly offended by sanguinary descriptions of the assault in *The Times* and noted English soldiers' violent treatment of civilians after storming Spanish cities held by Napoleon's forces during the Peninsular

War: 'Where is the holy indignation of *The Times* at these "barbarities, characteristic" not of the "fierce and destructive of volunteer and unpractised armies", but of the mild, humane, and skillful armies of Great Britain!' Badajoz, Ciudad Rodrigo, San Sebastian, as well as Copenhagen, and even Delaware and the Chesapeake during the Revolutionary War were cited as examples. 'We trust the philanthropic editors of *The Times*, before they treat us with another lecture upon our "barbarity" and "atrocity" ... will pass in review some few chapters of their own national history, of which they seem to be strangely oblivious.'[61]

Despite the death and destruction, the city quickly adapted itself to the American presence. General Worth, made governor of the city by Scott, ordered streets to be cleaned, and store owners and merchants who fled prior to the bombing returned to open their establishments to new customers. Arthur Middleton Manigault, a first lieutenant in the volunteer Palmetto Regiment from South Carolina who went on to become a Confederate brigadier general, wrote to his brother from a beach camp near Veracruz that hotels on the main plaza were opened for the generals and 'crowds of officers' and aides could be seen at all hours outside the main doors. Manigault was obviously referring to the Plaza de Armas, or *zócalo*, abutting the Municipal Palace and seventeenth-century Veracruz Cathedral, Nuestra Señora de la Asunción. It was a favourite place for watching patrols of dragoons crisscrossing the streets, and sailors, soldiers and officers idling in and out of recently opened coffee shops in anticipation of the march inland. Manigault also found time to attend the newly opened 'American Theatre' – which was 'much larger than, the one in Charleston'. Like other Mexican towns on the Gulf, Veracruz offered little resistance to its occupiers after being seized.[62]

Expeditionary Warfare

Was the 1830 French invasion of Algiers the inspiration for Scott's expeditionary joint forces operation at Veracruz? It is already known, based on the collaboration inherent in Henry Halleck's 1846 *Military Art and Science* and Scott's *Memoirs*, that the two worked to formulate the US Army's population-centric counter-insurgency doctrine, using Napoleon's failures during the occupation of Spain between 1808 and 1813 as a negative template. In addition, the strategy of keeping one single line of operation focused on the Mexican capital was informed by Henri Jomini's biography of Napoleon, which Halleck translated into English during his voyage to California when the war started, but appeared in numerous (uncited) excerpts in his 1846 work. Although Scott's written proposal to attack Veracruz (*Vera Cruz and its castle*) did not elaborate on precedents, he and Halleck undoubtedly consulted on the operation since Halleck was an expert in coastal defence and fortifications and examines them at length in his work. It is inconceivable that Halleck and Scott covered all the aspects of the military campaign without discussing how to take the Castle of San Juan de Ulúa – particularly with the recent experience of the French in Veracruz during the Pastry War. In addition, Halleck's statement that the future role for the Navy was 'in offensive operations' suggests they considered a coastal attack an option long before 1846. Although focus on the study of 'expeditionary warfare' – which includes land operations but often implies the use of naval forces – was still in its nascent stages, it is noteworthy that Scott first called it a 'water expedition' and Halleck used the term 'maritime expedition' – a term he probably acquired from the British when he visited Europe.[63]

In essence, the US Army was modelled along Napoleonic lines, emulating the most successful army in continental Europe, but much of the inspiration for US expeditionary warfare unsurprisingly originated from the British. In order to 'come to a proper conclusion' in evaluating the effectiveness of US coastal defences, Halleck examined various US states' coastal fortifications against a potential coastal attack and cross-referenced them with 'three or four great maritime descents attempted by the English during the wars of the French Revolution; a period at which the great naval superiority of England over other nations, gave her the title of *mistress of the seas*.' Halleck believed British efforts during the Napoleonic Wars offered the best and most useful examples of expeditionary warfare, and he concluded 'the whole history of these wars is one continued proof of the superiority of fortifications as a maritime frontier defence.' Examples included the 1795 expedition against Quiberon, France, a 1799 English-Russian effort against Holland, the 1801 attack by Admiral Horatio Nelson on Boulogne, and the 1809 Walcheren expedition on the Scheldt River near Antwerp. Halleck also dismissed an apparent belief among contemporary strategists that improving cannon and ship technology rendered coastal fortresses less effective. 'The opinions of military writers,' Halleck wrote, 'and the facts of history, fully accord with these deductions of theory.' Halleck strongly asserted that coastal fortifications in 1846 still posed a greater threat than the attacking force:

Some few individuals ... assert that modern improvements in the naval service have so far outstripped the progress in the art of land defence, that a floating force is now abundantly able to cope, upon equal terms, with a land battery. Ignorant and superficial persons, hearing merely that certain forts had recently yielded to a naval force, and taking no trouble to learn the real facts of the case, have paraded them before the public as proofs positive of a new era in military science. This conclusion, however groundless and absurd, has received credit merely from its novelty. Let us examine the several trials of strength which have taken place between ships and forts within the last fifty years.[64]

Halleck offered dozens of historical examples in which even small coastal fortifications repelled a more formidable attacker. These included: a three-day French assault on Cagliari in 1792, a 1794 British attack on a town in Martello Bay (Corsica), an attack by Nelson at Santa Cruz (Tenerife) in 1797, a French attack against the British on the Îles Saint-Marcouf in 1798, an 1803 French attack against Diamond Rock in Port Royal Bay (Bermuda), a British assault against the French at Cape Licosa in 1806, and a British assault against Antwerp in 1814. In Halleck's estimation, these assaults and others served as quantitative proof of the continued efficacy of coastal fortifications against naval assaults, even after the Napoleonic Wars. Moreover, despite 'intimate knowledge' of French harbours and bays, 'depth of water, and the resistance likely to be met' at each engagement, many targets of British expeditions were spared because 'the French knew how to defend their fortifications.' Thus, the lesson to be emulated from the British model was not based directly on attacking coastal fortifications, but on recognizing the outliers of success and finding a factor that made that success more likely. In the case of Veracruz, the idea to land the force and lay siege to the city while foregoing a direct assault on the fort protecting the harbour was informed by the British. In other words, the French landing at Algiers in 1830 mimicked the successful strategy of landing soldiers:

The British maritime expeditions to Quiberon, Holland, Boulogne, the Scheldt, Constantinople, Buenos Ayres, &c., sufficiently prove the ill-success, and the waste of life and treasure with which they must always be attended. But when her naval power was applied to the destruction of the enemy's marine, and in transporting her land forces to solid bases of operations on the soil of her allies, in Portugal and Belgium, the fall of Napoleon crowned the glory of their achievements.[65]

In the 2011 compilation work, *Naval Power and Expeditionary Wars*, historian Michael Duffy notes that the 1808 British expedition to Portugal during the Napoleonic occupation of Iberia 'was the first fully successful British expedition against the French on mainland Europe during the Revolutionary and Napoleonic Wars.'[66] The fact that Halleck recognized the efficacy of landing soldiers to undertake an assault, rather than attacking coastal fortifications directly from sea, bolsters the case that the Americans examined many aspects of the Peninsular War when formulating their strategy against Mexico. In addition, according to Robert Sutcliffe in his recent work *British Expeditionary Warfare and the Defeat of Napoleon, 1793–1815*, the assistance of the private merchant marine augmented the logistical support lacking within the Royal Navy during many of their 'more than fifty major seaborne expeditions ... involving hundreds of thousands of troops' voyages' over a wide range of geography. Sutcliff astutely notes that while thousands of merchant ships 'were essential to support the government's military operations', the state's initiative under the guidance of the Transport Board 'competed with the demands of trade by chartering ships in the open market'. In this regard, for the Americans, and Quartermaster General Thomas Jesup in particular, 'by purchase or charter' was the catchphrase for the procurement of hundreds of vessels and ships sent to Texas and the Gulf.[67]

Secrecy, Strategy and Scapegoats

As alluded to earlier, some historians have described the landing at Veracruz as a 'surprise', and no one is more guilty of perpetuating that myth than Scott. In his memoirs he wrote, 'Mexicans had never any apprehension of an effective invasion from that quarter [Veracruz] or from Tampico.' While it is true the US assault caught the enemy off guard, the statement that they 'had never any apprehension' of the attack or knowledge of the movement of American forces is incorrect. In fact, US activity in the Gulf indicated Veracruz was targeted at least three months prior to the assault. On 27 December, while arranging logistics in New Orleans, Jesup informed Marcy that 'secrecy in our country is out of the question. When I left New Orleans on the 6th instant the public seemed to understand, as well as the officers who are to conduct the operations, that Vera Cruz was the object of attack.'[68]

Rumours spread faster than facts in the Gulf, and nothing which occurred in New Orleans escaped the prying eyes and ears of Mexican informants. Beyond the port city, Mexicans could see troops massing at the island of Brazos Santiago at the mouth of the Rio Grande near Matamoros, and judging by the movement of ships and increasing number of troops moving towards Tampico, were capable of assessing Veracruz's vulnerability to attack as Santa Anna moved north to confront Taylor's army. A bulletin issued on 28 January by the Mexican Ministry of War and Navy noted the US 'threatens to invade us through Veracruz, where the garrison is desperate due to the lack of aid.' Indeed, the problem was not the lack of intelligence but that Mexican officials were having difficulties organizing two armies and could not 'provide the army of the North with the help it lacks, move the National Guard towards Veracruz, and create a large reserve corps.' Although Scott's strategy left Taylor vulnerable, Mexican inability to field two armies meant Veracruz was 'about to be invaded by North American troops'. The only recourse for Santa Anna was to re-march his exhausted and demoralized soldiers towards Scott after being defeated by Taylor.[69]

By early March, and after Taylor's victory at Buena Vista (23 February), everyone in the northern Gulf knew about the American plan to attack Veracruz. One article appearing in the Baltimore *Sun*, based on information received in New Orleans from Tampico on 24 February, informed the public of Scott's arrival in that port and his departure towards Lobos. Since anything happening in Tampico was known to those in San Luis Potosi, the information was readily available to Mexican authorities, who were 'convinced that it is the intention of the enemy to attack' Veracruz and were 'actively employed in devising and perfecting measures of defense'. American newspapers in the good graces of military planners noted, 'The destination of these troops is very properly left to the fruitful imagination of the public; for what is the value of a secret' – although everyone knew. Furthermore, additional reports from Mexican newspapers indicated there was 'no truth' in rumours of the evacuation of Veracruz, because 'authorities of the department, being convinced that it is the intention of the enemy to attack that city, are actively employed in devising and perfecting measures of defense.' In sum, the American attack on Veracruz was far from a surprise.[70]

After the war some Mexicans looked for scapegoats, and Santa Anna was the obvious candidate. Leading the charge 'to return for the honor of my homeland' was Deputy Ramón Gamboa, who compiled an extensive list of accusations against Santa Anna to present to a grand jury while the latter was exiled in Kingston, Jamaica – where he fled after his army was routed by Scott in the defence of Mexico City. Among a litany of charges amounting to treason, Gamboa accused Santa Anna of 'abandonment of Tampico, an important port, defensible and coveted by the Americans', who made it a launching point for their attack in Veracruz. Other charges against Santa Anna included focusing on a strategy that secured 'only San Luis Potosí' and abandoned other states, removing effective 'army chiefs of courage', and negligence at the Battle of Cerro Gordo in April of 1847 after the Americans seized Veracruz. Gamboa, who must have pleased the *caudillo*'s numerous detractors, also asserted that the inability to capture the American supply depot at Saltillo in the north had undermined the defence of Veracruz: 'the weapons and artillery of the Americans, everything would have passed to our troops,' Gamboa wrote, 'such would have been the terror that this encounter instilled in them, that undoubtedly ... if they disembarked in Veracruz they would be so intimidated that they would not dare to enter with the ease and contempt' in which they did.[71]

Santa Anna may have appeared politically inconsistent at times, but he was not going to let Gamboa make accusations without responding. In 1849, Santa Anna published a defence entitled, *Appeal to the good judgment of nationals and foreigners*. In it, he excoriated Gamboa and 'vile Mexicans' who 'accuse me of treason' and justified his wartime actions on the grounds of expediency and the limited resources available. In addition to compiling government bulletins demonstrating the shortage of men and material left behind to defend Veracruz, Santa Anna noted that 'symptoms of revolution ... beginning to manifest in the army' hindered operations in the north. Furthermore, the garrison left behind in Tampico was a scant 800 men – many of whom were sick: 'Do you know that there were no elements even for a regular defense,' he asked Gamboa rhetorically, 'and that with this knowledge, having to fight a weak garrison against a powerful enemy, in addition to being inexperienced, would be inhumane?' Santa Anna listed other hindrances, including long distances, 'fatal roads' and a shortage of funds – concluding, in view of the American victory at Veracruz, that resistance at Tampico would have meant the meaningless sacrifice of the garrison. How could Tampico 'hold its own against the attacks of the invaders, when it had been seen that the important plazas of Ulúa and Veracruz, perfectly armed, with more respectable provisions and garrisons, succumbed in a few days?' Criticism directed at him, after the war and coming from someone who was not even present, was particularly detestable to a man who lost a leg from cannon fire in 1838 while defending Veracruz from the French:

> Mr. Gamboa sees all things through the prism that he himself has invented, and without realizing that they forced me to leave San Luis Potosí ... almost at the same time that General Scott landed on the Veracruz coast, for which reason it now seems that I should have abandoned the North, even though General Taylor advanced in that part, and marched with the army, crossing the Republic, to oppose the new general, who was invading us from the East.[72]

Justifying his conduct further, Santa Anna questioned the inaction of other officials in the defence of Veracruz – highlighting the fact that the government supposedly ordered a division to Xalapa west of that city to check Scott's advance into the interior. 'Then why are someone else's crimes imputed to me,' he asked, 'and do they want me to attend to the errors that were committed more than two hundred leagues away from where I resided?' In the long litany of reasons given for the defeat, Santa Anna was also careful to admit that the American victory against him at Cerro Gordo was not merely the result of Mexican inability, but arose from the superiority of American artillery, weaponry and 'enthusiasm of victory, which instilled in our inexperienced soldiers faintness and discouragement.'[73]

Santa Anna did not only defend his actions during the war; his narrative discussing the period prior to 1846 demonstrates that Mexicans viewed the conflict with Texas as a prelude to a regional struggle lasting between 1835 and 1848. In essence, while many Americans may not have believed their country was at war with Mexico, many Mexicans believed it was. When Santa Anna was taken prisoner in 1836 after the Battle of San Jacinto in Texas he agreed to travel to Washington DC to meet President Andrew Jackson. 'I was able to observe in my transit through the United States of the North,' Santa Anna wrote, 'that the periodical press and the inhabitants in general manifested strong tendencies to widen the limits of their nation with a considerable part of our territory.' Internal conflicts preceding the larger war drained the Mexican treasury and prevented the country from uniting during a crucial period. 'The army was so diminished that the government of General Bustamante abandoned the Commander General of Yucatan,' Santa Anna argued, and thus federal forces had no choice but to surrender 'for lack of aid; an event with disastrous consequences that are still deplored'. Santa Anna also cited a handful of other uprisings in San Luis Potosi, Tampico, Michoacán and Tabasco: 'The same happened with the Commander General of Tabasco D. Ignacio Gutierrez, who succumbed to the adventurer Sentmaná[t], despite the long and vigorous resistance that he put up against him.' The internal rebellions and breakaways republics thus sapped the strength of the nation before the larger contest began in 1846.[74]

Isthmuses and the Second Battle of Tabasco

The situation on the opposite side of the Gulf continued to pose a dilemma to Mexico, but their preoccupation with Scott's army meant there was little they could do about it. In early 1847, Yucatan leaders in Campeche initiated a rebellion against political authorities in Merida who were positioning the peninsula to re-enter the federal system and sent Jose Rovira, a former consular agent of France at Laguna, to Washington to proclaim neutrality and negotiate concessions to alleviate the blockade which was damaging trade. Ancono claimed Rovira was 'a fanatical admirer of the homeland of Washington, and who … was not only in favor of neutrality, but even the annexation of Yucatan to that powerful republic.' American leaders, aware of the Navy's relationship with Laguna, acquiesced.[75]

On 22 February, Buchanan informed Secretary Mason of the change in policy but suggested enforcement and 'bona fide neutrality' should be determined by the commanding officer in the Gulf due to the discovery that Yucatecans 'under the guise of neutrality' were carrying on 'a contraband trade and furnishing Mexico with arms and munitions of war.' By mid-March Yucatecans were allowed to trade in American ports. Zuleta adds that Americans refused to sell weapons to Yucatan because the *campechanos*, who were controlling illicit trade in the Gulf, had been purchasing munitions in New Orleans and smuggling them into Tabasco. Ancono confirmed the origins of this relationship when he wrote that the Yucatecans first 'contacted Commodore Conner, who was in the waters off Veracruz, to ask him not to harass Yucatán, and he had acceded to their wishes – without prejudice to the occupation of Carmen.' It was Conner who granted Rovira safe passage to the United States to formalize the agreement.[76]

Executive decisions during early 1847 informed US action on the southern end of the Gulf, and Perry's return to Tabasco was not only motivated by his personal desire to fulfill unfinished business and stymie the smuggling of munitions and contraband, but had larger strategic objectives in accord with leadership in Washington. On 26 February, just before the invasion of Veracruz, Polk and Perry met twice to discuss the latter's orders to return to the war and relieve Conner of command of the Gulf Squadron. Two weeks later, Polk wrote that administration officials discussed raising the blockade 'to defray' war expenses and soon after granted Yucatan trading privileges in US ports. On 10 April, the Baltimore *Sun* received express news by way of Pensacola's telegraph station of the fall of Veracruz and its castle with minimal losses. 'In about two hours afterwards a more detailed account of the capitulation was received,' Polk wrote, describing it as 'joyful news'. That same day, the cabinet met to discuss appointing a commissioner to send to the army 'to take advantage of circumstances as they might arise to negotiate for peace'. The chief clerk at the State Department, Nicholas Trist, was chosen for the task.[77]

On 13 April Buchanan submitted his proposal to the cabinet for articles outlining a treaty. It was also decided that Trist's mission would be secret and only known to cabinet members. The administration wanted a border at the Rio Grande, was adamant about adding New Mexico and California, and addressed the issue about 'securing to the US the right of passage' over the Tehuantepec isthmus, which officials believed was accessible inland at Tabasco. Varying sums in the millions were offered as incentives to secure an agreement. Polk commented in his diary that Treasury Secretary Robert J. Walker 'attached greater importance to the free passage across the Istmus [*sic*] of Tehuantepec than to the cession of New Mexico & the Californias.' The cabinet discussed the issue further, concluding 'that if the passage across the istmus of Tehuantepec could not be obtained,' the financial incentive would be further reduced. Buchanan disagreed with this approach, and again 'Walker insisted that the free passage across the istmus of Tehuantepec should be a *sine qua non* to the making of any treaty.' It was here that Polk objected by explaining that the isthmus 'constituted no part of the object for which we had engaged in the war' and that the rest of the cabinet concurred with his views. Polk wrote that Buchanan, who seemed to side with Walker, was 'over ruled' and it was agreed that $5,000,000 would be set aside in the treasury and paid to Mexico if a road or canal was eventually constructed in that location. This prompted a debate regarding the financing of foreign infrastructure, which some believed the Senate would not abide, and thus the provision was omitted from the proposal. At the end of the day (11.00 pm), it was decided, against the wishes of both Walker and Buchanan, to add 'a simple provision securing to the citizens of the US a free passage across the istmus forever'. On 16 April, Trist departed for Mexico.[78]

Why was Walker, and to a lesser extent Buchanan, insisting on acquiring transit rights over Tehuantepec, and why were Polk and the rest of the cabinet objecting? The answer is illuminated by a treaty concluded by Benjamin A. Bidlack, the US chargé d'affaires in Bogota, New Granada, in December of 1846. Intended to forestall British and French intervention, the treaty not only guaranteed the neutrality of the Panamanian isthmus but obliged the US to defend New Granada in the event of foreign or domestic interference on the isthmus. Known as the New Granada, or Bidlack, Treaty, the pact was the first of its kind and controversial, given the traditional American policy of neutrality regarding the foreign affairs of other states. When the treaty arrived on Polk's desk, the president quoted George Washington's farewell address warning against foreign alliances: 'Serious doubts were entertained whether this stipulation was consistent with our long-settled policy to "cultivate friendship with all nations, entangling alliances with none".' Polk noted that he and Buchanan discussed the military obligation 'at some length' before deciding to forward it to the Senate on 10 February – a little more than two weeks before meeting Perry at the White House. In Polk's message to the Senate, he remarked that Bidlack made the agreement 'without instructions' with New Granada's Secretary of State, Manuel Maria Mallarino. However, because it was essentially in the spirit of a Senate resolution passed on 3 March 1835, requesting 'to consider the expediency of opening negotiations … with the Governments of Central America and New Granada,' for a permanent 'ship canal across the isthmus', Polk deemed it worthy of consideration. The president added that he was 'deeply sensible … of the danger of entangling alliances with any foreign nation' and that the United States 'should avoid such alliances', but that the importance of securing a route eliminating 14,000km (9,000 miles) distance around South America superseded those concerns. Furthermore, he informed the Senate, 'The guaranty does not extend to the territories of New Granada generally, but is confined to the single Province of the Isthmus of Panama.' The Senate shelved the treaty for the duration of the war but ratified it on 10 June 1848, and Polk signed it on 12 June, a couple of months before US soldiers began leaving Mexico.[79]

Among Polk's cabinet members, Walker had the most to lose if the United States focused its isthmian energies on Panama. Walker had inherited lands in Texas, and that state – along with shipping interests in New Orleans serving the wider Mississippi watershed – were proponents of the Tehuantepec route because it would have been a commercial boon to that part of the country. On the other hand, although Polk was from Tennessee, he and most of his cabinet – apart from Buchanan and Vice President George M. Dallas (both political rivals) – were aligned with the more powerful shipping and financial interests on the east coast favouring Panama or Nicaragua. In essence, geography, logistics, and money played no small role in the search for a favourable route connecting the Atlantic and Pacific. As the war entered its second year, powerful lobbyists began asserting their influence, with the result being that Tehuantepec was somewhat relegated as a priority. The other alternative, embodied in the political outlook of Polk's Democratic allies in the Senate, such as the Foreign Relations Chairman Lewis Cass, and Vice President Dallas, were proponents of annexing all of Mexico to the United States, which would have diminished the reliance on a Panamanian route.

The background of the Bidlack Treaty thus sheds light on Polk's seeming lack of interest in Tehuantepec (according to his account), but it is not known what he discussed with Perry in February prior to the commodore's return to the gulf to take over Conner's role. What is known is that Perry officially seized Laguna in mid-May and launched an expedition against Tabasco in June after US forces successfully seized Veracruz. Furthermore, although Polk and Buchanan were often at odds over policy and strategy, Buchanan believed, as did Walker and Dallas, that acquiring transit rights over Tehuantepec was important. One week after Trist left on his mission to Mexico, Buchanan sent a confidential letter to General James Shields in Mexico by way of Alejandro Atocha, a Spanish-born naturalized US citizen with extensive business in that country. The administration was using Atocha, unsuccessfully, as a back channel to get the Mexican leadership to renew negotiations and it is prudent to assume that Buchanan penned his letter knowing Atocha would share its contents with Mexican officials. Writing to Shields, Buchanan stated that he believed 'public opinion' was not in favour of annexing Mexican territory 'on this side of the Sierra Madre Mountains to the United States' – an idea that entailed nearly the entire Gulf of Mexico becoming an American waterway. He then wrote that it 'would be extremely desirable, if not indispensable, to obtain a right of passage across the Isthmus of Tehuantepec'.[80]

With that in mind, Griffis noted in his biography of Perry that the commodore 'was not personally in favor with the authorities' in Washington DC, including Secretary of Navy John Y. Mason, and mentioned the extremely poor relationship between Scott and Polk to make his point. Griffis wrote that Perry 'was not alone, for even Scott gained his brilliant victories without the personal sympathies or good wishes of the Administration.' Not knowing his legacy would be the missions to Japan in the 1850s, and thinking that perhaps the successful Veracruz landing completed by his predecessor would hasten the end of the war, Perry launched the expedition to Tabasco. Whether or not Polk told Perry in February that he need not acquire Tabasco, because the administration had ostensibly secured transit rights through Panama, is speculation, but if he did, it may have only served to harden his determination to win the wartime laurels he and his fellow naval officers were yearning for. Griffis believed, 'The very brilliancy of the victories of both our army and navy in Mexico blinded not only the general public, but the administration to the arduous nature of the service' – adding that armchair critics spoke of the army's role in the war as a 'picnic', and that of the navy as a 'yachting excursion'. In essence, Perry aimed to prove them wrong by making Tabasco his wartime legacy.[81]

However, unlike his first engagement there in 1846, the commodore would not enter the Grijalva River a second time without proper firepower and force. Accompanying Perry was future Rear Admiral Benjamin F. Sands, who cruised the gulf stream between Cuba and Key West and reached Veracruz two days after its capture, only to be ordered to Tabasco. 'We were elated at the prospect of a "brush" with the *Greasers* or Mustangs as they were euphoniously called,' he wrote, 'our vessel being ordered to blockade off Laguna until the Commodore should come down from Alvaredo with a force sufficiently large for the attack.' On 16 May, a few days after Sands attended a *fandango* at Laguna, Commodore Perry arrived, accompanied by marines, met local officials and dignitaries at the city hall, and formally took control of the port after raising the US flag over the city's fortress. Commander George A. Magruder, captain of the *Vesuvius*, was appointed governor. Perry then sent

Captain Samuel L. Breese, former military governor of the recently captured coastal town of Tuxpan, and Commander Alexander S. Mackenzie, known for his 1842 execution of mutineers aboard the USS *Somers*, as 'commissioners to settle the difficulties' that had arisen between the Americans and Yucatecans. It is not known what message Perry ordered Breese and Mackenzie to convey to authorities in Campeche apart from informing them of the US Navy's formal seizure of Laguna, but the commodore felt it important to do so before launching his attack on Tabasco.[82]

Again, Perry's actions just prior to the campaign to seize San Juan Bautista support the argument that Tehuantepec was a key reason for the assault. As mentioned in the introduction, American military engineers under the leadership of Major John G. Barnard, an officer entrusted during the war with constructing defences at Tampico in the event of a Mexican attack, led an exploration and survey of the Tehuantepec isthmus in 1850/51 after the war. One of the officers included in that survey was William G. Temple, the author who chronicled the logistical details of the Veracruz landing. Barnard's survey was partly based on Garay's 1844 *Survey of the Isthmus* and assertions of the navigability of the Coatzacoalcos River, but the first US survey of the river was conducted in May of 1847 under Perry's orders aboard the brig *Stromboli* – which was engaged in blockading duty near the mouth of the Coatzacoalcos in the Bay of Campeche. Barnard cited one weather observation report dated 24 May 1847, from the inland river town of Minatitlan, and confirmed the depth of the river was suitable for larger-draught vessels. Among a series of maps published in conjunction with the survey, Barnard included the 1847 *Sketch from the mouth of the Coatzacoalcos River to the town of Mina-Titlan; made by order of Commodore M.C. Perry.* The survey was conducted after Perry's arrival at Laguna and before the attack on Tabasco's capital. The *Stromboli* was also ordered to return in January 1848 to complete the survey of the river's mouth – indicating the US government's interest in the isthmus even after the battle.[83]

On 30 May 1847, a few days after US forces seized Frontera at the mouth of the Tabasco River, an anonymous report under the name 'Marinus' was sent from Veracruz to the editors of the New Orleans *Delta* and subsequently published in the *Daily Union* in Washington. The article entitled 'Canal of the Isthmus of Tehuantepec' was written by someone aboard the *Stromboli*. In addition to providing a timeline indicating the survey of the Coatzacoalcos was conducted following the seizure of Frontera, the writer asserted that the location, which someday might form 'a canal, or a railroad, or both', was 'destined to become at some future time the most important of any on the continent of America'. More importantly, it indicated that Commodore Perry's flagship the *Mississippi* and Perry himself accompanied the survey to Minatitlan. On or around 21 May, 'a considerable force was transferred from the *Mississippi* to the *Scorpion*, preceded by the commodore and staff.' After measuring the depth of the river as it emptied into the Gulf, the *Scorpion* proceeded 30km upriver. The forests with their exotic fauna were punctuated by prairies holding cattle, while nests hung from large trees reaching into the river, and there was a flock of flamingos in the distance. The *Scorpion* then reached the marshy town of Minatitlan:

> The barefooted *alcade*, with an assemblage of the principal citizens, stood firmly on the shore to receive and welcome us, apparently with open arms. The commodore and all the supernumerary officers landed; then a guard of marines, accompanied by seamen, with a staff and flag, which was raised and saluted in the plaza of the town by the marine officer of the Mississippi, pursuant to the orders of the commander-in-chief.[84]

The American flag planted briefly near the banks of the Coatzacoalcos River in Minatitlan represented the furthest southern extent of American forces in the Mexican-American War. The city centre of San Juan Bautista, the administrative capital of Tabasco, is nearly at the same latitude but US servicemen were stationed further north. In addition, the anonymous report from Marinus appearing in the *Daily Union* was sent back from Veracruz before Perry launched an attack on San Juan Bautista – indicating Perry left orders in Veracruz (Lizardo) for ships to move towards Tabasco. From around 12 June, US vessels began arriving at Frontera. Griffis wrote: 'From various points on the coast, the ships and steamers assembled like magic, and on Monday morning, June 14, 1847, the squadron came to anchor off the mouth of the Tabasco river.' It included the brigs *Stromboli*, *Vesuvius* and *Washington*, accompanied by Perry's Mosquito Fleet, the *Scorpion*, *Scourge*, *Spitfire* and *Vixen*. Towed behind the shallow-draught steamers were forty smaller ship's boats – seven of which were surfboats most likely used at the Veracruz landing. In total, around 1,100 men took part in the operation.[85]

Sands served as executive officer aboard the *Washington* as part of the attack, and was among many informed that 'the Mexicans were in considerable force'

– apparently bolstering their defences at San Juan Bautista in anticipation of another assault. After meandering most of the way upstream to a location known as the 'Devil's Bend', the flotilla encountered obstructions held by piles driven into the shallower parts of the river and met some resistance from Mexican fighters hiding in the chaparral lining the banks. The next morning, Perry landed the main force with batteries to support the removal of the blocking material, and a sizeable force marched along the banks towards the city. 'Such enthusiastic zeal could hardly be surpassed,' Sands wrote, 'and we at once commenced the march across the country to turn the flank of the forts which defended the city.' Perry led the force ashore, and 'pioneers' were tasked with cutting brush to make paths. The terrain was swampy, so particular attention was given to ensuring the cannons were kept dry as they were dragged. As the force cut their way towards San Juan Bautista, sounds of cannon fire from the steamers could be heard. When the group reached the city's defences the men charged. 'We gave them time to fire but a few guns before the sailors were over the parapets and into the fort,' Sands recalled, 'and on we went at double-quick towards the city, the enemy in flight before us.' By sundown on 16 June the US Navy was in command of the capital of Tabasco. Perry left Commander Gershom J. Van Brunt and a garrison of around 200 men to temporarily hold the city.[86]

Despite their immediate concern with Scott's army at Puebla, Mexico City officials were following events in Tabasco. The Mexicans also believed Perry's actions were intended to bolster the American position vis-à-vis Tehuantepec and a potential route over the isthmus. On 3 June, above an article discussing a nationwide implementation of guerrilla war against the Americans, *El Diario* cited a letter from Vice President Dallas to a constituent appearing in Philadelphia's newspaper *Spirit of the Times*. The letter, reprinted on 1 May in Washington's *Weekly National Intelligencer*, outlined his urging of 'the administration to enter into peace talks with Mexico' with the goal of acquiring 'the right to open a canal through the Isthmus of Tehuantepec.' Citing Garay's survey and the Gulf route as superior to Panama and Nicaragua, Dallas believed it was 'one of the most important points for the prosperity of the commerce of the United States and of the whole world'. An ardent expansionist, Dallas also expressed his opinion that the region could simply be purchased in the same manner the US had acquired Louisiana and Florida. Moreover, the Vice President stated that 'surveyors and engineers have already left for Mexico to reconnoiter the terrain and trace the line to open the canal.'[87]

Indeed, the blockade was making it difficult for federal officials in Mexico to follow events occurring in the southern Gulf, as there was no indication they knew of Perry's survey of the Coatzacoalcos before his attack on Tabasco. Dallas' letter obviously prompted them to pay closer attention, because the following month, on 8 July, they reported that 'it had been decided to send to Veracruz a considerable number of marines under the orders of General [Archibald] Henderson, with whom the engineers commissioned to reconnoiter the Isthmus' with a force 'believed to have exceeded 2,500 men.' The Mexicans likely learned of the expedition from an article appearing in Washington's *National Whig* – the mouthpiece of the administration's detractors in Washington. That article, which chided Democrats for their assertions that the war 'must be made' one of 'conquest of territory and treasures' of Mexico, indicated the decision to send the marines was the result of 'consultations of the President and his cabinet' following Scott's decisive victory against Santa Anna at Cerro Gordo. 'It is this expedition which was shadowed forth in the recent accounts from Commodore Perry. All the marines on shore have been ordered to the Home Squadron in the Gulf forthwith.' The article also noted that the 'force is large enough to ensure perfect safety to the exploring party, for the enemy, were he disposed, cannot offer any serious resistance in the section of the country proposed to be explored.'[88]

The only problem was that the force of marines sent to Veracruz – 300 of whom arrived on 29 June – was not intended to protect an exploratory party on the isthmus but rather to bolster Scott's forces in Puebla for a pending attack on the Mexican capital. Scott had recently dismissed around 4,000 soldiers whose enlistment periods were set to expire and desperately needed to refill his ranks. Polk met with the Secretary of Navy and Henderson in mid-May to formalize – 'with as little delay as practicable' – the transfer of six companies 'under the immediate command of Gen'l Scott'. Thus, the marines were rounded up from various naval bases on the east coast and sent to the Gulf. A small number of soldiers arrived from Pensacola, and together the group moved into the interior towards Puebla, but were delayed by poor weather and guerrilla activity. Marine historian Gabrielle Santelli notes that the battalion 'had only two days' rest at Puebla' before Scott began moving his main force on 7 August.[89]

While Dallas' views on Tehuantepec were probably sincere, it is evident that someone in the administration used the Whig newspaper to disseminate disinformation regarding the use and destination of the marines. Furthermore, the beleaguered (and infirm) garrison Perry left behind at San Juan Bautista – which was fending off attacks by Mexican forces on the edge of the city – added to the impression the Americans were attempting to seize the region to further their isthmian agenda. On 20 July, without knowledge that Perry had ordered a withdrawal from the Tabascan capital the day before, *El Diaro* reprinted a 6 July article entitled 'State of Oaxaca' from that state's *Nueva Era constitucional*. The article centred around Vice-Governor Francisco Ortiz de Zárate's efforts to rally a force to meet the rumoured exploratory party of Americans, and evinced local officials' concerns about a possible invasion. 'Mr. Zárate has the notable circumstance of belonging to the recommended military class,' the article read, 'to quell the internal war and pacify the point of Tehuantepec, where he has to direct his attention.' The Oaxacan newspaper also reported on what officials in Mexico City had come to believe regarding 'the projects that our enemies from the North have on that isthmus, and some signs of carrying it out are already announced; and so it is urgent to send some force to pacify and bring order to its inhabitants.'[90]

Adding to the intrigue, on 15 July Zárate received a report indicating 'Yankees in number of 500 had disembarked in the place named La Fabrica ... and headed for the town of Guichicovi.' Guichicovi, a small Zapotec community upstream from the Coatzacoalcos in the Sierra Madre del Sur, is located in the heart of the isthmus. A week later, after sending out inquiries into the veracity of the rumours, Zárate sent a letter to the central government indicating the reports 'were false' but likely related to the American force in the Tabascan capital. On edge, and seemingly unaware of activity in the isthmus, Zárate concluded that the 'supreme government should not concern itself that the state has been invaded by the enemy.' It was not until weeks later, just before Scott set out to conquer Mexico City, that federal officials learned San Juan Bautista had been abandoned by the Americans. While it may not have been an effort to seize the isthmus, it seemingly served as a diversion.[91]

With these concerns in mind, on 28 July *El Diario* printed a long article related to Garay's survey initiated by Santa Anna. Rather than harangue the Americans for contemplating a canal, the article coolly announced that Garay had formed an agreement the previous summer with interests in London to develop the project and facilitate 'European immigration' in Oaxaca to offset 'depopulation of the Isthmus.' The Mexicans were elated to learn what the Americans already knew – since the information about Garay's contract with a mysterious London company passed through the United States before reaching Mexico City. According to US reports, it was Dallas' letter that prompted New York engineer and surveyor Benjamin H. Wright to inform the public in mid-May that Garay had 'transferred his privilege to a company in London, who are waiting for peace between us and Mexico to commence operations .' One article in the *National Whig*, entitled 'Hands Off', boasted that 'Mr. Polk may now "hang up his fiddle" in this matter, for the right to the isthmus having been granted to a neutral before the war, cannot be taken away by this government.' One private citizen's assertion was obviously not enough to dissuade the Americans from conducting their own exploration – given that US military officers surveyed the isthmus after the war – but the episode demonstrates that the Mexicans were eager to announce in *El Diario* that British rights over a potential route (in their opinion) acted as an impediment to American designs:

> By virtue of this contract, an English commission came to make other reconnaissance, and the engineer ... was also dispatched again, in order to measure and designate the land for the settlers, and to form a provisional communication project between the two seas by a road, in the part where navigation is not now possible, thus preparing and facilitating the work of the great canal, since for it Mr. Garay has also contracted with English houses, the formation of a company that will take charge of its execution.[92]

That British interests potentially had a claim to rights over Tehuantepec added evidence to the argument by expansionists that Europeans were meddling in the war. Rather than acting as a deterrent, expansionists were emboldened by Mexican monarchists, who believed alliances with powerful European states would stymie the continental ambitions of the United States. There were still Americans who believed south-east Mexico, namely, Tabasco, Chiapas and Yucatan, could be split from Mexico. For republican-minded Mexicans such as Santa Anna, the juxtaposition presented a difficult problem. They likely applauded the possible thwarting of US acquisition of Tehuantepec, but the consequences entailed being beholden to a foreign power. The Mexicans had fought a long and costly war of independence to oust Europeans from their country and were therefore reluctant to rely on outside actors to moderate the impulses of their enemy.

Regardless, after August officials in Mexico City, given their preoccupation with Scott's army forcing its way to the capital, no longer had the luxury of following affairs in the Gulf. By mid-September the US Army headquarters was firmly seated in the large city, and directives were sent to naval officers to cease the seizure of Mexican ports. Bauer claims the 'American presence strengthened a movement in Chiapas and Tabasco states to secede from Mexico' and join in a confederation with Guatemala, which was the basis for Perry's submission in October 1847 to renew operations in the Tehuantepec region and thus 'cut Tabasco and Chiapas states off from the rest of Mexico.'[93] However, by that time yellow fever among sailors inhibited offensive operations and another war in the Gulf changed the dynamic of the conflict. Peace between the United States and Mexico was being negotiated, but as will be discussed, Yucatan was anything but at peace. Americans may have had total control over the Gulf, but their limitations would become manifest.

Texan and Gulf Intelligence

A factor vital in US military success was pre-war intelligence gathering. Since Texas was at war from 1835 to 1848, Texan and New Orleans smugglers, operatives, agents, spies, travellers claiming to be Americans, and others with intimate connections with Mexico collected and provided useful information that assisted US forces at land and sea when the United States became involved in the conflict. While it is true that many Texans entered Mexico to exact revenge for wrongs they believed were perpetrated against them in the years prior to 1846, the more important role these eager participants played in the outcome of the campaign should not be overlooked.

Many of them, especially those whose families had settled in Texas in the 1820s (and even earlier), knew the culture of Mexico, had travelled south of the Rio Grande countless times, married Mexican or Tejano women, often adopted the Roman Catholic religion to accommodate their spouses or in-laws (or both), and more importantly, read and spoke Spanish either eagerly or reluctantly. Thomas Jefferson Green, who was one of a couple of hundred Texans who were taken prisoner after a reckless effort in late

1842 to assault the Rio Grande town of Ciudad Mier, noted in his pre-war work chronicling the expedition and his captivity, that whites who became 'too intimate' with the culture often became 'Mexicanized', such as 'young men [who] had lived some time in San Antonio, and had acquired much of Mexican habit, with a consequent corresponding sympathy which outbalanced their Texian patriotism.'[94]

Green's ignorance of the forces of acculturation can be excused, given that he was a recent arrival from North Carolina and knew relatively little about those who had settled the frontier a generation before and sought accommodation with Tejanos. Nevertheless, his observations portray an obvious cultural schism between white newcomers and descendants of the earlier settlers who held a deeper understanding of Texas culture – many of whom adopted the ways of the *vaquero* to make a living. Green in this sense represents the wave of Americans who flooded into Texas after 1835 anticipating conflict with anyone appearing Mexican. Green wrote: 'I have remarked that whenever a citizen of the United States resides long enough in Mexico to discard his suspenders, and tie up his pantaloons with a red band around the waist, cover his shoulders with a blanket, and eat a gill of red pepper at a meal – beware of him!'[95]

Despite Green's uninformed observations, the men responsible for ensuring Texas independence benefited from acculturated white and Tejano patriots who gathered intelligence on Mexican activities – particularly as they related to a potential invasion. The ability to blend in, travel relatively unnoticed and speak Spanish was critical to their nascent nation's survival, and the information they provided to US authorities was used to the advantage of the army. One example was the American-turned-Texan A.S. Wright. Educated at St Mary's College in Baltimore before acquiring Spanish after living in Spain for many years, Wright eventually moved to Texas and did business with Mexicans. Beginning in 1838, he provided the authorities with information on the movements of native tribes, before catching the eye of Colonel Barnard E. Bee and becoming a special agent in Mexico City. Bee mentioned his initial encounter with Wright in a letter to Texas Secretary of State James Webb, writing that his new informant was 'on his way to Mexico ... to be promptly on the Rio Grande' to spy on the movements of natives in that area.

> He proffer[s] his services to keep us constantly advised, and wishes to know if we will recompense him. I have assured him he will

be compensated according to the importance and accuracy of his information. I am indeed not sorry to have met this man, if he is worthy. We ought to have at this moment an individual who will keep us informed of all Mexico's steps.[96]

In the initial years of Texas' status as a breakaway state, merchants were forced to be creative to avoid scrutiny from patrols in the Gulf or to avoid them entirely. The Texan and New Orleans merchants knew the Mexican ports better than anyone: Sisal, Veracruz, Campeche, Frontera, Carmen at Laguna, and even eastern Yucatan, where they attempted at one point to set up a naval station on the island of Cozumel and claim it for Texas. The idea of using Lobos Island – a known haven for piracy and smuggling – is a good example of the intelligence received in New Orleans while planning the Veracruz operation. Scott took credit for using the island and wrote in his memoirs that while in New Orleans he 'fortunately heard from old shipmasters that tolerable intermediate anchorage might be found in the terrible northers, behind the Lobos Islands.'[97]

Another example of the critical use of Texas intelligence to aid the US invasion were the connections made between Texans and the Mexican smuggling network between the capital city and Veracruz. The imprisonment of Texans in the 1840s in an old fortress at Perote, situated between Veracruz and Mexico City, ironically helped the campaign to seize the capital. The eighteenth-century prison, formerly known as the Castle of San Carlos, had an older history under New Spain's Viceroy as a 'second-line of defence' in the event that Veracruz was captured. The fortress was completed after several years of construction beginning in 1770 and later housed prisoners during the Mexican Revolution. A mid-twentieth-century summary of the notorious 'hellhole' describes the windy, high-altitude prison built atop an extinct volcano. 'Every force, either of nature's or man's making, combines to make Perote Prison one of the worst spots imaginable. Even the Aztecs called the place "*pinahuizapan*", or "something-to-be-buried-in".' For captured soldiers who fought for the Republic of Texas, Perote was the end of the world.[98]

Although the imprisonment was a cause of considerable anger among those who returned to Mexico during the war with the United States, their escape provided critical intelligence on the smuggling network in existence in Mexico. Most of the Mexican black marketeers were already on unfriendly terms with their government, and thus made perfect collaborators. George

Wilkens Kendall, a founder of and reporter for the New Orleans *Picayune*, chronicled his imprisonment in Perote in his 1844 *Narrative of the Texan Santa Fé Expedition*. The 1841 expedition, sent to New Mexico to trade with the Republic of Texas and seize the Santa Fe Trail, ended in disaster, and its members were taken prisoner and marched more than a thousand miles to Mexico City. Many of the prisoners who survived the march were held in Perote. According to Kendall, the 'butchery' of prisoners at the hands of the Mexicans made the entire group 'callous' and eager for retribution, but since Kendall was an American citizen, he was fortunate the US State Department worked to get him released. However, for most Texan prisoners, whose young republic was at war, waiting for help to arrive was futile.[99]

Green's experience in Perote and the intelligence his account provided before the war aided the US campaign to seize Mexico City more than the failed assault on Mier. Although one escape attempt in July of 1843 was thwarted, sixteen Mier prisoners managed to tunnel out and make their escape on 25 March 1844. In 1845, a year before the war began, Green published his account of the ordeal, noting how their previous escape attempt made their second attempt more difficult because guards checked their cells a 'dozen times per day' and examined the walls. The Mexicans, however, never conceived that the Texans would tunnel 40ft down through the floor 'underneath the main wall so as to reach the bottom of the great moat upon the outside'. According to Green, this arduous work was finished in forty days.[100]

More importantly, with the help of an elderly Mexican guide familiar with the smuggling trade, Green and a number of other companions made their way to the coastal city of Veracruz. Without this assistance Green would likely have been recaptured, as were seven of the other escapees. En route they passed Santa Anna's large estate near the Antigua River, and upon arriving in the port city lodged 'in the midst of the infected district, where scores died daily of the *vomito*, the worst kind of yellow fever, and where we were constantly under apprehension of discovery.' The small group stayed in hiding for nearly two weeks, and through a small opening from a window saw 'several officers of the Mexican army that we well knew ... Here in this death's hole we had to lay and sweat out the last days of hot July.' Green recalled a few American sailors offering 'their services' to the group, and it was soon 'ascertained that the steamer "Petrita", formerly the "Champion" of Mobile, would be the first vessel sailing for the United States.' The *Petrita* was the same vessel that plied the Grijalva River in Tabasco and assisted Perry in the US Navy's first attack on Tabasco's capital. And in 1843, it was aboard the *Petrita* that several former Perote prisoners were secretly stowed.[101]

As one of Scott's main intelligence officers, Colonel Hitchcock obviously took note of Green's account. On 20 June 1847, while in Puebla – the halfway point to Mexico City – he wrote that he was 'anxious to make an arrangement' with a group of Mexican smugglers, led by a man named Manuel Dominguez, who would act as spies and messengers along the corridor stretching between Veracruz and Mexico City. Hitchcock wrote that General Worth arrested the chief 'on complaint of his own people, and ... offered to take him into our service' after Scott approved. There is more to the story, since Hitchcock later worked diligently to have Dominguez and his family moved to New Orleans after the war. Apart from providing essential communications, the spies worked as guides for counter-insurgency forces that were needed to sweep the areas abutting the main logistics line between Mexico City and Veracruz. Years later, when Hitchcock penned his memoirs, he articulated why the spy company's significance in the war had gone unappreciated. The men

> were employed as runners from Puebla, and by means of them the General-in-Chief [Scott] was accurately informed of all Mexican movements in the towns adjacent to Puebla, and the highway was constantly explored, clear into the city of Mexico, at a time when everybody passing in and out of Mexico underwent the most rigid examination. These spies usually entered the city as market people from Chalco ... After the number of the spies was increased and the Mexicans suspected we had such persons in our employment some of them were detected and executed; but, notwithstanding this, Dominguez found others and continued to obtain information which could be had in no other way.[102]

Although Texans may have resented the fact that Taylor did not penetrate further into Mexico, or launch an attack on San Luis Potosi, their prior knowledge of the region contributed to victory. Despite being relegated in the conquest of Mexico City, for many Texans the US invasion into the heart of Mexico vindicated all the prior hardship they felt they had endured at the hands of their oppressors. This was particularly true of the Texas Rangers, who took on Mexican and Spanish guerrillas between Mexico City and Veracruz after years of defending their homes on familiar territory. Captain Samuel Hamilton Walker, a Texas Ranger and former prisoner of Perote, accompanied a brigade in 1847 to reinforce Scott in Mexico City and lift the siege of the small American garrison left behind in Puebla after US forces seized the capital. Walker stopped at Perote prison to visit his old cell and retrieve a coin he had hidden there – fulfilling a vow he had made to himself that someday he would return as a conqueror. The Rangers eagerly traversed the waters of the Gulf to bring the fight to the doorsteps of their enemy – to the seat of Mexican authority. For this reason, they rode triumphantly into the capital eschewing the US Army uniform and dressed as soldiers of the frontier, a gesture to the crowd of onlookers who knew exactly where they had come from and why they were there. For the most part, however, US officers, particularly those with formal training at West Point, attempted to keep retribution off the list of factors motivating their conduct.

Passing from one generation to the next, if left unmitigated, resentment festers to become a monster of obsession, blame, and finally vengeance. The Texans may have felt wronged, but by comparison, the Maya of Yucatan harboured a longer and deeper resentment against their masters that, for a number of reasons, was unleashed in 1847. The success of the US campaign to seize the Mexican capital only fuelled the ambitions of those in power in Washington who believed that Mexico, and thus the whole North American continent, belonged under the hegemony of the Stars and Stripes. However, the politicians and pundits far removed from the Gulf had little understanding of the practical efforts the US Army and Navy had made to accomplish what they did despite the many obstacles they faced. Unlike the coastal cities of Mexico that had long enjoyed interaction with the other principal Gulf ports, New Orleans, Havana, and even Galveston – Tabasco would not acquiesce to American dominance or hold *fandangos* to accommodate the invader. Owning the seas was one thing, but subduing a people staunchly independent and weary of strangers was another. Similarly, the Maya were indifferent to US aspirations to unite two oceans by way of a canal severing the peninsula from the mainland. To them, and to other non-Mayan indigenous peoples in the region, those concerns were the fanciful notions of outsiders who knew little about them or the world they lived in. As we will discuss, the Caste War and bloody conflagration that ensued thus represented a vicious clamour against the bold pretensions of the white man's world.

Chapter 3
The Caste War

For the last night of the fiesta the neighbouring villages had sent forth their all; the ball was larger and gayer of whites and those in whose veins white blood ran, while outside ... natives of the land and lords of the soil ... people in whose ruined cities I had just been wandering, submitting quietly to the dominion of strangers, bound down and trained to the most abject submission, and looking up to the white man as a superior being ... At no time since my arrival in the country had I been so struck with the peculiar constitution of things in Yucatan. Originally portioned out as slaves, the Indians remain as servants. Veneration for masters is the first lesson they learn, and these masters, the descendants of the terrible conquerors, in centuries of uninterrupted peace have lost all the fierceness of their ancestors. Gentle, and averse to labour themselves, they impose no heavy burdens upon the Indians, but understand and humour their ways, and the two races move on harmoniously together, with nothing to apprehend from each other, forming a simple, primitive, and almost patriarchal state of society; and so strong is the sense of personal security ... so little apprehension was there of robbery, that we slept without a door or window locked.[1]

John L. Stephens, *Incidents of Travel in Yucatan*, 1843

The Caste War of Yucatan (1847–1901), which erupted at the height of the Mexican-American War due to a myriad of internal and external events impacting the Gulf region, marks a particularly tragic chapter in the history of ethnic conflict in the Americas. To the Americans, those of the growing North American power who sought to aggrandize their young nation at the expense of their older, weakened neighbour, Yucatecan independence appeared at first as an opportunity to realize the lofty ambitions of expansionists who believed Latin American states could simply be grabbed in the same manner as the sparsely populated western territories. Pivoting south, however, proved more challenging.

In 1816 Americans officially began fighting the Seminoles in Florida, and that conflict – fought in unfamiliar territory that favoured guerrilla tactics – endured until 1858. The Yucatan peninsula, with its similarly humid lowlands, rain, mud and terrain that mitigated the effectiveness of the cavalry-centric warfare fought in much of northern and central Mexico, was larger and included a borderless frontier abutting the neighbouring states of Guatemala and British Honduras (Belize) that facilitated migration and trade in munitions and contraband. For US observers relying on reality more than rhetoric, for those that understood the logistical requirements of operating and projecting military power over the Mexican Gulf, the forested shores of Yucatan and the long-term war of attrition waged there represented a green wall and a southern limit to American empire.

The portrait of the Maya that American John L. Stephens drew in his popular 1843 *Incidents of Travel in Yucatan* was one of contented servitude, and he asked himself, 'Could these be the descendants of that fierce people who had made such bloody resistance to the Spanish conquerors?' However, underneath the outward appearance of tranquillity lay generations of anger waiting to be unleashed. For no apparent reason other than relegating the brutal and atrocious nature of the violent whirlwind that began in early 1847 and lasted more than fifty years, the term *caste* could have easily been replaced with the less subtle word *race*. However, 'caste' (*castas* in Spanish) appeared appropriate because one side of the conflict consisted of natives, while the other included both *criollo* and *mestizo* – people of mixed Spanish and indigenous heritage. And yet, Stephens was aptly qualified to witness the first rumblings of discontent by an ancient people who once built pyramids and developed systems equal to many of the esteemed cultures of the Old World. The Mayan civilization undoubtedly went through cataclysmic disruption and conflict on the eve of the Columbian Exchange beginning in the late fifteenth century, but the forces that brought Spanish conquistadors to Yucatan in the mid-1500s hastened their decline. Indeed, below the surface lay a long bitterness.[2]

According to Nelson A. Reed, one of the early historians of the Caste War, of the 300,000 Maya who remained after the conquest, only 150,000 survived the smallpox that swept the region. By 1845, the combined population including Yucatecan (Spanish), Mayan, and *mestizo* recovered to around 580,000 people. Roughly 440,000 of those, or 75 per cent, were Mayan. Reed notes the 'total war' that erupted forced the Yucatecans (or 'Ladinos') to arm roughly 17 per cent of their population to forestall destruction and forced exodus from the peninsula. Furthermore, census data between 1846 and 1850 indicates the population fell by an astonishing 40 per cent, meaning the peninsula lost nearly 200,000 people. Of those, some 120,000 were displaced, having fled to the safety of the neighbouring states of Tabasco, Belize, or Cuba, leaving historians with an estimated death toll of around 80,000 people, or 16 per cent – a numerical testament to the unmitigated violence that occurred between racial factions. This violence emanated from the eastern side of the peninsula and swept west in a wave of death that nearly pushed the non-Mayan people into the Gulf of Mexico.[3]

Stephens' work was the second series of a more comprehensive picture of a region Americans and Europeans other than the Spanish knew little about but were just beginning to understand. His earlier two-volume work on travels in Chiapas, Guatemala and Yucatan was published in 1841 and reprinted several times before and after the war to provide eager readers with an insight into the unknown parts and peoples of southern North America. Stephens spent much of his time describing the exotic fauna, temples and intriguing natives and their alien culture to fascinated readers in northern climes, but the name that ran through both volumes was that of Guatemalan mestizo Rafael Carrera (1814–1865) – leader of a rural rebellion in the late 1830s who went on to become Guatemala's president for much of the 1840s until his death.[4]

In the early 1840s, Carrera sent forces into the frontier region of Petén, to the largest settlement of Flores, south of the famed ruins of Tikal, and claimed the region for Guatemala. Yucatan and Mexico, with their ongoing struggles, were in no position to contest this claim politically or militarily. Today, this vast and borderless wilderness abuts the territories administered by Tabasco, Campeche, Chiapas, and Belize, but in the early 1840s Petén represented one of the last unexplored swathes of North America. Stephens called it the region of the 'unbaptized Indians', adding that the people there lived 'precisely in the same state as before the discovery of America'. Indeed, even in colonial times few Europeans ventured into the heart of this forested frontier, and Stephens attested that among the intellectual classes in Merida 'there was a universal belief that beyond the Lake of Peten there was a region of unconverted Indians of whom nothing was known.' In essence, Carrera may have planted the Guatemalan flag in Petén, but it made little difference to life among a people who had long lived outside of the boundaries of formal administrative authority.[5]

However, Carrera left a legacy that later defined Central America among military analysts. The increasing use of guerrilla warfare during his tenure as leader of a three-year insurrection beginning in 1837 hastened the demise of the Guatemalan-led Federal Republic of Central America. When not the scene of fighting amongst its various factions, the republic spent much of its political capital attempting to oust the British from the east side of the isthmus – where they were firmly ensconced through their proxies. Nevertheless, Carrera's involvement of peasants in successfully overthrowing the establishment was a blueprint for Mayan leaders who dreamed of an independent ethnic-Mayan nation. When Stephens travelled there in the early 1840s he admitted that – although he was 'most intimately acquainted with Central American politics' – he 'had not the remotest idea' what Carrera's revolution against the government was about, nor was his political insight of 'more use to us than a knowledge of Texan politics would be to a stranger in the United States'. He did, however, witness 'the horrors of this partisan war' when he entered the town of Ahuachapán, in present-day El Salvador, amid rumours that Carrera's forces were coming to ransack the town. 'It was the first time I ever saw terror operating upon masses,' he wrote, 'and I hope never to see it again.' Much of this internecine warfare resulted in El Salvador (known at the time as San Salvador) breaking away from Guatemala's grip in 1841 after the collapse of the federation and becoming an independent state.[6]

Political upheaval and civil strife had plagued most of Central America since the late 1830s, but the northern Maya, who lived closer to the colonial *criollo* population in the northern and western part of the peninsula, received a taste of the efficacy of guerrilla warfare during the Mexican invasion in 1842/3. One of the main instigators of the Caste War was Jacinto Pat, a *batab* (tribal chief) from Tihosuco in the present-day state of Quintana Roo who fought against the Mexicans in the early 1840s. Cecilio Chi, often referred to as the most ruthless of the warring *batabs*, was originally from Tihosuco but hailed from Tepich in the same region and was active in the defence of Campeche during the Mexican siege of that city. Both men are often cited as being *caciques* – denoting a certain level of wealth and political prestige – and must have felt their efforts betrayed when Yucatecan officials began talking about reintegration with Mexico in 1846 during the war. Ancono noted that 'until the year 1840 there existed a hatred of three centuries between the two main races' but the Maya 'lacked the means to shake off the yoke that weighed on them. The caste war would always have broken out in a more or less distant era.' According to him, it was the 'imprudence' of putting 'weapons in the hands of the Indians before assimilating them to the rest of their fellow citizens' that led to the disaster. This was likely correct, but it would have been extremely difficult to win the war against the Mexicans without Mayan assistance and their irregular tactics.[7]

Reed discusses guerrilla tactics employed by the Maya in his history of the war. These included using back trails to attack the enemy's rear, building and moving walls made from loose limestone for cover before and during engagements, barricading trails to set up ambushes, and digging and hiding pits containing sharpened stakes. Accompanying these lethal methods was a tendency to kill prisoners – many of whom were raped and tortured in indescribable ways. Women and children not murdered were often sent into the unreachable regions of Yucatan. The Yucatecans were not immune from committing atrocities either – particularly after witnessing the aftermath of the annihilation of a village or town.[8]

Outbreak of the Caste War

Even cannibalism appeared in the opening act of this ethnic turmoil. On 8 December 1846, shortly before the US Navy increased its presence at the nearby Ciudad del Carmen, the government in Campeche issued a pronouncement entitled the 'Yucatan Act' – proclaiming its neutrality in the US-Mexican conflict and objecting to Merida's decision to reincorporate the republic back into Mexico. 'The resolution on the reincorporation of Yucatan to the republic is postponed', the Act read, pending settlement of Mexico's 'relations with foreign powers and their subjects' – a euphemism for the war with the United States. Ancono commented that although 'no express resolution was made on neutrality, it was clearly indicated in the preamble.' The resulting political schism between Yucatan's two main centres of authority 'spread with electric speed throughout the Peninsula.' Civil war erupted, and officers aligned with the Campeche faction accepted Mayan volunteers from Tihosuco – the region from which Pat and Chi hailed. Merida was soon surrounded, and martial law was declared.[9]

The Yucatecan historian was critical of the Campeche faction who, he believed, 'flattered the egoism' of elites who claimed that neutrality was 'preferable to the country being involved in the American war; and thus, as the elements of the rebellion increased, those of the government diminished considerably.' While Merida was under siege, forces heading west from Tihosuco under the command of Antonio Trujeque and an 'adventurer named Juan Vázquez' entered the city of Valladolid and besieged the local garrison in the main plaza. The particular time and place involved a caustic blend of social and ethnic anxiety, for 'since time immemorial in Valladolid there was a constant struggle between the population of the city center and that of the neighbourhoods.' In the centre, where the besieged were forced to retreat, lived 'a kind of aristocracy, which based its vanity on descending from the conquering race and on having better education and greater wealth than the inhabitants of the neighbourhoods.' On 15 January, after two days of back-and-forth threats and insults – fuelled by looted stores of brandy and uncontrollable insubordination – the plaza was rushed by 3,000 men, and a massive slaughter ensued:

> They immediately uprooted from their homes the people against whom they had some resentment, and they murdered them barbarously without respecting sex or age. What could not be stolen was destroyed, in which task the Indians mainly distinguished themselves, and the trees themselves, the flowers and even the domestic animals were victims of this savage instinct. But this was not the last act of that scene of cannibals. The corpses were paraded in triumph through the streets, and when their executioners had had enough of desecrating them, they threw them into bonfires where the torn pieces of furniture and papers taken from public offices served as fuel. The Indians were agitated around these bonfires, manifesting with savage howls the pleasure that the crunching of meat caused them, and taking some of them to their mouths, after tearing them from the bodies of their victims. These horrifying scenes lasted eight days, during which attacks occurred that modesty resists stamping on paper. It is assured that there were eighty-four victims sacrificed by the accused, and that the massacre extended to the farms and towns near Valladolid.[10]

When news of the Valladolid massacre reached Merida, Governor Barbachano, disclaiming responsibility for additional deaths, acquiesced to the revolutionary government in Campeche led by Domingo Barret and left for exile in Havana. It was during the unrest, and before the massacre, that the Barret government made appeals of neutrality to US naval authorities at Laguna and sent Rovira to Washington under assurances of safe-conduct. The US government acceded to his requests for neutrality and lifted the blockade, but was still noncommittal when it came to official recognition of Yucatan as an independent republic. Nevertheless, the Rovira meeting made the administration's officials – many of whom were ardent expansionists such as Walker and Dallas – aware of the pro-American faction on the southern end of the Gulf. As the war progressed, voices for incorporating Yucatan into the United States grew louder. In his 22 February letter to Mason, and without knowing the revolt was on the brink of becoming a race war, Buchanan outlined the American position on the warring factions, noting that the 'revolutionary movement of the people of Yucatan for the purpose of restoring her to her former neutral position in the war … has not yet to our knowledge proven completely successful.' According to Buchanan, Merida was still abiding by the commitments made on 25 August 1846 to return to the federal system. Thus, the American position was one of wait-and-see:

> The revolutionary struggle, so far as we have learned, has not yet terminated successfully for the partisans of neutrality. Under these circumstances, all that this Government can do with propriety is to instruct the officer commanding the US Naval forces in the gulf of Mexico to treat Yucatan again as a neutral state.[11]

Meanwhile, as the new Yucatecan government attempted to weed out 'Barbachanistas' operating overtly and covertly to restore the former governor, Mayan leadership was on the verge of committing itself to total eradication of the non-Mayan population from Yucatan. The flashpoint for the transition from political to ethnic struggle arose from the arrest and execution of *batab* Manuel Antonio Ay in Valladolid on 26 July 1847. Ay was arrested on suspicion of instigating a racial revolt much like the one that occurred in French-controlled Haiti, but his execution only exacerbated the violence of the Caste War because other *batabs* believed if they did not unite to conquer the peninsula, they might be next. Rugeley also believes the Campeche faction's decision to temper their revolt and pivot towards the arrest of Ay may have been influenced by their concern over the US presence on the coast and the growing power of the *batabs* used to oust Barbachano. Ancono blamed the Campechans for the Mayan uprising: 'The ill-fated revolution of December 8, which proclaimed neutrality in the North American war, finally provided them [the Maya] with the first opportunity to wage open war against the white race.'[12]

One influential Barbachanista who immediately changed sides was Colonel José Dolores Cetina. Cetina initially accompanied Barbachano to Havana and returned with munitions to aid a counter-revolt against the Campeche regime, until Ay's execution completely altered the dynamic on the peninsula. Reed notes that Cetina 'made his declaration on the day of the execution.' News spread quickly because in a matter of days the Maya began moving men and weapons from the east for the coming assault on the *criollo* and *mestizo* population centres. On the morning of 30 July, Mayan guerrillas led by Chi launched an assault on the white inhabitants of Tepich – located in the centre of the peninsula. All of the whites were murdered in revenge for Ay's execution, and thus the thirst for vengeance intensified. The following month, *criollo* officials in Tihosuco learned first-hand from a number of Mayan peasants that discussions had indeed taken place among the *batabs* of Tihosuco and Tepich to kill all the whites and establish an independent Mayan nation. Ancono commented on their meeting at a ranch named Xihum, north-east of Tihosuco, 'The place could not be more suitable for the object that the Indian conspirators had proposed, [and] it was there that they met for the first time to discuss the insurrection of their race.' After two major massacres, it appeared they had passed beyond a point of no return:

> This cabal was attended by Manuel Antonio Ay, Cecilio Chi and several other Indians from the towns of that region ... Cecilio Chi was without any dispute the most bloodthirsty of all ... His program consisted of exterminating all individuals who did not belong to the pure indigenous race, so that the descendants of the Mayas would remain absolute masters of the country of their elders. Manuel Antonio Ay believed that so much blood was not needed to achieve the same goal, and he believed that the Indians could get rid of their enemies, expelling them all from the peninsula.[13]

Ancono noted that it was unknown whether Jacinto Pat attended the Xihum meeting, because at the time he was still believed to be a supporter of Barbachano. However, none of that mattered after Pat, Chi and a handful of other principal *batabs* met in Culumpich (east of Valladolid) immediately after the Tepich massacre and formalized their campaign. Ancono wrote that 'Jacinto Pat's aspirations were less ignoble, because although he aspired to dominate his race over the others, it was not with the aim of exterminating or expatriating them, but with the aim of replacing the whites in the government of the country.' Nonetheless, for those such as Bonifacio Novelo, who played an active role in the massacre at Valladolid, total eradication of the whites was the primary objective. 'Despite the mystery in which the first steps of the conspirators were involved,' the chieftains who plotted the takeover of the peninsula 'found powerful support in Bonifacio Novelo, the most ferocious of the Valladolid murderers, who lived with a few of his own in the forests, removed from the obedience of the government.' When the plan was agreed, Bonifacio headed south to Belize to purchase more weapons and use Pat's holdings at Culumpich as a staging area for the offensive.[14]

Wood, Weapons and Proxy Wars

The Mayan cabal emanating from eastern Yucatan received much of their munitions and materiel through their trade in mahogany with merchants in the British Honduran region of Belize. Native to the Americas, mahogany was a much-sought-after timber among the British because it was sturdy, dense and resistant to the cold and humidity of northern Europe. It is also beautiful, as its reddish-brown colour displays a sheen when polished, and it ages well over time. In the sixteenth century, the Spanish were the first to appreciate its qualities, but it was the English, and later American colonials, who established a flourishing mahogany trade in the seventeenth and eighteenth centuries. In the early eighteenth century, after all of the easily obtainable wood was logged from the islands of the Caribbean, the British moved their cutting operations to the Bay of Honduras. British claims to Honduran and Nicaraguan territory along the Mosquito Coast were further cemented following the 1763 Treaty of Paris ending the Seven Years' War – a war known in North America as the French and Indian War. It was a war that redrew the map of colonial America and allowed the British to obtain a foothold in a contested isthmus the Spanish claimed as their own. Administered from Jamaica, Belize became the centre of an expanding trade that continued into the nineteenth century.[15]

Most of that trade was centred around the port town of Bacalar, in present-day Quintana Roo. Bacalar had been a Mayan city before the Spanish arrived but later served as a logging centre connecting entrepreneurial Mayan chieftains to a profitable mercantilist system focused on the exfiltration of the valuable timber. With British complicity, the Mayan used mahogany to fuel their war against the Yucatecans. In Thomas Young's 1842 account of travels through the region he noted that good Anglo-Mayan relations dating back more than a century were informed to a degree by their mutual opposition to Spanish dominance over the region, and that 'many of our old English voyagers speak of the regard and reverence these Indians had for the English, and of their willingness at all times to fight against their mutual enemies, the Spaniards; witness Dampier, Falconer, Frobisher, and a host of others.'[16]

The official often cited as responsible for arming the Maya was Charles St John Fancourt. Born in 1804, Fancourt served as a Member of Parliament for a few years in the 1830s before being appointed Superintendent for British Honduras in 1843. In his 1883 history of British Honduras, Archibald Robertson Gibbs described Fancourt's initiatives to 'subvert the influence of the people' in that colony by suspending elections of local magistrates as 'Machiavellian' – noting that he was 'a diplomatist by training, and a courtier, [who] knew well how to conceal the iron hand of arbitrary authority under the silken glove of a bland and courteous manner.' Gibbs added that when the Caste War began both Maya and Yucatecans 'sought the British of Honduras as allies, and each watched closely our dealings with the other.' More problematic for Fancourt was that refugees began entering Belize in the hope that it would prove a safe haven, and 'alarm prevailed throughout the settlement that the sheltering of these refugees would bring upon it Indian raids and reprisals.'[17]

Violence pouring over the border into Belize eventually forced Fancourt to rethink his policy, but in the conflict's initial period the Maya exchanged looted goods and valuables to fund their campaign. Ancono wrote that the 'English knew very well that the Indians had enough treasures to buy these effects with the wood they cut in our forests and with the jewelry and other objects they stole in their raids.' Moreover, Fancourt 'treated and respected' the Mayans 'as the subjects of any other friendly nation of Great Britain'. Although there was no direct evidence, it was claimed Fancourt established 'official relations with the ferocious Cecilio Chí, flattering his brutal passions'

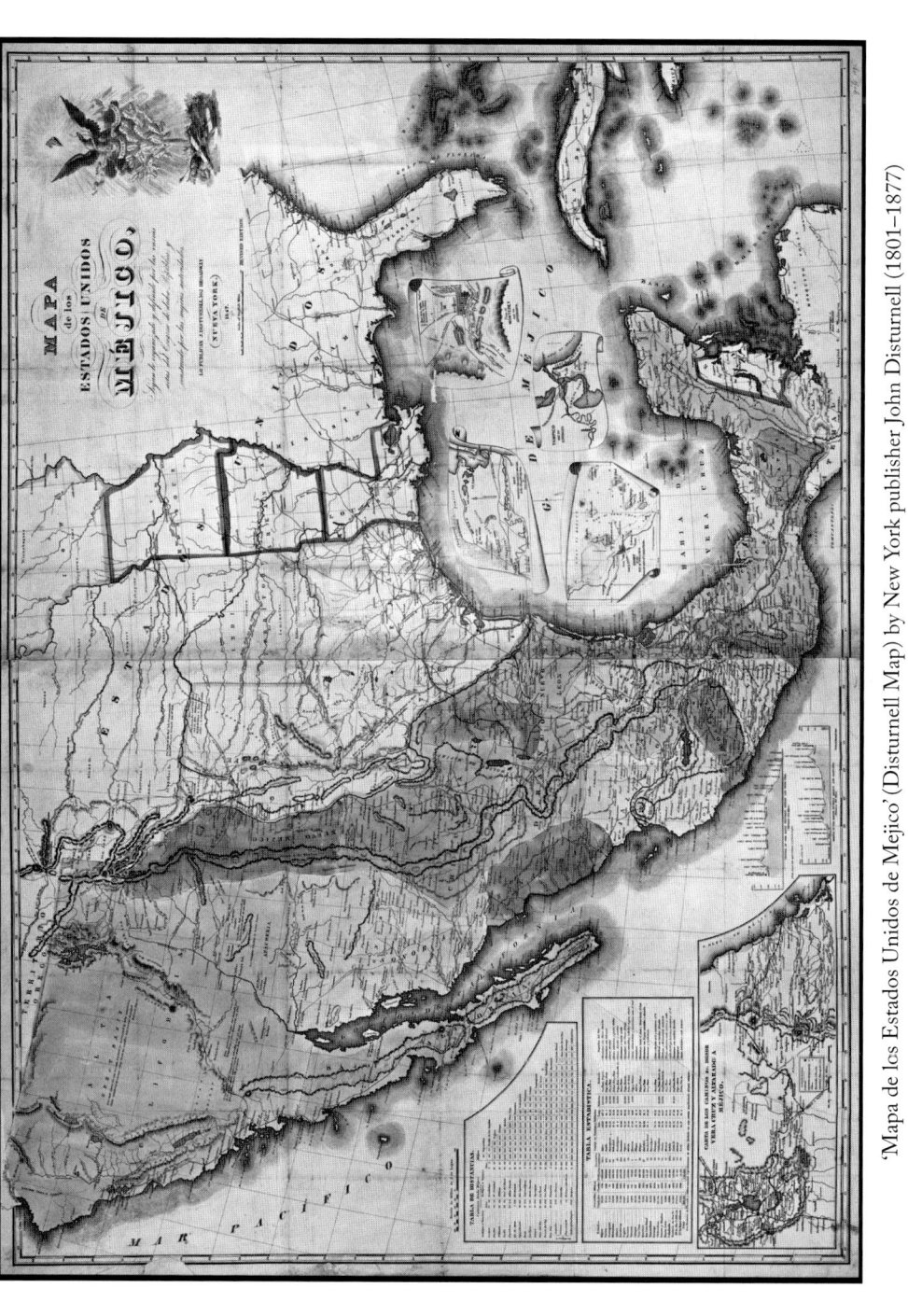

'Mapa de los Estados Unidos de Méjico' (Disturnell Map) by New York publisher John Disturnell (1801–1877)

Commodore Matthew Perry, c. early 1850s. Exhibit in the Sanada Treasure Museum, 4-1 Matsushiromachi, Matsushiro, Nagano, Japan.

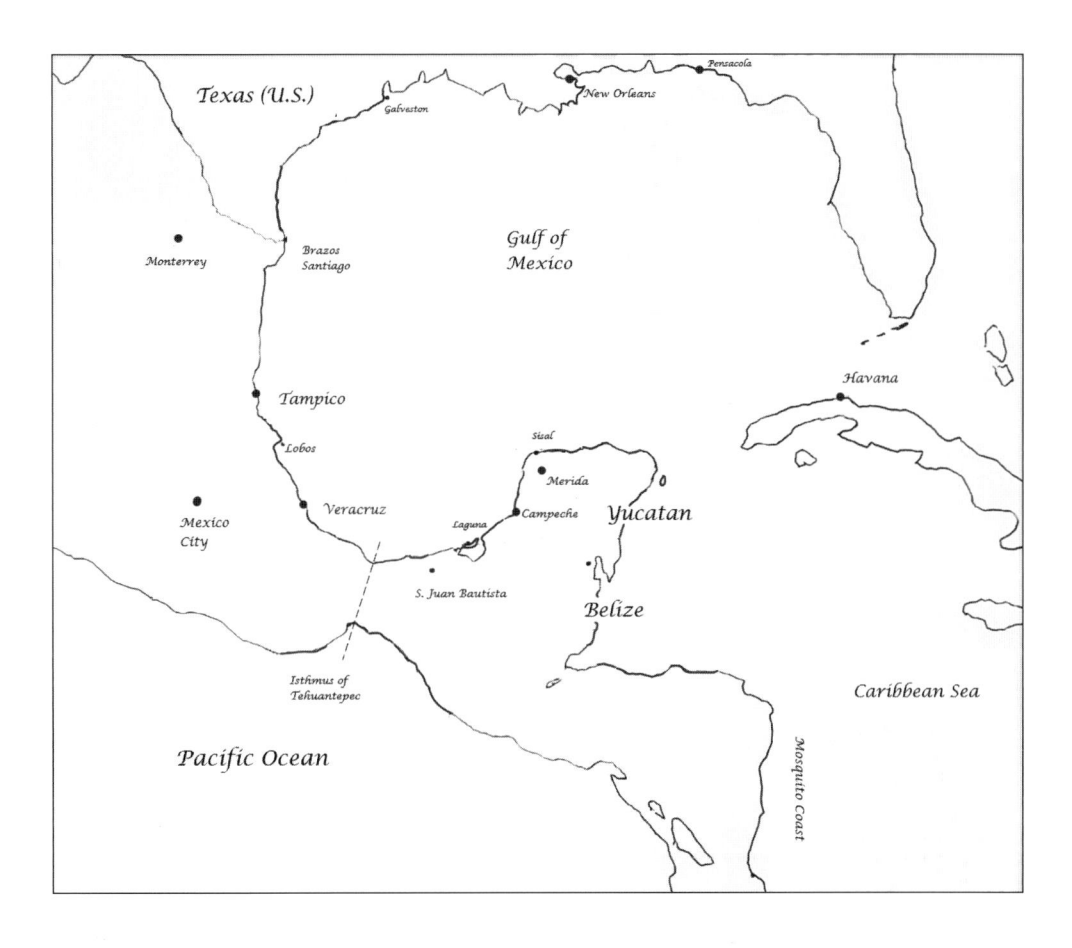

The Isthmus of Tehuantepec – being the results of a survey for a railroad to connect the Atlantic and Pacific oceans, made by the scientific commission under the direction of Major J.G. Barnard. (*New York: D. Appleton & Company, 1852*)

'Bombardment of Vera Cruz and Castle'. In Edward D. Mansfield, *The Mexican War*, 1850.

1847-8

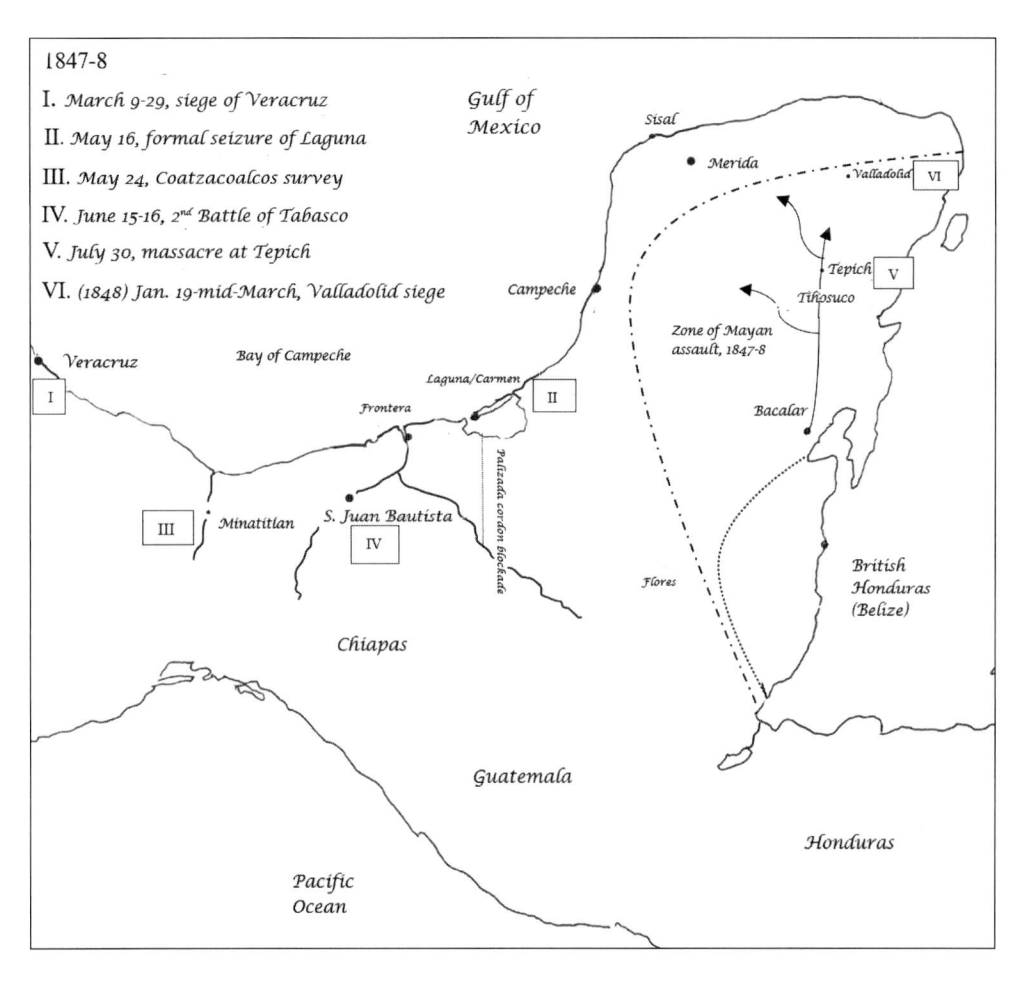

I. March 9-29, siege of Veracruz
II. May 16, formal seizure of Laguna
III. May 24, Coatzacoalcos survey
IV. June 15-16, 2nd Battle of Tabasco
V. July 30, massacre at Tepich
VI. (1848) Jan. 19-mid-March, Valladolid siege

Mexican-American War. Landing of the U.S. Army under General Winfred Scott, assisted by the U.S. Navy, on the beach near Veracruz, Mexico, March 9th, 1847. (*Library of Congress, National Museum of the U.S. Navy*)

Ruined church at Pisté, Yucatan, 1889. The town had been abandoned in 1847 during the Caste War, and in 1889 was starting to be repopulated.

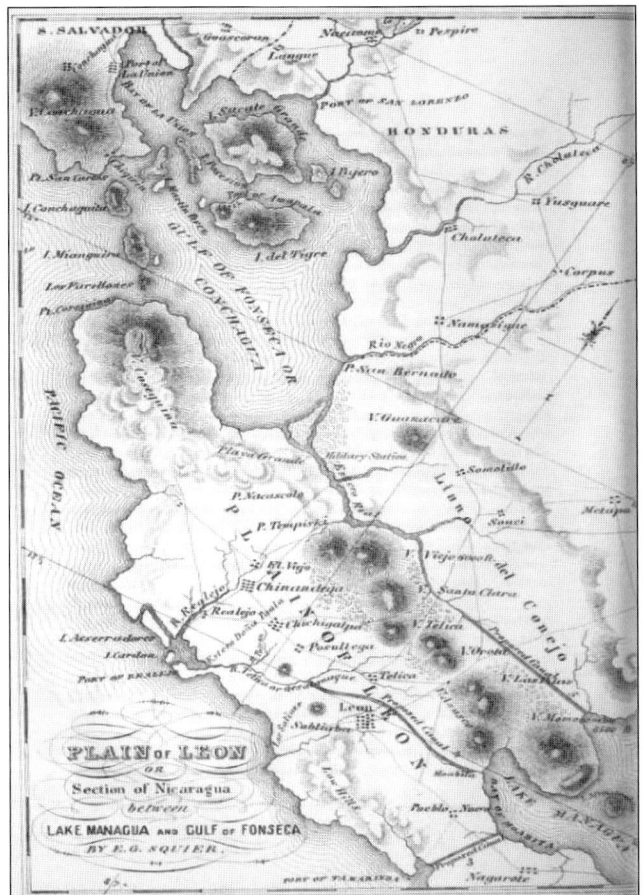

'Plain of Leon or Section of Nicaragua between Lake Managua and Gulf of Fonseca', by Ephraim G. Squier, in Squier, *Nicaragua; Its people, scenery, monuments and the proposed interoceanic canal*, vol. 2 (New York: D. Appleton & Co., 1852), 238.

'The U. States Steamers, Scorpion, Vixen, Spitfire and Scourge; with 40 barges in tow, crossing the bar at the mouth of Tobasco [*sic*] River, Mexico.' Lithograph drawing by Lt Henry Walke, USN, appearing in: *Naval Portfolio: Naval Scenes in the Mexican War* (New York: Sarony & Major, 1847), No. 3. National Museum of the US Navy, Library of Congress.

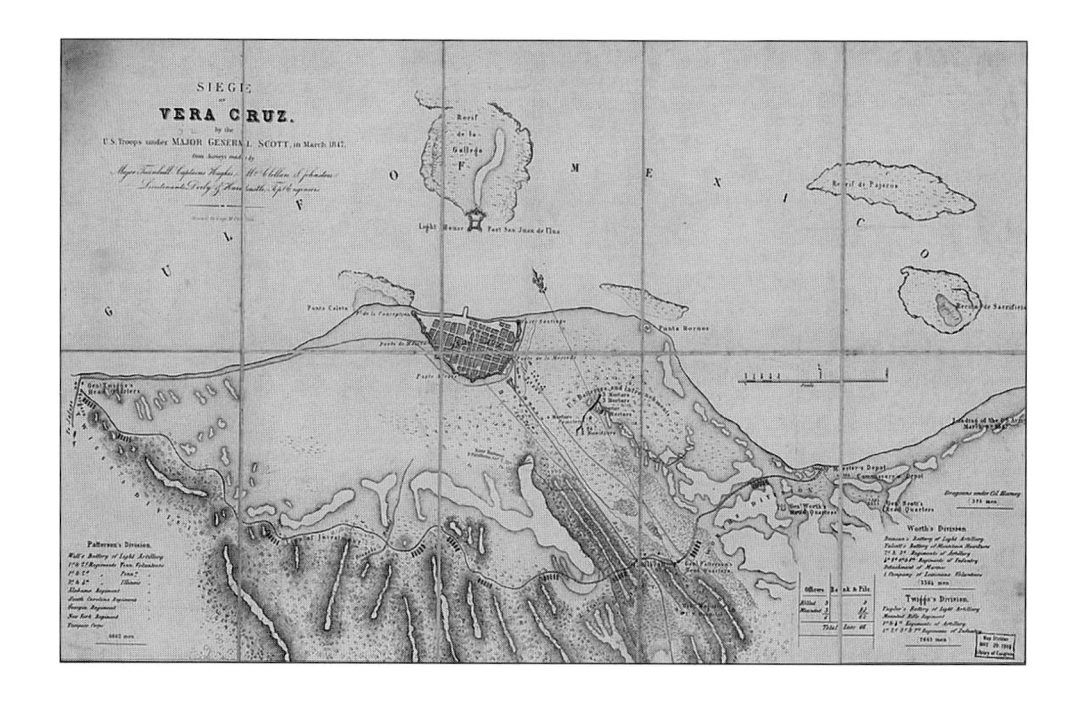

'The Capture of the City of Tabasco'. Steamer *Spitfire* and Schooner *Bonita*, Second Battle of Tabasco, 15 June 1847. Lithograph drawing by Lt Henry Walke, USN, appearing in *Naval Portfolio: Naval Scenes in the Mexican War* (New York: Sarony & Major, 1847), No. 7. National Museum of the US Navy, Library of Congress.

– the result being 'that weapons and gunpowder depots were established in the town of Bacalar itself, in order that the rebels could acquire these items more easily.' Rugeley asserts that a separate political insurgent economy developed, adding that a system of passports and 'mule team trails' emanating from Bacalar north towards Valladolid supplanted the economic influence of Merida and Campeche. With their own source of contraband, the Maya were capable of waging a long-term war of attrition.[18]

Another important point that Rugeley makes is that Mexico City's war against Texas after 1836 changed a long-held tradition relating to service in the armed forces. Prior to the war, Mayans (and other indigenous peoples) were generally excluded from recruitment, and most natives reciprocated by refusing to serve. Reforms initiated in the 1840s designed to incorporate rural and indigenous soldiers thus contributed to the development of a martial spirit and political identity that had long lain dormant. Local militias with Mayan members ultimately gave their loyalty to their tribal identity. In other words, attempts to bring young indigenous men into the military system backfired, because the social bonds at the local level superseded those of the state or nation. Therefore, when the *batabs* decided to launch a racial campaign, there were obviously few objectors in the local militias.[19]

The arming of the Maya was not the first time the British had engaged in such activities in the Gulf region. During the Creek War (1813–1814), which overlapped the Anglo-American War of 1812 (1812–1815), the British armed and even trained Creek soldiers at the Spanish port of Pensacola. The idea was to check the expansion of US forces in the lower Mississippi Valley and specifically the strategic port of New Orleans. The fighting that took place in present-day Alabama and the Gulf climaxed on 27 March 1814 at the decisive Battle of Horseshoe Bend, where roughly 2,000 soldiers, including several hundred Cherokee and Choctaw allies, under the command of General Andrew Jackson, confronted 1,000 Creek warriors (known as Red Sticks) at a bend in the Tallapoosa River. Remnants of the Creek force, who wanted to continue fighting the Americans, fled over the border into western Florida, where they joined the Seminoles, already hostile to the Americans.

Although the British armed the Creeks after the engagement, historian Thomas Kanon notes that they 'planned to use the Indians to divert American forces from the defense of the sought-after prize of New Orleans on the frontier.' For this reason, Jackson seized Pensacola in November of that year when he discovered the British scheme – a move that gave the Americans victory against the British at the Battle of New Orleans in early 1815. In 1966, historian John K. Mahon took a more comprehensive view of British support for native tribes during the war, noting that the 'British promised war supplies and other assistance' as early as 1811 to tribes along the frontier in the upper Mississippi Valley, and that in May of 1814, in Pensacola, British officers Hugh Pigot and George Woodbine began assisting the 'Indians willing to oppose the United States'. Jackson had long suspected British intrigue, writing to the Governor of Tennessee in late 1812 that American 'volunteers have drawn their swords, and shouldered their muskets' to defend their homes against 'the British, and their savage and barbarous allies, the Indians, and may they never be returned to their scabbards until the enemies of America of every denomination, be humbled in the dust.' Jackson, whose popularity was crucial to the establishment of the Democrat party, was in many ways the personification of the opprobrium often directed by that party towards the British long after the war ended.[20]

A generation later, during the Mexican conflict, much of the contraband trade between the Maya and Belize initially went unnoticed by Americans waging war and maintaining the blockade on the opposite side of the Gulf. American officials likely learned of British involvement when they began investigating the riverine smuggling between Yucatan and Tabasco. Conner wrote that before Tabasco was captured 'an undisturbed trade had been carried on to that and the neighbouring ports and the whole country was supplied with every necessary article of provision.' That trade included materiel 'directly' from New Orleans and even Europe. That much was known, but it was not until about mid-May of 1847, when Perry appointed Benjamin Sands as Governor of Laguna, that Americans understood the extent of the problem when they realized a network extended into the Usumacinta River – which today defines the boundary between Tabasco and Chiapas, and further upstream, Chiapas and Guatemala. The Usumacinta is navigable for nearly 400km and meets the Grijalva before it arrives at Frontera. To sever this illicit trade, the Americans patrolled the Palizada River entering into the large Laguna de Términos south of Carmen. In those days, the Palizada met the Usumacinta near the municipality of Jonuta, south of the town of Palizada located on the river with the same name. Semmes wrote that a 'cordon of boats was then established in the bay, and up the principal river, as far as *Palisada* [town], to cut off all communication between the eastern part of the peninsula, and the department of Tobasco.' It was believed that this effort to cut off the movement of materiel flowing west through the Usumacinta River would 'prevent the enemy from supplying himself with arms and other munitions of war, through Campeachy, Sisal, and the adjoining province of British Honduras.'[21]

Mosquito Kingdom

Americans were surprised to learn that a race war was unfolding on the peninsula, but the British were not about to let the Americans dictate the outcome of the war by acquiescing to US designs in Tehuantepec or Panama without their own initiatives. Mahogany may have initially been the primary reason for British interest in the region, but American expansion threatened their position on the continent. Consequently, sometime in the early 1840s, during the period where the US was focused on annexing Texas and contemplating war with Mexico, Great Britain, under the guidance of Belizean Superintendent Colonel Alexander MacDonald (Fancourt's predecessor), began treating the Kingdom of Mosquitia, or Mosquito Kingdom, as a protectorate. The Anglo-Miskito relationship was invigorated when the British formally established a consul at the port of Bluefields on 6 July 1844. 'The British government has taken formal possession of the Mosquito kingdom,' *Niles' National Register* reported from Baltimore. A flag-raising ceremony was conducted, and afterwards the king was escorted to Belize 'to be crowned in presence of the governor of the British settlements.' Since the kingdom claimed coastal territory stretching from northern Honduras to southern Nicaragua, the designation essentially made them masters of the Caribbean coast between Belize and Costa Rica. Neither Honduras nor Nicaragua recognized the kingdom, and US officials were understandably interested in what they were doing. 'Great Britain attaches great importance to this portion of the American continent … In case of war between the United States and Great Britain, this possession might prove a great detriment to this country.'[22]

However, while the Americans were occupied with Mexico, there was little they could do to prevent the British from expanding their influence in Central America. Formalization of the kingdom as a protectorate – opposed by the small Central American states – not only allowed the British to strengthen their claims to the eastern side of the isthmus, but gave them a clear advantage in controlling the route of a potential canal believed to be feasible through the southern San Juan River and coastal settlement of Greytown. Foreign Secretary Henry Palmerston's official position was that the kingdom's boundaries extended 'as far as the southern branch of the St. John [or St. Juan]' – the British name for the San Juan River. Nicaragua vehemently opposed the claim. In November 1847, Jose Guerrero, the Supreme Director of that country, issued a proclamation directed at the British. 'Thus it is a civil war stirred up by the savage against the civilized part of Central America,' the proclamation read, 'to tear away by force from Nicaragua the only and best port [Bluefields] in the north, possessed from time immemorial with dispute.'[23]

Guerrero's protests were similar to those issued by the Yucatecans incensed by Fancourt's role in the arming of those seeking their destruction. In September 1847, just as American soldiers triumphantly entered Mexico City, Justo Sierra O'Reilly, the son-in-law of Santiago Méndez Ibarra, Governor of the Campeche faction, was sent to the United States to seek recognition and possibly annexation. The occupation of Mexico City forced the Mexicans to the negotiating table, but American leadership – particularly Polk's Democrat allies in the Senate – were working to prolong the conflict and seize as much territory as possible. Underpinning their intentions was the administration's mid-November recall of Nicholas Trist from Mexico. No one predicted Trist, at the behest of Scott, would disregard executive orders and stay to fulfil his initial role as peacemaker. In essence, between November 1847 and 19 February 1848, when the treaty landed on the president's desk in the White House, the leadership in Washington believed the Texan-Mexican-American war would continue. Moreover, observers, including O'Reilly himself, were just beginning to understand the horrible nature of the Caste War.

Chapter 4

'Savage and exterminating war'

This savage and exterminating war has assumed such a formidable aspect, that I can ... no longer refrain from invoking, frankly and conclusively, the sympathy and humanity of this highly civilized republican government in favor of that people ... In the name of humanity and civilization I am compelled to demand that this government will dictate all such measures as may be within its power; and, if possible, by a prompt intervention, put an end to this war, which threatens to produce the most lamentable consequences to the American policy.[1]

Justo Sierra O'Reilly to Buchanan, 7 March 1848

Late 1847 and early 1848 marked the end of formal hostilities against Mexico, but for Yucatan the crisis continued. Mayan gains against Yucatecans were leading to desperation – as the envoy sent from Campeche, Justo Sierra O'Reilly, pleaded for US intervention. In theatre, US naval officers, whose blockading duties were diminished as the result of an armistice between Mexicans and Americans, found it necessary to provide humanitarian and limited military assistance to besieged Yucatecans fleeing their homes as the enemy pushed them further to the coast. On 19 February, while American lawmakers deliberated on expanding the war in Mexico, the Treaty of Guadalupe Hidalgo unexpectedly arrived in Washington. More than three weeks later, on 10 March, the US Senate voted to ratify the agreement officially ending the war. However, pending ratification of the treaty in Mexico, the war and US position regarding Yucatan remained in limbo. The result of the timing of ratification in Mexico (which sceptics believed might not occur) and the ongoing chaos in Yucatan was that US authorities contemplated sending soldiers to the Gulf state and even annexing the territory.

Justo Sierra O'Reilly

In many ways, novelist and envoy Justo Sierra O'Reilly reflected the features and frustrations of Yucatan and more specifically Campeche. When O'Reilly was born in 1814, during the Mexican War of Independence against Spain, Yucatan was still an intendancy, or captaincy general (*capitanía general*), and its rule from afar afforded the peninsula relative autonomy. In the colonial period following the conquest, captaincy generals were military-administrative units usually designated in areas where unsubdued Indians lived, such as Guatemala; but Yucatan's geographic isolation from the administrative core of New Spain's Viceroyalty made its *criollo* class staunchly independent and – given its minority status among the population – culturally conservative. Like many aspiring members of the peninsula's intellectual and ruling class, O'Reilly studied law in Mexico City before returning to complete his studies in Merida. In 1842, after centralists' failed invasion and siege of Campeche, he married the daughter of Santiago Méndez Ibarra, a wealthy *campechano* businessman and the disputed governor when O'Reilly was sent on his mission to the United States.

O'Reilly's cosmopolitan outlook was informed by his preference for Campeche over Merida. Merida was the larger of the two cities, the capital, and the crossroads of all the other principal cities of the interior such as Valladolid. But its connection to the outside world was tentative until the early nineteenth century when the small port of Sisal, located further north, was allowed to facilitate trade to Merida. Before that, Campeche was the only port that serviced Merida, via the *Camino Real*, and thus dictated its interaction with the rest of Mexico. Campeche is an ocean city, surrounded by walls protecting it from whatever exists beyond them, firmly attached to the Gulf of Mexico, and thus commercially and geographically inclined towards the more worldly ports of Veracruz, Tampico, New Orleans, Havana, and the Spanish homeland. To O'Reilly's imaginative mind, marrying into Campeche's ruling elite complemented his predilection for the less provincial.[2]

That is not to say he did not consider the Indians who had long coexisted with whites on the peninsula. Like the Americans, O'Reilly was intrigued by John L. Stephens' popular travelogues depicting lost Mayan cities and his romantic elucidations of ancient pre-Columbian history. In 1848, this fascination resulted in O'Reilly publishing a Spanish translation of the American's *Incidents of Travel in Yucatan* to promote his anti-insurrectionary periodical, *El Fenix*. Within the work O'Reilly meticulously corrected Stephens's false assumptions with footnotes, but he was essentially attempting to reconcile one outsider's popular interpretation of a people with events that ultimately laid waste to much of the peninsula.[3] One example of that devastation is found among the ruin of formerly notable convents, monasteries and churches in the interior. Like countless others, the abandoned convent of San Juan Bautista in Tixcacaltuyub, in the heart of the peninsula, was built atop an old Mayan temple and destroyed during the war. Remnants of its seventeenth-century arches can still be seen today, but on the map the location may appear as 'Tixcacal de Justo Sierra O'Reilly' – renamed in the 1970s because it was his birthplace. He was probably baptized there, but like many whites, could not return because the Maya toppled the largest monuments of the colonial culture in the interior and turned places like Tixcacal into no-go zones for upper class *campechanos*.

Even so, Stephens' romantic accounts contributed little to O'Reilly's opinions on the political tsunami in the Gulf during the war years. Rather, O'Reilly's perspective on his role in the larger conflict was informed by another Yucatecan and statesman, Lorenzo de Zavala (1788–1836). O'Reilly looked upon Zavala's life and accomplishments as a model for his mission to the United States. Zavala was born in Yucatan, represented the peninsula in the Madrid Cortes, and played a prominent role in the drafting of the 1824 national constitution, revered and invoked by Yucatecans as the basis for their struggle against centralist forces. Like other secular liberals of the day, he spoke French.

During the late 1820s, when conservatives seized power, Zavala left for the United States and occupied his time perfecting his English and managing *empresario* grants to American emigrés interested in settling in Mexico's frontier department of Texas. When Zavala became the Mexican Ambassador to France, he published a work in Paris on his time among the Americans entitled *Journey to the United States of North America*. At home, centralist and federalist divisions resulted in the alternating presidencies of Santa Anna and Valentín Gómez Farías, until Santa Anna seized power to centralize the government under a conservative banner. As a result, Zavala fled to Texas and fostered a movement that ultimately led to that state's independence. The Yucatecan even designed the breakaway republic's first flag – cementing the mutual history of the two Gulf republics. Although the Campeche faction that O'Reilly represented was more conservative than Zavala – and like many blamed him for fracturing the national polity by supporting Texan independence – he was nevertheless admired for defending the 1824 Constitution and taking a stand against centralists.[4]

In early October of 1846, around the same time that US naval officers began forming relationships with officials at Laguna, O'Reilly published Zavala's *Journey to the United States* in Merida. In the introduction he staunchly defended Zavala by affirming that it was 'natural that a public man who has played a notable role in the history of our political revolutions is judged by his contemporaries in very different ways.' He blamed factional tendencies for making people 'blind even among the most enlightened.' Although Zavala died suddenly from an illness in Texas in 1836, O'Reilly claimed he was destined to play 'a brilliant role' in American affairs despite the forces working against him. These assertions, amidst a war consummated in part by the actions of Zavala himself, appeared perfidious given that Mexico's enemy lay immediately off the coast of Yucatan. Yet, O'Reilly remained unapologetic, and in a way confessed to the analogous role he himself would play in the ongoing dispute when describing his predecessor:

> So that man beaten by so many enemies, on pain of always walking on the edge of a precipice, into which his honesty, fame and power can very easily sink, must do good for the good's sake, serve his country ... It will not be strange that in the end he is belittled and forgotten; because in political factions the recent converts are generally preferred to the most loyal affiliates, and more than once it has been seen that the election of a man in public life is counted from the opportune change of a weather vane. This has been of all times and places.[5]

O'Reilly's admiration for Zavala extended to his subject's appreciation for the qualities of the ascendant constitutional republic during a period when Mexico was rife with internal conflict. Washington DC, small and nominal in those days, was the perfect expression of limited government and Jeffersonian egalitarianism – an outlook that complemented classical liberal views underpinning the belief in sovereignty among states seeking protection and commercial benefit in joining a larger federal system. In such a system, states were free to manage their own affairs. It was a system that appeared both politically stable and conducive to enterprise. 'The "Voyage to the United States" is a most precious book,' O'Reilly wrote, 'worthy of being read, studied and meditated by all those who wish their country the social improvements.' Indeed, just as in Zavala's time, O'Reilly looked upon the United States as an emulative, albeit intimidating, template for Mexico:

> The powerful neighbouring nation, colossal in size and progressing to a degree of inconceivable prosperity, certainly deserves an examination that will make us aware of its means of aggrandizement and power. A republic that is at our gates, invading the national territory today, must undoubtedly be the object of our observation. From now on, the United States cannot be indifferent to us. Strength is to see the giant up close, measure its proportions and take advantage of the fruit of this exam. Zavala knew the value of these considerations a long time ago, and he has given his country a present whose price has not yet been fully known.[6]

O'Reilly's assertion that 'Zavala knew the value of these considerations a long time ago' was based on his belief that his predecessor understood the complicated geopolitical dynamics in the Americas. Some of these dynamics involved the ever-present concern among Mexicans and Americans about a resurgence in monarchism, along with a preoccupation concerning the premier naval power of the Atlantic – Great Britain. In Zavala's time, American independence only became a certainty after 1814, even though the war fought between the United States and its former colonial master resulted in the burning of Washington towards the end of that conflict. In his *Journey*, Zavala observed how the nascent US Navy 'has given unequivocal proof, in the last war with England, of its ability, courage and discipline.' Zavala referred to the Americans' growing prowess at sea – citing figures such as 'Stephen Decatur the American Nelson, Paterson, Baimbridge, and Porter' – while observing a completely new power relationship in the western world. 'What nation has been able to meet the proud Albion, sole mistress of the Ocean, but her emancipated daughter, that enterprising nation, which rises yearly to a height that will one day surpass the mightiest nations?'[7]

Thus, the United States, despite its expansionist impulses, was viewed by many as a bulwark against monarchist revanchism, European dominance in American affairs and centralist despotism antithetical to republican principles. The 'Monroe Doctrine' of 1823 forbidding European interference in the Americas – although nearly impossible to enforce at the time – was the expression of that commitment. For most Mexicans, the US invasion of their country was flagrantly imperial, but given the alternative of monarchists seeking to resubmit their nation to the yoke of a foreign power, incorporation into the United States appeared the lesser of two evils. This is the international and domestic interplay with which O'Reilly interpreted Zavala's actions. His predecessor fought against the Spanish and helped draft a constitution granting hitherto-unheard-of rights to Mexicans, only to have that document replaced by a military junta.

The motivations of centralists such as Santa Anna were unclear to many observers before Texas declared independence, but the bitter irony of Zavala's passion to protect that which he fostered in 1824 was the fragmentation of his country. Yucatan, for its part, allied with Texas for the same reason that Zavala did, and successfully fought off a difficult invasion by centralist forces in the early 1840s. O'Reilly himself had made overtures to Sentmanat in 1842 to consider a Yucatan-Tabasco-Chiapas federation to thwart Mexico City's dictates. This led to O'Reilly's conclusion, that 'Lorenzo de Zavala loyally served his country. It was to him that Yucatan owed its first notions of freedom.' Moreover, O'Reilly's 3 October 1846 statement that Zavala's contribution 'has not yet been fully known' and still 'awaits' judgement goes to heart of his own mission. He was careful to iterate this point because he was not only referring to his predecessor, but awaiting the outcome of the war and his possible role in Yucatan's future:

> I will repeat it for the last time ... The present generation cannot impartially judge the character and public life of this character, whose name is linked to the great times of the people. His distinguished career has given him an honorable place in national splendors ... This must have brought him admirers and enemies. 'I only wish [Zavala himself says in his Essay] to be judged with the impartiality and decency with which I do when I speak of my fellow citizens, and about facts, and not about slander. What more just thing can you ask for? The one who has had the misfortune to play a part in the bloody scenes that have torn apart his country? If party spirit is mixed in this trial, it will deserve the contempt of posterity.'[8]

Journey across the Gulf

On the calm Friday morning of 17 September O'Reilly went on deck aboard his US naval escort to see the summits of Orizaba and Perote looming behind his destination. Despite landing at Veracruz on Mexican soil, he received the diplomatic courtesies afforded foreign dignitaries – including a military band. O'Reilly and his travelling companion Rafael Carvajal, the progeny of a wealthy family and future Governor of Campeche, stayed in Veracruz for ten days meeting officials such as Perry and Henry J. Wilson, the US Army Governor of Veracruz. A few days after arriving, rumours that Scott had attacked Mexico City trickled into the port. Indeed, between 8 and 13 September, Scott's forces engaged the Mexicans at Churubusco, Molino del Rey and finally at the critical stronghold of Chapultepec Castle outside the capital. On the 18th, O'Reilly noted in his diary that he saw a convoy of 3,000 men readying to 'march into the interior'. Those forces, under Brigadier General Joseph Lane, had recently arrived from Texas and were assigned to reinforce Scott's army of occupation. Lane's brigade would battle Spanish and Mexican guerrillas coalescing along the road between the coast and Puebla. The following day, O'Reilly commented that people were 'nervous about the news' from the capital, adding that 'nothing was certain', only to be informed later in the day that Scott had indeed entered Mexico City a conqueror.[9]

O'Reilly's voyage to Veracruz, rather than directly to New Orleans, served two purposes. One was to submit official letters of intent and receive formal invitations from Washington through Perry. The other was to connect with first-hand information coming from Mexico City on the outcome of the assault on the capital. O'Reilly's timing in this regard was not coincidental. Once it was learned that Scott was seated in Mexico City, formalities proceeded between US officials in Veracruz and the Yucatecan envoy. On 21 September O'Reilly boarded the recently built sloop-of-war USS *Germantown*, Perry's command centre. Through an interpreter the two discussed 'political business concerning Yucatan' over drinks. The following day, they met again, and O'Reilly submitted a memorandum highlighting the 'neutrality of Yucatan and occupation of Carmen Island and its dependencies'. While the Yucatecans understood the blockade was designed to intercept 'smuggling that could be done with the neighbouring towns of Tabasco', their protest was that it was damaging commerce. The memorandum also indicated, without identifying specifics, that the Yucatecans had taken steps to 'cut off the contraband trade'. Lastly, the memorandum noted that in the event of peace between Mexico and the US, Yucatan wanted 'the protection and shelter of the US government; and there is no doubt that Mr. Commodore Perry will do everything' to help obtain these ends.[10]

The Spanish words used in the memorandum for 'protection and shelter' were *protección y amparo*. It was a major concern that following the conclusion of the war, Yucatan, and officials involved in proclaiming that state's neutrality, might be subject to retribution from centralist officials. While it is true that other Mexican states outside of the theatre of war contributed very little to the fight against the invaders, Yucatan was the only state to issue declarations of neutrality. The Spanish word *amparo* was particularly legalistic and could also be interpreted as 'refuge' – implying a desire among the Campeche faction not only to obtain security from US naval forces in control of the Gulf, but also to arrange some type of legal guarantee they could rely on to prevent their being arrested and prosecuted for their wartime conduct. In addition, O'Reilly did not mention in his diary that he was meeting Perry for the first time, and it is likely the two previously shook hands at some point while the commodore was in Laguna. This is speculation, but Perry undoubtedly knew better than anyone the political dynamics of the region, which included Tabasco.

After the two met on the 22nd to discuss the memorandum, O'Reilly came away confident. 'We discussed its content at length and he offered us what he would do in favor of Yucatan,' he wrote. 'Everything depended on him.' Perry was obviously inclined towards Yucatan since they provided his navy with food and supplies during the war, but getting officials in Washington to accede to their requests was another matter. The day before O'Reilly set off on the *Alabama* to New Orleans, a banquet was held by senior officers and 'Perry toasted to the prosperity and aggrandizement of Yucatan and to the success of our mission to the United States.' O'Reilly obviously knew about the deteriorating situation in Yucatan because two days before he and Carvajal steamed to the Crescent City, the *American Star* in Mexico City reported that after the execution of Antonio Ay in Valladolid 'a conspiracy had been entered into among the Indians of various villages for an insurrection.' If the information from Campeche reached Mexico City, it came through Veracruz before O'Reilly's departure. 'The details of their excesses are horrible. The white race at once united in self-defense. The government has appealed to the people to forget the animosities and join for common protection. Seventeen Indian villages are involved in the insurrection.'[11]

O'Reilly may have felt optimistic about his prospects after meeting Perry, but following his arrival in Washington DC in mid-November news that Yucatan was falling apart was reaching the United States. On the 22nd, as he was preparing for the first of several meetings with Secretary of State Buchanan, O'Reilly wrote, 'The fate of our country is so sad and precarious that a long time here is needed to deal with matters relating to it.' Later that morning, introductions were held, and O'Reilly submitted his memorandum outlining the objectives of his mission. Those objectives, however, would ultimately undergo continuous amendment as the position back home worsened. Two days later, while the administration was considering the requests, an impatient O'Reilly penned a long letter to Buchanan outlining Yucatecan history against Mexican centralists, monarchists, and even Santa Anna. He also noted that the US occupation of Laguna was inhibiting 'great interests there invested in commercial houses and industrial enterprise'. More revealingly, however, O'Reilly mentioned that Laguna's 'relations extend to all the neighbouring towns and farms in the territory of Yucatan, and even to those situated in the province of Petén, and the republic of Guatemala.'[12]

That O'Reilly specifically mentioned Petén was telling. Although Buchanan may not have been aware of the details of Yucatecan riverine geography, Perry would have understood that O'Reilly's appeals to permit the flow of goods between the Guatemalan region adjacent to Belize and Laguna was a protest against the American blockade along the Palizada directed at contraband heading west from Peten into Tabasco via the Usumacinta. There were other trafficking routes, to be sure, but it confirms that the cordon set up along the Palizada that Semmes referred to in his 1851 work had an impact. At any rate, as the severity of the Mayan assault against the white inhabitants of the peninsula became known, O'Reilly's requests regarding Yucatecan commercial interests were quickly put aside and replaced with a more urgent plea for direct military assistance. This shift in dynamics was partly informed by Polk's Message to Congress on 7 December stating that Trist's peace mission had failed and that the war needed to be expanded by sending more soldiers. Polk stated, 'We should secure and render available the conquests which we have already made; and ... we should hold and occupy, by our naval and military forces, all the ports, towns, cities, and provinces now in our possession, or which hereafter may fall into our possession.'[13]

Polk did not specifically mention Yucatan in his message, but O'Reilly could easily interpret the intention behind the statement 'hold ... all the ports' taken by the US Navy. The argument expansionists regularly used to seize as much territory as possible was that if the United States did not do it, some other European power would. Polk was no different in this regard.

'Besides, there is danger,' the president stated, 'if our troops were withdrawn before a peace is concluded, that the Mexican people ... might be inclined to yield to foreign influences, and cast themselves into the arms of some European monarch for protection.' In essence, O'Reilly arrived in Washington at the same time as a movement to annex all of Mexico was gaining speed. Yucatan would undergo a special role in that debate because many pro-war advocates looked upon it as a separate country – an opinion formed from its wartime pronouncements and pre-war struggles against centralists.[14]

O'Reilly eagerly awaited the administration's reply to his memorandum, and it finally arrived on Christmas Eve 1847. In it, Buchanan explained 'pressing duties' with Congress had caused the delay and acknowledged O'Reilly's 'interesting historical sketch' of Yucatan's history. More importantly, Buchanan conveyed Polk's desire to 'cultivate the most friendly' relations with Yucatan, but his decision was that he could not relinquish Laguna because it was 'impossible for the authorities of Yucatan' to stop the contraband trade. According to Polk, surrendering Laguna would 'furnish the means to Mexico of seriously annoying the forces of the United States and prolonging the existing war.' Buchanan also noted that the 25 August pronouncement by the Barbachano government to re-enter the federal system 'had thus made herself our enemy' because it 'converted her neutrality into open war against the United States.' Essentially, the administration was saying that Yucatan's factional infighting prevented the US government from acceding to O'Reilly's requests. 'The position of Yucatan is peculiar. The president cannot recognize her as a sovereign, independent state. She must still be considered as a portion of the Mexican republic, but yet as neutral in the existing war.' For the Americans, the infighting in Yucatan and shifting allegiances were major impediments to initiating deeper involvement – representing a very different scenario to that of Texas:

> Had she preserved her neutrality, from the commencement of hostilities until the present period, it is more than probable the naval forces of the United States never would have taken possession of Laguna ... It is true that Yucatan has again become neutral; but it cannot be denied that she has ever since been distracted by civil dissensions, and that the enemies of neutrality and partisans of Mexico are in open rebellion against her government.[15]

'The white population are removing'

Such a response would normally have ended O'Reilly's mission to Washington, but news of the deteriorating situation in Yucatan changed objectives. On 19 January, Valladolid once again became the centre of the Caste War when it was besieged by a massive army of 12,000 to 15,000 men. The *American Star* in Mexico City reported that Veracruz newspapers 'are crowded with news from Campeachy' that white officials among both factions (previously 'fighting among themselves') were beginning to realize the extent of the revolt directed at them. The report stated that on 29 December Governor Santiago Mendez was 'in company with Barbachano [the person whom the insurgents wanted for the governor] to check the revolution of the Indians against the whites – this revolution having taken a more alarming aspect.' Making matters worse, civilian militia were not only unprepared but 'destitute of troops and all necessary means of sustaining a war'. The leadership in Merida and Campeche were thus forced to set aside their disputes and focus their energies on the existential threat. 'Since the successful affair for the Indians eight towns have united to them, raising their number, it is said, to 15,000 men.' The article also indicated that economic activity was 'paralyzed', farms and estates 'abandoned' out of fear, and Yucatecans 'were awaiting with great anxiety the arrival of Com. Perry, and they look upon him as sole proprietor of their lives and property.'[16]

Perry was following events closely. On 30 January, while at the naval yard in Veracruz, the commodore sent a short message to Mason explaining affairs remained 'unsettled' there. Reports from the other side of the Gulf painted a dire picture. 'The Indians, receiving their arms from the settlements in the bay of Honduras,' he wrote, 'are gaining strength and the white population are removing towards the coast.' A week later, Governor Mendez issued a desperate decree granting amnesty for the 'crime of revolt' to 'insurgents who submit to the government's obedience'. The decree, issued from the town of Maxcanu, located between Campeche and Merida, was an attempt to gain the favour of 'Indians who with their own means make war on the rebels' by offering exemptions from taxes and other incentives. Threats of forced labour, prison sentences and stern punishments accompanied the forlorn plea for assistance that generally came in the form of non-action. For the most part, Yucatecans were fortunate that the majority of the Mayans who lived nearer to the *criollo* population centres on the western side of the peninsula were not taking up arms against them.[17]

On 15 February, with news that Valladolid was still holding out, O'Reilly penned a long letter to Buchanan outlining 'orders and instructions' accompanying 'new considerations' from the Yucatan government. Frustrated with the slow response to the crisis, O'Reilly vented his angst against the 'hatred, the envy, and the savage ferocity of the eastern Indians, who have declared against us a war of extermination.' O'Reilly's appeals had now changed to asking for humanitarian assistance, and he believed that the United States represented 'the vanguard of freedom and civilization of the American nations, and from the immense power which they possess ... to prevent the Yucatan from becoming the prey of rebellious savages.' Moreover, he blamed the British for the state of affairs, noting that perhaps through some 'occult of mysterious power, which, nourishing a deep and ancient hatred to the sacred cause of those American countries, who are endeavoring to cast off the yoke of European dependence, are engaged either directly or indirectly in fomenting revolt among the Indians.' O'Reilly further outlined to Buchanan the history of Belize and conspiracies between the Mexican and British governments, and even cited muskets found among Mayans manufactured in the Tower of London to conclude it was the moral obligation of the United States to preserve the 'future destiny of the American nations' from their mutual enemy:

> The weakness or impotency of the first Spanish government, and, subsequently, the neglect and culpable heedlessness of the general government of the Mexican, patiently tolerated the successive invasions of that colony [Belize] ... but now it is a vast depository of contraband, which annihilates Yucatan, and invades the states of Tabasco, Chiapas, and Guatemala. Day by day these men are penetrating to the very heart of the peninsula ...[18]

On the same day that O'Reilly penned his letter to Buchanan, Perry was readying to leave Veracruz. The insurrectionists 'were still in great force,' the commodore wrote to Mason, 'and had carried their excursions of rape and rapine still nearer the coast.' With minimal duties in Veracruz, Perry informed his superior he was headed to Laguna and Campeche in the hope that 'the appearance of two or three vessels of the squadron upon the coast will doubtless check the advance of the Indians upon the principal towns, and give them time to bring a larger white force into the field.' Meanwhile,

US soldiers in the Mexican capital, who soon learned that Nicholas Trist had secretly left that city later than reported and arrived in Washington with a treaty to end the war, were reading excerpts from New Orleans newspapers about 'mingling in the contest' with Central American states fearful the US would compensate Mexico for its lost northern territories by allowing it to enlarge itself southward at the expense of its neighbours. According to the report, Honduran president Juan Lindo contacted 'states composing the old confederacy' asking them 'to co-operate in resisting any attempt the Anglo-Americans might make upon the Central Americans'. However, Guatemalan president Rafael Carrera reportedly stymied the effort by proclaiming Guatemala's neutrality and amicable relations with the United States. By the end of February, and for the remainder of the war, reporting in the *American Star* on events in Yucatan and Central America abruptly ceased.[19]

Spain also played a role in the Gulf crisis. At the end of February, Abraham Bigelow, the governor at Laguna, informed Perry that the commander-general of the naval station in Havana was readying the schooner *Churroa* with weapons and supplies to assist the Yucatecans. *Churroa*'s destination was the port of Sisal but he was awaiting a 'written answer' from Sisal's authorities – who were obviously obligated to request approval from the leadership to allow foreign soldiers on their soil. The report that Bigelow forwarded also indicated the Spanish were aware of how their limited mission might be perceived by the international community, particularly the Americans, and thus pledged not to 'advance more than ten yards from the shore' – even if coming under fire from hostile forces. Shelters for refugees would be set up near Sisal's fortifications and possibly further down the coast at Cape Catoche – located off the mainland and nearer to Cuba. The report cited Merida's newspaper *Union*, which in addition to asking for 2,000 muskets and powder, was no short of praise for the 'worthy sons of Cid and Pelayo!!!' Perry sent Bigelow's report to Washington out of concern 'that the Spanish government had interfered in the affairs of Yucatan', but expressed his understanding that the 'object of the rumored offer of aid from Cuba, is solely to assist the ... war against the Indians.'[20]

Bigelow's report to Perry also indicated news of a treaty had reached Laguna and residents there were 'apprehensive of a withdrawal of our forces, and that they will be left without protection.' The desire by Laguna officials to seek security guarantees from US officials towards the end of the war mimicked O'Reilly's requests in Washington. Laguna's relationship with the

US Navy had been particularly fruitful, both socially and financially, especially since naval officers paid well for goods and materials supplying the Gulf Squadron. Like Puebla's role in assisting Scott's army before the advance on Mexico City, in the eyes of many of their compatriots the residents of Ciudad del Carmen at Laguna had been collaborators. 'The people of this place consider themselves compromised in the eyes of their countrymen,' Perry wrote, 'in consequence of having submitted quietly to our occupation, and having consented to serve in civil offices under our authority.' For that reason, there was an effort among the citizenry to 'draw up a petition that a force may be left here as long as is necessary for their protection.'[21]

Back in Washington, O'Reilly was attempting to further his collaboration with the administration. While the US Senate's pondering of Trist's treaty took the wind out of the sails of the All-Mexico movement, it was somewhat mollified by an effort to involve the US deeper into Yucatan's affairs by using the Caste War as an opportunity. Whig war sceptics, like Indiana's Richard W. Thompson (later Secretary of the Navy) were still debating the origins of the war and chastising expansionists for continually seeking ways to enlarge the United States. 'We are told that the people of the northern states of Mexico, not embraced in the treaty,' he asserted on 4 March in the House of Representatives, 'are petitioning for admission into this Union.' His statement was partly conjecture, but Thompson did mention O'Reilly specifically: 'It is known that a commissioner from Yucatan is asking protection of this government. Looking to South America, we see even they are throwing themselves into the arms of this administration for protection ... Where are we to stop?'[22]

O'Reilly was running out of patience with Washington, noting that the treaty under consideration had 'complicated' Yucatan affairs 'in an alarming way'. His obvious concern was that if the United States concluded a treaty of peace with Mexico without including Yucatan, they would be at the mercy of both the Maya and the centralists. 'Sometimes I get the most flattering hopes,' he wrote in his diary, 'but there are times when I really despair of seeing the remedy for our maladies. This has me in continual agitation ... As it was discussed in the Senate behind closed doors ... anxiously awaiting the end of this noisy treaty.' On 6 March, O'Reilly spent two hours with Buchanan discussing Yucatan, only to follow up that meeting with another letter castigating the 'barbarous' Mayans, invoking the humanity of the United States, mentioning Yucatecan acceptance of aid from Spain, and requesting 'two thousand troops, and a half million dollars'. More than any of the above mentioned, O'Reilly's reference to the 'lively sympathy of Spain in favor of her ancient colonies' and their aid 'in munitions of war belonging to the Spanish crown' prompted an immediate response from the administration. Ultimately, the threat of European involvement in Yucatan motivated US officials to act, and O'Reilly understood as much when he mentioned how such an action might result in 'lamentable consequences to the American policy' – a direct reference to the Monroe Doctrine.[23]

Mentioning European involvement worked. That same day, after Polk conferred with Senators who mentioned the treaty was likely to be ratified in a matter of days, he held a cabinet meeting at which the Secretary of State read O'Reilly's application 'requesting that the US would afford assistance to the white population to save them from destruction ... against the Indians'. O'Reilly's conversations had apparently persuaded Buchanan because, according to Polk, he was 'petulant' when it was suggested that gunpowder sent to the Yucatecans might end up in Mexican hands. After further discussion, it was decided to send 10,000lbs pounds of powder to the peninsula to be distributed at Perry's discretion. Polk also deemed Yucatan to have returned officially to 'a neutral attitude' in the war.[24]

On 13 March, three days after the US Senate formally ratified the treaty and sent it back to Mexico for approval, Perry penned a dispatch to Mason from Campeche. In addition to bringing his flagship *Cumberland*, Perry brought the *Mississippi*, *Scorpion*, *Iris*, *Water Witch*, and *Vesuvius*. The commodore was hoping to make 'as imposing a demonstration [as possible] ... in the probability that the appearance of such a force on the coast might have some influence' in dissuading the Maya from further advances towards the coast. Perry met with Governor Mendez 'several' times and believed that the 'panic-stricken' people there – who had, in fact, gladly accepted aid from Cuba – would eventually acquiesce to a foreign occupier in exchange for security. Moreover, Yucatecans were pleading with Perry to provide them with weapons, and he assured them he would return to Veracruz to see what was available. He also received an official request from the civil authorities in Laguna to maintain the US naval presence there until the end of the crisis. 'The statements set forth in these newspapers are not in the least exaggerated,' he wrote to Mason, 'and, unless assistance is received from some quarter, the whole country will be laid waste.' In addition, the Europeans were beginning to focus their attention on the conflict:

> The French consul expresses the opinion that England may, in view of obtaining an increase of territory in the bay of Honduras ... on the east coast of Yucatan, be induced to furnish aid in troops and munitions from the settlement of Balize [sic] ... Governor Mendez has declared to me that, failing to obtain aid from the United States, he should apply to other powers, and as a last resort the people of Yucatan would offer up the sovereignty of the state to whatever power would consent to take it under protection.[25]

By March the besieged in Valladolid were desperate. Yucatecan officers attempted a rescue from the outside on a couple of occasions, only to be repelled by the massive force of Mayans led by Cecilio Chi who had surrounded the city. Inside were nearly 10,000 citizens and refugees from other locations on the peninsula – many of whom unfortunately believed Valladolid would be safe. Of those who came from other areas devastated by the revolt, many were too tired to continue to Merida. Negotiations also proved futile because the Mayans simply locked up those who attempted to parley with them – including O'Reilly's brother and curate of Valladolid, Manuel Antonio Sierra O'Reilly. Most of the prisoners were later executed, but O'Reilly's brother managed to escape. By mid-March supplies and ammunition were exhausted, and thus it was decided the inhabitants needed to break the siege themselves.[26]

On the morning of 14 March, a column of 500 soldiers led by Colonel Pastor Gamboa charged the fortifications of their captors. Behind them came civilians of all stripes, some with wagons, but most on foot. Ancono wrote that Gamboa did his best 'to take a great number of precautions so that the withdrawal would not degenerate into a disorder', but panic quickly 'seized all the spirits' and the breakout turned into a free-for-all. Most of the supporting units assigned to the flanks and rear of the convoy broke formation. For a moment the Maya kept their distance due to enemy cannon fire, but when discipline was abandoned, butchery ensued. Reed writes that congestion among the wagons caused a fatal bottleneck, and the disorder turned into 'an orgy of revenge'. The nearby village of Popóla became a scene of carnage as desperation forced many to leave the convoy, 'dragging the young children behind them, hoping that, fleeing singly or in small groups, they would be able to better escape.'[27]

Horror stories from survivors spread throughout the peninsula. *Vesuvius*'s captain Murray Mason, the younger brother of Virginia Senator James

Murray Mason, assigned by Perry to protect Campeche while Perry was in Veracruz rounding up spare weapons, relayed reports from Merida that 'the Indians mustered about forty thousand men, and were within fifty or sixty miles of Merida.' The numbers were a wild exaggeration born from fear, but like nearly all non-natives on the peninsula, Mason believed 'that unless Yucatan can get more troops from some foreign power, she is lost.' The captain also witnessed multitudes who fled their farms and homes for the safety of Campeche's walls. 'The Yucatanos are already scared ... Every night carts, wagons, stages, &c., are coming from the interior ... These people are in great distress; but if they have not the courage to defend themselves, what can they expect?' Others were asking similar questions of the Americans, hoping they would get involved. Abraham Bigelow, the Governor of Laguna, put the question to the commodore: 'Why could not a few thousand troops, who will remain idle during the armistice, be sent here to roll back the tide of victory?' According to Bigelow, the dire situation presented the Americans an opportunity to demonstrate their abilities. 'The war-whoop of these ruthless Indians would have no terrors to those who have conquered the red man in our own territory ... three thousand of our troops, either regulars or volunteers, would in a month, drive every Indian in Yucatan into the bay of Honduras.'[28]

Most of the survivors from Valladolid fled to Merida, while others took the shorter route to the coast, where US naval vessels picked up people from sand bars wedged between the ocean and enemy. John F. McGregor, the consul at Campeche, sent word from Captain Mason that 'three to four thousand souls' who escaped from Espita and Tizimín made it to the coast, and that Tekax would soon fall. 'If you can possibly spare me a steamer,' Mason asked Bigelow, 'you will be doing a great act of charity. There are now thousands of men, women and children on the beach, suffering and in want.' The request was granted, and Captain John J. Glasson of the *Falcon* began rescuing people along the coast near Dzilam. Europeans also assisted. An English vessel, the *True Blue*, captained by James Smith, ferried refugees to the island of Cozumel. The Spanish sent others to the safety of Cuba. 'Laguna, in consequence of American protection,' Perry informed Washington, 'is now considered by the Yucatecos the only safe place of refuge in Yucatan to those who are flying before the infuriated Indians.' Captain Mason, emotionally absorbed by the rescuing of civilians, relayed an urgent request to the American capital: 'Yucatan is lost unless some foreign power comes to her assistance.' These pleas were apparently coming from 'ex-governor, Mendez, through our consul' who 'was desirous that I should forward a dispatch to the United States, and, as you will see, that the government of Yucatan desires to be annexed to the United States.' According to Mason's request, the situation was becoming so precarious that the Yucatecan authorities were appealing for a simple solution. 'All they ask is this – hoist the flag of the United States, annex us to your government, and we are satisfied. Now it comes to this – unless we do, Spain will.'[29]

'Dominion and Sovereignty' and British 'Encroachments'

On 25 March, more than two weeks before resigning his position as governor, Sierra Mendez, with the blessing of the Yucatecan Secretary of State and Secretary of War and Marine, issued a declaration offering 'dominion and sovereignty of the country to the nation which will assume the charge of saving it'. The offer was extended to the governments of Great Britain, Spain and the United States. 'I find myself obliged, in like manner,' Mendez addressed Buchanan, 'to apply with this object to the Spanish and English governments, through their respective ministers in Mexico, and the captain general of Cuba and the admiral of Jamaica.' O'Reilly was equally dejected by the obligation of forwarding a letter relinquishing Yucatecan autonomy. 'In the sacred name of the living God,' he wrote, 'the affrighted people of Yucatan appeal to the humanity of their happy and more fortunate neighbours, the people of the United States, to save them from utter extermination.'[30]

Perry believed Mendez's resignation in favour of reinstating Barbachano was 'disgraceful cowardice', adding that 'men who make no effort to defend their own firesides, have no claim upon the friendly aid of others.' On the other side of the peninsula, the inhabitants of Belize, long comfortable with their beneficial relationship with the Maya, began to seriously re-evaluate the conditions of their security. On 19 April, the town of Bacalar fell. Although the English were under no serious threat of attack from their business partners, the authorities agreed to put the colony in a state of defence.[31] In addition, American newspapers were beginning to realize the extent of British involvement in Yucatecan affairs after excerpts of Perry's correspondence to Secretary Mason regarding a potential 'increase of territory in the bay of Honduras' and trade in munitions was made public. One article in Baltimore's *Sun* requoted speculation of 'annexation of Yucatan to

British Honduras' – noting the 'grave charge' amounted to 'a most infamous, double-dealing policy on the part of Great Britain, to further her schemes of territorial aggrandizement.'[32]

Although the fact was not widely publicized, the Europeans were not simple observers of a contest most people assumed lay solely between the United States and Mexico. Ever since Carlist guerrillas from France and Spain began appearing in the spring of 1847 on the logistics lifeline separating Scott's army in Mexico City from Veracruz, US leadership had been concerned about European intervention in the war. Information that many of the Carlists may have received aid in Great Britain facilitating their passage over the Atlantic, as well as the mid-summer revelation that a British company held proprietary rights to the isthmus of Tehuantepec, painted a picture of duplicity. Furthermore, the trade in contraband emanating from Belize added evidence to suspicions that US war efforts were being thwarted, and – for those with longer memories – resembled exactly what the British did to oppose American expansion during the War of 1812, when British officers armed the Creeks in the southern gulf states. Like others who accused the British of conspiratorial schemes, O'Reilly was a believer. Just before forwarding the Mendez letter, he outlined to Buchanan Yucatan's efforts to stop the arming of Mayans by sending a commissioner to Belize, and that Belizean officials 'answered that this should be done'. However, the problem was that the 'British government of Balize [*sic*] may act as it has promised; yet without diminishing, in any way, the resources of the Indian. Recollect, sir ... the unworthy and intolerable farce of the kingdom of the Mosquitos.' With Bacalar in Mayan hands, it was obvious the contraband trade was still being conducted on Yucatecan soil.[33]

Again, O'Reilly touched upon the 1823 'Monroe Doctrine' when 'applying in preference to the United States', and cited it specifically in relation to Polk's previous message to Congress and the possibility of British or Spanish involvement. 'Thus, if such intervention should take place,' he wrote, 'as it is more than probable that it will, Yucatan would be involved in difficulty.' The dilemma, in his estimation, was the possibility of there being a 'theatre of another war' in the region 'since, though these doctrines of Mr. Monroe and Mr. Polk may be a declaration of the principles of the United States, the other powers may, or may not accept them, according to their own political views and objects.' O'Reilly understood the American passion for the Monroe declaration before his arrival in Washington, but his friendship with Senator John Dix of New York no doubt contributed to his knowledge. On 10 March, O'Reilly met with a handful of senators, including Daniel Webster, John C. Calhoun, Lewis Cass and Dix. Among them, Cass was the most ardent expansionist and, as Chairman of the Committee of Military Affairs, supported Polk's policies. However, Dix spoke Spanish, French, and Italian and met with O'Reilly on several occasions.[34]

It was Dix, more than any other senator, who was sounding the alarm about European involvement in the conflict. In early 1848 he publicly accused French Foreign Minister François Guizot of meddling in the war, and two days before meeting O'Reilly and Senator Thomas Benton to discuss Yucatan, Dix addressed the senate, asserting that 'Mr. Monroe's declarations have not been maintained.' On 29 March, it was not the French who were the subject of Dix's scrutiny, but the British. 'While discussing the bill to raise an additional military force in January last, I stated some facts in illustration of the encroachments of Great Britain on the southern portion of the North American continent.' Dix argued that the Americans had been so preoccupied with the war in Mexico, that they did not see what the British were doing elsewhere:

> I alluded particularly to her movement on the Mosquito coast, where she is establishing herself under the pretense of giving protection to an insignificant tribe of Indians ... But it is not through her connection with the Mosquito coast alone that Great Britain is extending herself across the continent. Through her establishment at Belize she is penetrating to the very heart of the peninsula of Yucatan.[35]

The day after submitting the 'dominion and sovereignty' letter to Buchanan, O'Reilly went to see his 'respectable friend General Dix, who is the one who has more warmly taken things concerning Yucatan, although unfortunately still without success, despite the fact that he is a senator highly regarded by the current administration.' Three days later, Sierra met President Polk to discuss the future of his homeland in the Gulf of Mexico. The Americans were ready to reaffirm their commitment to the Monroe Doctrine, but whether they would annex Yucatan, or go to war with Great Britain to maintain their dominance over the Gulf, remained to be seen.[36]

Chapter 5
'Eagle and lion watching the same prey'

Our own security requires that the established policy [Monroe Doctrine], thus announced, should guide our conduct, and this applies with great force to the peninsula of Yucatan. It is situate in the Gulf of Mexico, on the North American continent, and, from its vicinity to Cuba, to the capes of Florida, to New Orleans, and, indeed, to our whole southwestern coast, it would be dangerous to our peace and security if it should become a colony of any European nation. We have now authentic information that, if the aid asked from the United States be not granted, such aid will probably be obtained from some other European power which may hereafter assert a claim of 'dominion and sovereignty' over Yucatan.[1]
President James K. Polk, Message to Congress, 29 April 1848

Towards the close of the Mexican War and before news of the ratification of the Treaty of Guadalupe Hidalgo in Mexico reached Washington DC, US expansionists in the American capital were faced with a tempting proposition to intervene in the Caste War at the request of Yucatecan authorities. Informing their deliberations was the failed effort by prominent All-Mexico advocates to expand the war in central Mexico and accomplish the complete annexation of that country. The consequences of military intervention in Yucatan were clear, and thus proponents of assisting the Yucatecans – including President Polk – were the same figures who sought to send more soldiers to Mexico and offered bills to acquire Mexican states as spoils of war. Ever present in the argument for aiding Yucatan was the belief that if the United States did not do so, another European power would. This assertion, bolstered by the 1823 Monroe Doctrine forbidding further European colonization in the Americas, was not unfounded given British arming of the Maya through their contraband trade in Belize. Although the US decided not to occupy Yucatan, American mercenaries, inspired by pleas and the pro-war press, volunteered to fight in the former breakaway republic.

Events moved quickly after the 'dominion and sovereignty' letter was received in Washington. Although O'Reilly initially struggled to gain the attention of the American leadership after his arrival in the capital, he was finally the centre of discussion. On the evening of 22 April, after holding a morning cabinet meeting discussing affairs in Yucatan and the appointment of a commissioner to send the recently ratified treaty back to Mexico, Polk met with the Yucatecan commissioner. Polk believed O'Reilly's written appeal was 'earnest and eloquent', and there is no indication the same message was not conveyed properly through an interpreter. The president also promised a formal response in a matter of days. O'Reilly felt the president had listened with 'considerable deference' and was assured he would 'do everything within his constitutional powers, and since they were not enough, he would demand intervention of the Senate.'[2]

For the next few days Buchanan and Polk prepared a draft message for Congress. 'The subject is environed with difficulties,' Polk wrote, adding, 'We could never agree to see Yucatan pass into the hands of a foreign monarchy ... and that sooner than this should take place the US should afford the aid & protection asked, but that this could only be done by the authority of Congress.' During the preparation period, Polk conferred with Indiana senator and expansionist Edward A. Hannegan, chairman of the Foreign Affairs Committee, and discussed the 25 March letter and draft proposal 'to save the white race from extermination by the Indians, and offering ... dominion & sovereignty of Yucatan to the U. S.' More than once Polk noted it was 'an important subject' and the message invoking the Monroe Doctrine as 'one of great importance.' Treasury Secretary Robert Walker, who favoured acquiring Tehuantepec, was also in favour of annexing Yucatan, and Polk's diary entry of that conversation noted the president 'concurred with Mr. Walker, rather than see it fall into the hands of England.' Buchanan was opposed. On Saturday, 29 April, while O'Reilly was waiting in the Capitol, the message arrived and was referred to Hannegan's committee for consideration. Senator John C. Calhoun, the All-Mexico movement's most vocal opponent and a critic of the expansionist war (despite being a Democrat), immediately called the intent of the message 'a broad and dangerous principle ... It goes far beyond Mr. Monroe's declaration. It is difficult to say what limits can be fixed to it ... if reduced to practice.'[3]

Polk's short message concerning Yucatan and invoking Monroe's principle was also a declaration proclaiming US hegemony over the Gulf of Mexico.

Polk argued that since Yucatan was part of North America and located close to Cuba and Florida, 'it would be dangerous to our peace and security if it should become a colony of any European nation.' Although Polk admitted Yucatan was a 'portion of Mexico' and considered neutral for most of the war, 'if we had troops to spare for this purpose, I would deem it proper, during the continuance of the war with Mexico, to occupy and hold militarily possession of her territory, and to defend the white inhabitants against the incursions of Indians.' He believed it could be done 'in the same way we have employed our troops in other states of the Mexican republic in our possession, in repelling the attacks of savages upon the inhabitants, who have maintained their neutrality in the war.' Philadelphia's *Public Ledger*, sympathetic to the administration, summed up Polk's position by stating, 'If we mean to prevent European intervention we must intervene ourselves,' while noting that the US remained in 'imminent peril' because the House of Representatives, which was controlled by the opposition Whig party, was refusing to address the Ten Regiment Bill asking that more soldiers be sent to Mexico.[4]

However, the Senate was controlled by Democrats aligned with the expansionist policy. On 5 May, after it easily passed committee, Hannegan submitted a bill in 'accordance with the recommendation' of Polk's message. The proposal allowed Polk 'to furnish to Yucatan munitions of war and all necessary means of defense and protection ... to allow him to abstract from Mexico, or from any part of the United States, sufficient force to meet and drive back the savages.' To assuage sceptics, Hannegan added that 'No man has dreamed as yet, so far as I know, of the permanent occupation of the territory of Yucatan. There are motives, however, which may lead to such a result.' To add urgency to the proposal, the senator suggested Merida might have already fallen, and that it was not his or the president's intention to seek 'the permanent occupation of the territory of Yucatan'. Nevertheless, with the British lurking in the shadows, such an outcome remained within the realm of possibilities. It was obvious to observers that expansionists were keeping their options open:

> Considerations may arise which will lead us beyond our first intentions, and render it imperative that we should convert this temporary occupation into something more. Sir, there is a most formidable power in Europe menacing American interests in that country, and let me add

American institutions too. That power is hastening with race-horse speed to seize upon the entire Isthmus. Heretofore, by slow degrees, according to her usual policy, England has got possession of various points along the Gulf coast of the Isthmus.[5]

As the sponsor of the bill conveying the intentions of the presidential message, Hannegan was essentially promoting Polk's position, and in doing so, rehearsing the argument used in the debate over Texas annexation and war by employing the (yet) unnamed 'Monroe Doctrine' as justification. 'England cherishes the design, at this moment,' he stated, 'to secure the most practicable route for an artificial means of communicating between the two oceans, and to effect that object she is gradually and rapidly absorbing the entire Isthmus. Unless we act she will accomplish her purpose.' Thus, on the eve of US continental hegemony, Yucatan was conflated with a larger argument concerning American geopolitical and geostrategic concerns. Hannegan stated that 'the miserable traffic in dye-woods' was merely a pretext for a 'higher object' and that British presence on the peninsula served 'a double purpose'. One of those purposes, he argued, served commercial interests, 'but the second strikes directly at us.' Hannegan was referring to the location of Yucatan vis-à-vis the Gulf. 'Look at the position of Yucatan. Look upon the map – see how she stands out in almost juxtaposition with Cuba. She shakes hands with Cuba. The possession of Yucatan by England would soon be followed by the possession of Cuba.' In his mind, allowing the British to intervene in Yucatan was tantamount to giving up Cuba and control of the Gulf itself. 'Cuba has been called the key to the Gulf. Yucatan and Cuba combined are the lock and key.' The senator also accused the British agent in the region, Patrick Walker, of supplying the Mayans with arms and establishing a trading depot to control the Isthmus. 'If we interpose the great principle laid down by Mr. Monroe, reiterated by Mr. Polk, England will hold her hands off.'[6]

Opponents of the Yucatan bill, such as Delaware Whig Senator John M. Clayton, argued that the 'principle of intervention' was entirely 'inconsistent with the farewell admonitions of the Father of his Country [George Washington], and with our earlier presidents. If we adopt it now, it will react upon us at some future day.' Any action directed at Yucatan, he believed, should not only be conducted 'with the consent' of the Mexican government, but was in 'direct conflict with the treaty' still under consideration in that country. In essence, it was 'bad faith' to contemplate military action while the war was still technically under way. Jefferson Davis, who also advocated annexing Mexico, was eager to promote the initiative, saying, 'The subject of the future annexation I leave to the future.' Employing Hannegan's argument, Davis also claimed Britain was continually 'extending her naval stations, until by a line of circumvallation, she almost surrounds the Gulf of Mexico ... Yucatan and Cuba are the salient points commanding the Gulf of Mexico, which I hold to be a basin of water belonging to the United States.' Davis then put forward an amendment allowing Polk to enlist more soldiers 'for the purpose of holding posts in Yucatan' and declared 'that the cape of Yucatan and island of Cuba must be ours.' Supporting his Whig colleague and the opposition, Senator John Crittenden called it a 'perilous step' and indicated the United States was about to abandon long held traditions:

> How far ought we to go? Are we not transgressing altogether that principle of non-intervention which lies at the foundation of the security of nations? ... If this doctrine of the right of intervention be generally admitted, the ambitious nation which seeks aggrandizement and extension of power will employ every pretext and be satisfied to act upon the principle. The consequences must be apparent. The violation of the principle of non-intervention is calculated to fill the world with distress, discord, and war.[7]

A few days later, the debate continued. Lewis Cass, the future Democrat Party choice for president in the 1848 election, asserted that the United States held a duty to ensure 'that the states of this continent should be republican as well as independent' and that no one believed the 'doctrine of non-intervention' meant that it 'prohibits us from preventing' interference by European states. Like other expansionists, he reiterated that the 'Gulf of Mexico is the reservoir of the great river of the North American continent' and 'must be practically an American lake for the great purpose of security.' Citing Gibraltar and other strategic ports, Britain's designs in Belize in conjunction with 'her tortuous policy' of arming the Maya and Native American tribes in the War of 1812, her position in the Bahamas and perceived desire to acquire Cuba, Cass argued, 'It should be a cardinal principle in our policy, never to be lost sight of, that the command of the Gulf of Mexico must never pass into foreign hands.'[8]

Two days later, Polk wrote that the ratification of the treaty in Mexico 'may be regarded as doubtful' and prepared two statements depending on the outcome of the procedure. On 13 May, New Jersey Whig and war opponent Jacob W. Miller addressed the Senate with an attack on the proposal to send US soldiers to Yucatan. He was also critical of O'Reilly's mission, the authority of Mendez to make an offer handing over Yucatecan sovereignty, and assertions made by Cass. 'To sustain his opinion,' Miller said of Cass, 'the honorable senator asserts that Yucatan is now politically separated from Mexico as much as China.' Moreover, Miller stated that the war was technically ongoing and that peace was jeopardized by 'bad faith' in discussing military intervention in Yucatan while Mexico debated ratification. Passing the bill would entail 'either continuing the present war, or the cause of a new war with Mexico'. Miller noted that 'on several occasions on this floor, by the friends of annexation, that the annexation of Texas was, if not the immediate, yet the remote cause of the war with Mexico. Is there not a similarity in the two cases?' According to the senator, the proposal to occupy Yucatan was not about humanitarian assistance, but part of a larger contest:

> In this race for dominion, the exercise of our philanthropy towards the white race of Yucatan is to end in a contest between England and the United States, over the graves of the Yucatecos, for the possession of a depopulated country. In what a strange and false position do gentlemen place England and America. The two great Christian and civilized nations of the earth gazing with covetous eyes upon a defenseless and woe-stricken country, and each, under the pretense of giving aid to its wretched people, seeking an opportunity to establish dominion. The eagle and lion watching the same prey, and whether the eagle shall strike before the lion has time to leap is the question which now fearfully agitates the minds of honorable Senators.[9]

Ever present during the debate over Yucatan's future, O'Reilly wrote that 'Senator Miller has resorted to the authority of a kind of Sancho Panza to decide the fate of Yucatan and from there form various other arguments.' He was critical of the Whigs in general, and their opposition to the administration's allies in the Senate. 'The Democratic senators are extremely indignant,' he wrote in his diary, 'and I am with them, at the strange twist that has been given to the question, which is already decidedly partisan.'

O'Reilly believed from the moment of his arrival in Washington that 'the question of Yucatan is a matter of party,' but had obviously dismissed, or overlooked, Democrat John C. Calhoun's role as the most vocal and effective opponent of the war. He finally had his chance.[10]

Born in 1782, Calhoun was not only an accomplished orator, but was also the US Secretary of War when Monroe issued his message in 1823. 'Yucatan does not come within this declaration', Calhoun said, explaining that Monroe's message was originally directed at the four powers of the 'Holy Alliance' assembled following the Napoleonic Wars – Austria, Russia, Prussia and France. Their objective 'to sustain and extend monarchical principles as far as possible' was in conflict with the establishment of republican governments in the Americas, and Calhoun noted that – while England initially supported it 'in the early stages of the alliance', Prime Minister George Canning 'became alarmed' when 'the alliance turned its eyes to this continent in order to aid Spain in regaining her sovereignty over her revolted provinces.' The result of that change of heart, Calhoun said, was assurances given to the Americans that if the Holy Alliance's efforts to reinstall monarchy in North America (i.e. Mexico) was 'sustained by the United States, Great Britain would resist' in favour of the republicans. Calhoun recalled that when Richard Rush, US Minister to the United Kingdom, sent word of Canning's decision, it 'was received here with joy.' The senator also noted the recent political turmoil in Europe undermining monarchies was directly related to the British shift in policy regarding the Holy Alliance. Calhoun was not an Anglophile, but he demonstrated from first-hand knowledge that the British played a crucial role in the endurance of Monroe's message:

> The cabinet met. It deliberated. There was long and careful consultation; and the result was the declaration [Monroe Doctrine] which I have just announced. All this has passed away. That very movement on the part of England, sustained by this declaration, gave a blow to the celebrated alliance from which it never recovered. From that time forward it gradually decayed, till it utterly perished. The late revolutions in Europe have put an end to all its work, and nothing remains of all that it ever did. Now, by what ingenuity of argument, by what force of sophistry can it be shown that this declaration comprehends the case of Yucatan, when the events which called it forth have passed away forever?[11]

As to the trade in munitions in Belize, Calhoun noted that O'Reilly 'speaks with some degree of uncertainty, however, and is unable to say whether the arms were given or not, and cannot state how they were obtained by the Indians.' In essence, Calhoun was saying that it may have been true that the Maya obtained their weapons from British agents but there was no certainty if arming them was official policy based on aggressive designs towards Yucatan by the British leadership. 'England does not interpose as a hostile power. She does not come to oppress Yucatan.' In his opinion, the Yucatan situation was entirely different from Texas annexation, which Calhoun supported 'even at the hazard of war'. If conquered by a foreign power, Cuba would also have to be discussed, but he believed conflating that island, owned by Spain, with Yucatecan geography meant nothing when the Royal Navy was still the dominant force on the seas – especially in the Caribbean, where 'Great Britain has the complete command' from Jamaica and other regional ports. Therefore, taking possession of Yucatan 'would impose on us a very heavy cost' in American blood and treasure, and at the same time do nothing to improve the strategic position of the United States. On the contrary, Calhoun argued, annexation of Yucatan could spark another Anglo-American conflict, or result in a long-term war against the Maya akin to 'another Seminole affair'.[12]

Although Calhoun argued eloquently against the Yucatan bill, O'Reilly was still impressed with the speech. According to him, the South Carolinian 'is such an outstanding speaker that it moved me to listen to him even though I already foresaw that he would make me very uncomfortable.' To assuage fears of abandonment, O'Reilly indicated he was working on 'a large colonization plan in order to attract foreigners to Yucatan', but was startled by reports from New Orleans by way of Veracruz's *El Arco Iris* indicating Barbachano had made a peace agreement with Jacinto Pat. 'The terms of the treaty', he wrote, 'if there is such a treaty and it can be called such, cannot be more offensive and degrading to the government of Yucatan.' The Yucatecan commissioner also vowed that 'if such a thing happens, I will finish convincing myself that Yucatan is cursed forever and that there is no hope left for it and from the moment ... prepare my departure from Washington.'[13]

On 17 May, O'Reilly's mission unravelled. At twelve o'clock that day, he entered the room where the Senate Foreign Affairs Committee met to find Buchanan and Hannegan engaged in a quiet 'confidential' conversation. O'Reilly surmised that rumours of a treaty between the Maya and Yucatecans were the reason. 'His presence seemed to me a very bad omen because if there is indeed a treaty … it is possible that Commodore Perry will stop being informed of everything … Under these apprehensions that I harbored, the session of the Senate began.' O'Reilly fears were allayed for a few moments while Senator Dix made a speech in support of the bill before Hannegan stood and informed the body that indeed 'a fair and liberal treaty' between the Yucatecan government and the Maya had been agreed upon. 'Cold I was left with such an announcement … and such has been the unexpected outcome of all my efforts and eagerness to obtain aid from this government.'[14]

O'Reilly liked Dix's speech but what he overlooked was an admission from the senator that he 'would not charge the British government with a design to aid the Indians' and a statement 'that British agents may have taken this course from a desire to extend the British dominion.' Following his exoneration of the British government, Dix expressed his friendship towards the English and lamented that the US 'had taken away the means which would have enabled Mexico to assist Yucatan.' Hannegan, the sponsor of the bill, noted that 'no harm could result from a little delay', advised a wait for more details from Yucatan, and indicated that 400 marines were being ordered by Mason from Alvarado to reinforce Laguna. 'It will be judicious to strengthen your forces at El Carmen,' Mason informed Perry. 'In addition to those already those sent by you to Laguna, it would appear to me to be proper to send the entire detachment of marines now at Alvarado, with instructions to repel the Indians if they approach that point.' This was as far as the Americans were willing to go, and O'Reilly's mission was over.[15]

In his diary, O'Reilly accused Hannegan of being 'Machiavellian', blamed Buchanan and Barbachano, lashed out at the US press for their misinterpretation of events and their unwillingness to publish his 'notes, in which all the facts were authentically established', and expressed general frustration with Washington and party politics. Adding insult to injury, the New Orleans *Delta* mischaracterized Jacinto Pat as some type of Irishman turned native freedom fighter. To its credit, the *New York Herald* allowed O'Reilly to contest those and other claims that the whites had already violated the terms of the treaty. 'This arbitrary and absurd report … of New Orleans is spreading over the country.' It was becoming obvious that O'Reilly was overwhelmed by the forces acting against his mission. 'The extravagant invention of the *Delta*,' O'Reilly fulminated, 'saying Pat is an Irish descendant, is a ridiculous one … Jacinto Pat never has been either a saint (San Jacinto Pat as called by the *Delta*) nor an educated man. He is, and has been, a savage ... and progeny of banditti and murderers.'[16]

More importantly, O'Reilly intuitively understood better than anyone in the US capital that the 'treaty' was nothing of the sort, but merely a temporary agreement to buy the Yucatecans time and an effective way of dividing the Mayan leadership – since the treaty ostensibly recognized Pat as 'governor over the indigenous captains' on the peninsula. The *National Intelligencer*, which reported on the agreement after the Senate dropped the bill, called him the 'principal chief of the revolted Indians'. This designation flattered Pat but would have wounded the pride of his co-conspirator Cecilio Chi, who continued to slaughter non-Mayans in an effective display that proved Pat controlled nothing beyond what he could see. An *El Arco Iris* correspondent from a 25 April report indicated, 'The other chiefs ... deny Pat had any right to make this treaty. His troops are abandoning him, and committing the worst sort of excesses.' Moreover, as soon as Pat left Tekax, where the treaty with Barbachano was agreed upon, Mayan officers executed those (on their side) in charge of negotiations. In other words, there was no treaty, but US leadership used the supposed existence of one to prudently avoid entering and inheriting a war it knew very little about. Texas was one matter, but Yucatan was another world altogether and far from fertile ground as an American frontier fit for colonization. In addition, Washington's *National Intelligencer*, which was often critical of the war, printed an excerpt from the *Baltimore Clipper* entitled 'The Yucatan Question' outlining similarities between Yucatan, Texas and potential war with the British:

> The plea urged to justify intermeddling in the affairs of Yucatan, that Great Britain will seize the territory, is pure humbug. This was the plea used in the annexation of Texas, and it is brought forth on all occasions. England has enough at home to occupy her attention without seeking to grasp Yucatan or the Island of Cuba. There seems to be an inveteracy of feeling against England, with certain politicians in the United States, which can never be satisfied until the two nations are brought into collision.[17]

Twentieth-century Mexican statesman and historian Marte R. Gomez, familiar with O'Reilly's diaries written during his visit, believed that, while the commissioner was a talented and capable man, 'Mexico should celebrate the fact that Sierra O'Reilly had difficulty communicating' in English. Gomez also asserted that – although Polk rarely revealed his annexationist tendencies in his diary – he would 'have had no qualms about entering Yucatan.' The result 'was fortunate for Mexico,' he wrote, 'and for the United States itself – because ambitions of conquest are always costly, as history repeatedly teaches – that President Polk's political opponents tied his hands.' Just like the failure by the All-Mexico movement to annex Mexico, O'Reilly misunderstood the opposition because it was not only a partisan effort led by Whigs who opposed the war, but a bi-partisan endeavour whose main and most effective protagonist, John C. Calhoun, was a member of the same party as the expansionists. 'As for the Yucatecan commissioner,' Gomez wrote, 'when the United States Senate opposed intervening in Yucatan, Justo Sierra O'Reilly had nothing to do but sit back and suffer the final onslaught of the newspapers.'[18] O'Reilly was an accomplished man, but ultimately, for better or for worse, he could not live up to the achievements of Lorenzo de Zavala. Both men were irreversibly separated by time and circumstance.

Bacalar and Belize

While news of the treaty smashed Yucatecan hopes for American intervention, officers there were planning (despite the treaty) to recapture Bacalar from the Mayans. All of the principal northern roads were under Mayan control, and it was therefore decided to launch a coastal attack. Funding for the expedition was provided by selling captured Mayans, including women and children, as slaves to Cuban merchants. The 7th Division, under the command of Colonel José Dolores Cetina, was organized in Sisal and arrived near Bacalar lagoon in late April. Although the Maya were waiting for the Yucatecans, Cetina pushed forward until they recaptured the town on 2 May. It was only a matter of time before the Maya regrouped and counter-attacked, and so Cetina quickly put his men to work digging defensive trenches and adding fortifications to a perimeter centring around the eighteenth-century San Felipe fortress abutting the lagoon. Assisting these efforts were hundreds of civilians who had more to fear by being on the outside of a siege than on the inside of Bacalar. Most were local men who sent their wives and children to the safety of Belize.[19]

The Yucatecans knew a counter-attack was imminent, and at one point during the preparation Cetina said to his men, 'Anyone who wants a passport to the English colony of Belize, speak up.' When a few raised their hands, he had them shot in a demonstration of his determination. At dawn on 14 May, roughly 4,000 Mayans under orders of Jacinto Pat appeared just beyond the perimeter, and the defenders began a barrage of fire and artillery that lasted all night. To keep the enemy from closing in, any building or structure beyond the line was destroyed. The Yucatecans held the fortress, but the trade in arms and munitions simply moved to places like Ascension Bay further north or Rio Hondo to the south. The nineteenth-century Caste War historian Serapio Baqueiro wrote that the Mayans attacked Cetina's line 'every day, until after a few months, Bacalar found itself completely surrounded by walls, bastions and ditches, and trenches, with a well-organized artillery that was the terror of the rebels.' The expedition took the pressure off the forces defending Merida by forcing the Maya to address the strategic point in their rear essential to the financial and material interests of their campaign. Thus, Baqueiro credited Cetina with helping to save Yucatan from destruction – noting that the plaza fronting the fortress of Bacalar became 'one of the strongest places in the country, thanks to the heroism of the worthy chief of the memorable 7th Division'.[20]

Because the Fortress of San Felipe abutted Bacalar lagoon and was originally intended to protect the town from pirate attacks, the division was able to re-supply itself with excursions to Belize. Baqueiro noted that when supplies ran low, Cetina was able to provide 'abundant meat ... biscuits, coffee, sugar, butter, and other things that remedied the needs of the garrison'. The position was so formidable that the division was sometimes able to mount guerrilla forays outside the perimeter. However, while the campaign was technically a strategic success, turning Bacalar into a war zone resulted in thousands of people fleeing to the safety of British territory. Most reports in the US indicated people were fleeing because the Maya had seized the city, but in actuality they were fleeing the battlefield that ensued and the subsequent hostilities directed against non-Mayans in the area who were blamed for collaborating with the Yucatecans. Reports from the *Picayune* appearing in Washington depicted a humanitarian crisis. 'The men, to the number of from four to five hundred, retired to the forts, where they are now. The women and children (poor creatures), with hardly any clothing, and no money or food, are flying in all directions.' Rumours also indicated the Maya – many of whom obviously believed Cetina received aid from Belize – were considering an attack on that territory.[21]

The US Consul in Belize, Christopher Hempstead, sent a 'heart rendering' [*sic*] report back to Buchanan on the turmoil, confirming that 'several thousands are in the most disrupted state imaginable but few of them have any money, property, or clothing.' He also stated that a large number of whites had fled to the island of Cozumel off the coast but did not confirm the rumours of a Mayan attack on the colony. Rather, Hempstead believed the Maya 'have applied to her majesty's superintendent at Belize for protection and have desired him to take possession of the territory they now occupy and take them under his protection as British subjects.' Hempstead cited a letter by Fancourt in Belize's *Central America Times* stating he would 'be most happy to maintain friendly relations' with the insurrectionists, and that he believed 'Col. Fancourt has forwarded their request to his government and strongly urged ... granting their request.' The Consul admitted his speculation, but added that if it were true, the British 'will then have possession of the entire coast ... to San Juan de Nicaragua.' British reporting indicated Fancourt was more interested in protecting the colony from potential Mayan incursions and had sent a request to Jamaica for more soldiers. Nevertheless, Hempstead's report is indicative of the conspiratorial suspicions Americans held of the British.[22]

Hempstead's theories mimicked those of the *Weekly Delta* of New Orleans, which confidently stated British 'designs' were 'transparent' to any observer. 'The only wonder was that they should escape the notice of our wise men in Washington ... England has always had a hankering after some possession on the neck of land which divides the Atlantic and Pacific.' The *Delta* cited previous surveys in the region conducted by the British, their presence in Belize, and their support for the Mosquito King as evidence of a long-term strategy. The newspaper was also critical of Washington leadership for neglecting the region for ten years by failing to provide 'a minister or consular agent in the neighbourhood of the English intrigues'. The *Delta* defended Polk for 'repeatedly' requesting a diplomatic representative for Central America and blamed both partisan politics and the constant regime changes and fluctuations in the states of that region. 'It would have been better to have appointed a Consul General for the States of Central America.' The larger goal was ensuring the British did not control 'the most important' geography in North America. 'The canal across the isthmus must be possessed by the United States. It is the grandest enterprise of the age, and the nation which executes it will be the mistress of the world ... The

Yucatan affair is a bold move for that end.' The *Delta*'s argument was that British machinations in Belize and elsewhere in Central America mimicked the 'fixed policy' used in India

> to set the native princes by the ears, and when the conflict between them has grown hot, to interfere ... and dispossess both. So, we have no doubt, San Jacinto Pat has been stirred up by English agents, to war against the whites of Yucatan, for the purpose of giving them an excuse for interfering and getting a foothold in Yucatan, and thereby commanding the route of Tehuantepec.[23]

The British, for their part, followed the Yucatan debate, but as American opponents of expansionists often argued, the British had other, more pressing, concerns. The *Morning Chronicle*, one of London's Whig organs for Palmerston's Foreign Office, was seemingly more interested in the upcoming US presidential contest than in defending American accusations over British activities in Central America. 'It is really painful to observe the attempts made in the debate on this bill,' the *Chronicle*'s correspondent wrote, 'to make it appear that England, or rather certain persons with the connivance of the British Government, had supplied the Yucatan Indians with arms.' The newspaper disavowed any intention on the part of the British to seize Yucatan, but did admit that the situation was getting out of control. 'The flame of the Indian is also spreading southwards ... the natives of Honduras are in arms, and even the town of Belize was threatened ... Similar outbreaks have also occurred at Guatemala.' They also pointed out that the 'revolutionary spirit ... pervading the new world' among indigenous peoples was 'a different kind from that of Europe' and that more 'Indian revolts are anticipated on the withdrawal of the American troops – perhaps before.'[24]

Cuba and Caribbean Pivot

The administration was more responsive to US criticism of inaction than to British denials. On 9 June, news that Mexico had ratified the Treaty of Guadalupe Hidalgo reached Washington. With the war officially over, and the prospects of acquiring Yucatan temporarily shelved, the administration was freer to discuss the more lucrative and strategically important island of Cuba. On 17 June, Buchanan wrote a long letter to Romulus Sanders, US

Minister to Spain, in which he articulated the administration's views: 'We are content that it shall continue to be a colony, [but] 'we can never consent that this island shall become a colony of any other European power.' This was the same position Polk held concerning Yucatan. 'In the possession of Great Britain or any strong naval power, it might prove ruinous both to our domestic and foreign commerce, and even endanger the Union of the States.'[25]

In addition to advice on how to broach the subject of purchasing Cuba, Buchanan detailed the importance of the island's location, which could 'be enabled in time of war effectively to blockade the mouth of the Mississippi and to deprive all the western States of this Union, as well as those within the Gulf.' He cited a litany of reasons to be concerned with British actions in the region, including: 'plausible pretexts' prompting them to wrest control of or purchase Cuba from the debt-laden Spanish government, the recent expulsion of their minister, Sir Henry Bulwer, from Madrid as an indication of souring Anglo-Spanish relations, and their 'uniform policy throughout her past history to seize upon every valuable commercial point throughout the world whenever circumstances have placed this in her power.' Buchanan also noted how the British recently seized 'the harbor of San Juan de Nicaragua, probably the best harbor along the whole coast … to obtain the control over the communication between the Atlantic and Pacific Oceans by the route of the Lake Nicaragua'. To an American leadership concerned with British intentions, the events painted a picture of a strategic rival:

> The disposition of Great Britain to extend her dominion over the most important commercial positions of the globe has been clearly manifested on a recent occasion. Tempted by the weakness and disunion of the Central American states, and acting under the mask of a protector to the King and Kingdom of the Mosquitos … she is endeavoring to acquire permanent possession of the entire coast of the Caribbean Sea from Cape Honduras to Escuda de Veragua [Panama].[26]

More than any other document in the immediate aftermath of the US-Mexican War, the Romulus letter outlines the pivot the administration made towards the British and the fact that American officials – despite securing transit rights over the isthmus of Tehuantepec – felt they still needed to pursue Cuba and (as the *Delta* advocated) launch diplomatic initiatives in Central America. In that regard, what the British were doing in Belize (although it was denied) was alarming because it not only affected Yucatan and possibly Tehuantepec, but Central America as well. Washington observers were keen to keep an eye on Yucatan, but they were also forced to pay attention to ongoing events in Nicaragua. While the Bidlack Treaty with New Granada meant that the US potentially acquired two transit routes connecting the Atlantic and Pacific, the agreement meant nothing (particularly to New York shipping) if Great Britain controlled access to the Gulf or denied the right of passage to American vessels in the Caribbean. Buchanan informed Romulus that 'the acquisition of Cuba would greatly strengthen our bond of Union. Its possession would secure to all the States within the valley of the Mississippi and Gulf of Mexico free access to the ocean.' Lastly, he wrote that Cuba was 'ready to rush into our arms.'[27]

Buchanan's opinion about Cuban desire for incorporation into the United States was misguided, but his general concerns with British intentions in Central America were warranted given their (unofficial) arming of Mayan insurgents and belligerent attitude towards Nicaragua on behalf of the Mosquito Kingdom. In essence, the attention of the Polk administration began shifting away from Mexico proper and south towards Yucatan and beyond. There was also another reason why US officials did not press the British too publicly on their activities in Belize. Although the British controlled the port leading into the interior of eastern Yucatan, American merchants were also engaging in the mahogany trade. Most US ships doing business there were from New York, New Orleans or Boston, and carried 'provisions' traded for the lucrative wood supplied by either Belizean middlemen or natives, some of whom undoubtedly contributed to the ongoing insurrection. Although Hempstead reported on the munitions trade and activities of Fancourt in Belize, his patience was also tested by unscrupulous American merchants.[28]

Reincorporation and rebel setbacks

Polk, who seemingly never rested and died shortly after his term in office, kept Buchanan so busy that the Secretary of State, who indulged in his own dreams of inhabiting the White House and was granted his wish in 1856, was too busy to solicit the Democrat nomination for the 1848 presidential election. That honour was instead bestowed upon expansionist and ardent Polk ally Lewis Cass. In other words, important post-war affairs were ongoing and urgent. In early August, Buchanan wrote to Nathan Clifford – the American envoy to Mexico who conveyed the treaty after ratification – informing him that his business was concluded at his discretion and that the 'irritation of feeling' from the 'disastrous war ought to be soothed.' That was easier said than done, as many Mexicans remained bitter about the loss. More importantly, however, Buchanan told Clifford that the request by Francisco de Paula de Arrangoiz, former consul at New Orleans appointed by President José Joaquín Herrera to Washington to ask for 'three or four thousand' US soldiers to be sent to Yucatan to put down the rebellion, was denied. As Dix noted in his speech before the US Senate dropped the Yucatan bill, the war inhibited the Mexican government from aiding the Yucatecans when the Caste War began – which was the rationale the Mexicans used when they asked that US soldiers 'be employed to sustain the present government against the revolutionists'. As the *Morning Chronicle* reported, the Mexican government, dealing with several revolts, were so desperate they were willing to use one of the $3m treaty instalments to pay for the military operation. US leaders were sympathetic, wanted to keep the defeated government as stable as possible, and thus provided it with surplus weapons previously used in offensive operations. Buchanan told Clifford that he had, that very morning, discussed the issue with Arrangoiz, and wanted to explain to the Mexicans that Polk did 'not possess the power to employ the army beyond the limits of the United States, in aid of a foreign country, without the sanction of the treaty-making or war-making power.' Furthermore, with the Yucatan bill dropped during the last remaining months of an election year, there was very little political will to support it. Lastly, Buchanan noted that 'to employ the army in this manner would be contrary to our established policy not to interfere in the domestic concerns of foreign nations, and this ought not to be violated unless under extraordinary circumstances.'[29]

In his 2005 work, *Wars within War*, Irving Levinson highlights many of the internal divisions plaguing Mexico and the ethnic conflicts that erupted there prompting US assistance. The Caste War – albeit the most serious of the indigenous conflicts – was merely one example of the wars plaguing Mexico in the aftermath of the US-Mexican contest. Levinson cites a number of areas where turmoil erupted 'before, during, and after the invading army of General Winfield Scott marched inland to Mexico City'. These locations included Chiapas, Guanajuato, Baja California, Sonora and places in the central states. Levinson writes, 'Many of México's most powerful and propertied citizens evinced a greater fear of their fellow Mexicans than of the invaders from the north.' Although it would seem counter-intuitive to ask a former conqueror for assistance – like Perry sending weapons from Veracruz to Yucatan – this was the context in which Arrangoiz solicited Buchanan for soldiers. In essence, federal officials were too busy stamping out opposition in the heart of their country to address the revolt on the other side of the Gulf.[30]

Back in Yucatan, Barbachano had little choice but to re-embrace the Mexican government and appeal for aid. The success of Cetina at Bacalar helped to stymie Mayan momentum against the principal cities, but the leadership remained cautious about their gains. On 17 August 1848, Yucatan officially rejoined 'the other states that make up the Mexican confederation' and recognized the 'federal regime adopted by the nation' as the 'supreme national power'. Article 8 of the decree also declared the Yucatecan government would 'continue to use its extraordinary powers, for everything related to saving the country from the war waged by the rebellious indigenous people.' Needing no decrees to motivate him, Cetina kept up forays from his citadel and recruited local spies unsympathetic to the Mayan cause. The Merida government attempted to persuade the Mayan leadership to desist by offering limited clemency, but there was still a movement among the influential eastern *batabs* to recruit the British to negotiate something more beneficial to them – including the creation of a protectorate-like state (à la Mosquito Kingdom) stretching north from Bacalar to the Gulf.[31]

In October it appeared the Yucatecans were finally making progress against the tide that had nearly swept them into the sea. Thrusts penetrated as far into the interior as Sabán, Tihosuco and even Tabi – Jacinto Pat's former forward base. Starvation also became a factor limiting Mayan successes, since many of the soldiers were obliged to return to their homes and assist in the cultivation of crops neglected for more than a year. In mid-November, Belizean superintendent Charles Fancourt held a meeting with various *batabs* in Ascension Bay at which they asserted their desire for a separate enclave. Fancourt was obviously in a difficult position, given that Great Britain and Mexico were officially on good terms, and did not want to provoke American involvement by making agreements with Mayan leadership without the consent of the Foreign Office. Nevertheless, the fact that the Mayans were willing to negotiate was a good sign that an armistice could be reached. Essentially, both sides, Yucatecan and Mayan, were exhausted. In his 2009 work on the Caste War, *Rebellion Now and Forever*, Terry Rugeley writes that the result of the temporary lull in violence, effected in part by Barbachano's restoration to the office of governor and his willingness to negotiate, resulted in the establishment of 'what came to be known as the *línea*, or line.' This imaginary but important border extended 'southeastward from Valladolid through Tihosuco and Peto, and westward to the Chenes region of Bolonchén' and for three decades 'served as both a defense mechanism and as a launching point for various excursions into rebel territory.' In other words, although hostilities subsided, the conflict was far from over.[32]

On 1 December 1848, less than a month after war hero General Zachary Taylor was elected president, a small article entitled 'Expedition to Yucatan' appeared in the New Orleans *Picayune*. It stated that a bark named *Florida* had been towed to sea carrying a number of officers 'and three hundred and eighty men; all bound for Yucatan'. Prompted by the news of suffering and the loss of interest by the American leadership in the former breakaway republic, the expedition was on its way to wage war against the Maya. The short article finished: 'The Indians had better look out. These boys are hard customers to deal with.' The war with Mexico was over, but the contest in Central America remained.[33]

Chapter 6

Limits of Empire

[T]he plan of the British Government to extend its influence over the peninsula has approached consummation ... though the people of Yucatan, who have already suffered from the machinations of the English, are bitterly opposed to it ... In such an event, the whole coast of the continent, from Mexico to the Isthmus of Panama, would be transferred to a power hostile to our interests, and even now every means to prevent the accomplishment, by American citizens, of a communication between two oceans.[1]

The Republic, Washington DC, 3 October 1849

Elija Hise's journey to Guatemala in 1848 was the embodiment of the obstacles expansionists faced south of the Rio Grande and the reason Americans needed to deal diplomatically with the British to avoid a war centering around the isthmian contest that intensified after the Mexican conflict. In essence, the Clayton-Bulwer Treaty of 1850, designed to mitigate hostilities arising out of Central America, amounted to a geopolitical and continental epilogue to the 1848 Mexican-American War and Treaty of Guadalupe Hidalgo. Imperfect as it was, the agreement was successful in that it prevented an immediate confrontation over a region both sides believed was essential to their future geostrategic and commercial interests. Furthermore, in O'Reilly's words, although the Americans may have invoked 'the doctrines of Mr. Monroe and Mr. Polk', which emerged out of the Yucatan debate and became known in 1849 as the 'Monroe Doctrine', it was during the post-war period that Americans realized they could not dictate terms to their British rivals. In the end, American expansion southward was not only restricted by British actions affecting Yucatan, but Central America as well.

In the spring of 1848, the US Senate confirmed Hise's nomination as chargé d'affaires to Guatemala. That summer, the Kentuckian boarded the US Navy's schooner *Onkahye* in New York for Fort San Lorenzo at the port town of Chagres (Panama), New Granada. It was Hise's intention to cross the isthmus, charter a vessel on the Pacific side and disembark on the coast somewhere closer to the capital. On 21 June, less than two weeks out from New York, the *Onkahye* was wrecked on a reef in the vicinity of Blue Hills, Caicos, on the western edge of the British-controlled islands. According to State Department correspondence, Hise managed to find a ship to Chagres, but did not cross the isthmus because he fell ill. After recovering, he secured a passage to Kingston, Jamaica, where one American traveller bound for Lima noted in a letter that the island 'appears to be the refuge of distressed ex-Presidents. Gen. Santa Anna and three Haytien ex-Presidents are now residing on the island.' The traveller also stated that 'before my arrival here, Mr. Hise ... visited Jamaica on his return home, after fruitless attempts to reach Guatemala, and after experiencing many privations.'[2]

Rumours of Hise's return were inaccurate, as he was determined to reach his destination. Although the British took care of him in Caicos, it appears they were not eager to convey a potential diplomatic competitor to his revised destination, Belize – even though there were frequent vessels between the two colonies. For that reason, Hise travelled to Havana and took a Spanish ship there – whereupon he travelled inland and up into the Guatemalan highlands cradling the capital. The tenacious diplomat arrived at his post sometime in mid-November – five months after leaving New York. Buchanan later wrote that Hise's delay 'was a cause of severe mortification to us all: & necessarily prevented Mr. Polk from laying the whole subject before Congress.' Had Hise attempted the same journey to Guatemala via Chagres a year later, he would have found it a great deal easier, since the first reports of the discovery of gold in the hills of California were just beginning to trickle into the eastern papers when Hise reached his post.[3]

Hise's eclectic journey was gruelling but informative, given that the entire region was in turmoil and up in arms against itself and the British. After he arrived in mid-November in Guatemala City – one of the former capitals of the Federal Republic of Central America – he wrote to Buchanan that both Nicaragua and Honduras had publicly protested against 'the British occupation of the Mosquito country and the port of San Juan', and that he expected the Guatemalan government to do the same 'when there is one in being' – as that country was currently 'in the midst of anarchy, revolution, and civil war'. He also informed Buchanan that the British had blockaded San Salvador's port for refusing to pay back loans given during the Federal Republic period, and that Costa Rica was diplomatically aligned with the British. Another observation based on Hise's journey through the Caribbean was that the British had 'almost entirely monopolized' commercial trade in the region, and thus he requested 'that an American man-of-war should occasionally make its appearance in the ports of Central America to inspire the people and governments of these states with due respect for our country.' The problem was not a lack of goodwill from Central Americans towards the United States, but that there was very little US attempt in the region to prevent the British from acting arbitrarily. 'It is clear to my mind that Great Brittian [sic] designs to become the owner and occupant by force or stratagem of the ports on the Atlantic and Pacific coasts of Nicaragua which will be the points of termination of the canal communication between the two oceans.' Based on its activity in San Juan, Hise speculated that Nicaragua was Great Britain's preferred route and that the acquisition of California from Mexico prompted them to hasten their Central American endeavours.[4]

Hise also recommended the same remedy advocated by the New Orleans *Delta* in the spring of 1848 – that it was 'advisable' to grant him 'authority to make treaties with each and all the states of Central America especially with Nicaragua.' He believed he could accomplish that feat through correspondence centred at Guatemala City, but that journeying to each country would incur enormous travel expenses. Hise was confident the request would be granted, but two days later, the Nicaraguan Minister of Foreign Affairs, Sebastián Salinas, contacted him expressing 'pleasing relations of brotherhood' and continued 'fraternal communication' between the two countries. This seemingly coincidental gesture by Salinas, who was vehemently opposed to British interference on the east coast on behalf of the Mosquito Kingdom, was the result of information provided to him by a somewhat enigmatic US 'official' by the name of Henry Savage, who had been living in the region for years providing various US Secretaries of State with information relating to internal events and British activities.[5]

The Nicaraguans believed improved relations with the US might help to halt the unopposed British activities. Salinas had unsuccessfully appealed to British consul Frederick Chatfield to desist, and when the British seized the port of San Juan in early January of 1848, he contacted Viscount Palmerston indicating their encroachment in the San Juan River and seizure of their flag amounted to a 'declaration of war'. Much of the activity in 1847 preceding open hostilities was conducted under the guidance of Her Majesty's agent Patrick Walker, the same man Senator Hannegan accused during the Yucatan debate of arming the Mayans. Acting as an adviser to the Mosquito King in Bluefields, Walker accidentally drowned somewhere in the vicinity of Sarapiquí on 11 February after leading a force of 260 men in twelve boats upriver. Hise forwarded Nicaragua's statements related to 'Patrick Walker professing to be Consul Genl of Great Britain for the pretended Mosquito Kingdom ... guardian of their infant King (crowned at Jamaica)' – but the Polk administration was already aware of events based on updates from foreign consuls and reporting in the US press, much of which factored into the Yucatan debate. Nevertheless, Hise's presence in the region was well received by Nicaragua's desperate officials.[6]

'A sanguinary struggle'

Meanwhile, around the same time that Hise gained his first view of Guatemala City, more than 900 American mercenaries arrived in Sisal under the command of a certain Captain George W. White. As with Sentmanat's expedition, and subsequent others following the Mexican War, the men believed their success would result in prized land (320 acres each) and fiefdoms with allegiance to US interests. Those aspirations were considerably tested, however, when reports began emanating from New Orleans that a couple of key officers commanding 'The Gallant American Regiment' were killed around Christmas time near Tihosuco after attempting to take on a vastly larger Mayan army. In addition to the officers, thirty-eight others were killed when the Maya employed their traditional tactic of erecting 'barricades of rock and large masses of stone, at intervals across the road, leaving loop-holes to fire through'. This strategy, which was used to stunning effectiveness until the Yucatecans adopted guerrilla tactics to flank positions, was devastating to the US mercenaries. 'As the Americans stormed one barricade,' the *Delta* reported, 'the enemy retreated to another, and so on.' Jacinto Pat was also apparently involved in directing the 'great force' opposing the Yucatecan-American effort to regain lost territory. 'This has been, no doubt, the scene of a sanguinary struggle, where our gallant fellows have gained fresh laurels.' Another report from the same issue (indicating White had mysteriously become a colonel) confirmed the American charge against the Mayans. 'The whole of Col. White's command, each man of which was eager for a glimpse at the elephant, rushed forward and charged the enemy, Col. White taking the lead, and gallantly waving his men on, sword in hand.'[7]

Reed's account of the Caste War also relies on New Orleans reports to explain what happened to the American mercenaries, and calls the stone walls the Mayans (and Yucatecans) used *trencherias*, and their 'little forts' or 'enclosures' *plazuelas*. He also cites a first-hand account of the fighting recorded in 1905 by Edward H. Thompson, who was intrigued by John Lloyd Stephens's depictions of the ancient Mayan civilization and embarked on his own multi-year inquiry in Yucatan in the late nineteenth century. Most of Thompson's work involved dredging the fabled *cenote* of Chichén Itzá, but during his time there he learned much about its people, language, and history, and recorded an account by a farmer named Dionisio Pec, who had fought against the Americans:

> They fought like very brave men and caused us many deaths. We had guns and powder from Belize but we had few balls and so we often had to use small stones; also we made balls of red earth, well mixed with honey and hard dried in the sun. These balls made bad wounds and hard to heal. The stranger white men fought close together and for that reason it was easy to kill them. But they were brave men and laughed at death and before they died they killed many of our men.[8]

Reed also cites another account from Thompson by a man named Leandro Poot, who retold 'Cresencio Poot's account of the battle' with the Americans. In it, Poot claims the Mayans were at first 'perplexed' by the arrival of the American *dzulob* (whites) because 'they spoke the language of Belize, and Belize was not against us, so we waited to see what was meant.' When informants told them that the Americans were aligned with the leadership in Merida, they were obliged to wage war against them as well. 'Then we fought them,' the account reads, 'but we had rather they had not come, for we only wanted to kill those that had lied to us and had done us great harm ... and even these we had rather send away across the water to where their fathers came from, and where they would cause us no more harm.' Poot's account also corroborates Pec's recollection that the Americans used a close formation when charging 'as if they were marching', while the 'white men from T'Ho' (Merida) used guerrilla tactics and natural cover for protection. Despite their unwillingness to adapt to the tactics used in the Yucatan, Poot's story is similar to Pec's and lauded the bravery of the mercenaries who had come from the other side of the Gulf. 'But all the people said that the stranger white men were the bravest men they ever saw. They laughed at death and went toward it with joy, as a young man runs to a handsome woman.' Some of the Americans wore uniforms, others resembled the frontier fighters of the borderlands, but according to the Maya, they all appeared rather alien to them, with 'big bodies ... pink and red in the sunlight and from their throats came their strange war cry, Hu-Ha! Hu-Ha! (evidently a Hurrah).' These men were different to the descendants of the Spanish who had coexisted uneasily with them since the Conquest:

> They were brave men and shot keenly. Some of them were such good shooters that no man could hope to escape when once they pointed at him; no, whether he ran or walked or crawled, it made no difference unless he could hide behind a tree before the shot was fired, and even then some of those who reached the tree were dead as they fell behind it, for the balls had found them ... So for a time we greatly feared these strange white men and only sought to keep out of their reach. Had they stayed behind their defences and only used their guns as they could use them, no one knows what might have happened, for our people were so scared of the big, pink-skinned men with their terrible cries and their death shots, that they could not be made to stand up against them. But the stranger white men were too brave, for they threw their lives away.[9]

Indeed, routing the Mayans on their own territory without utilizing tactics best suited to the terrain began sapping the fighting spirit of the Americans. Nor were the Maya, like the Seminoles, about to engage them directly when ambush was better suited to their style of fighting and the environment. Following the Christmas battles around Tihosuco, Colonel White accepted the resignations of several officers who may have objected to charging fortified positions or simply pined for the luxuries they had ostentatiously received in Merida upon their arrival, rather than eating 'cats and dogs' while under siege for eight days in Tihosuco. Water was also hard to find on the peninsula. Adding insult to injury was the ten dollars they earned for their efforts from an empty Yucatecan treasury (and no land) – a paltry sum compared to expectations assuredly enhanced by banter aboard the *Florida* as she sailed to Sisal. Hundreds left and a few hundred remained, but by early February even Colonel White had reached his breaking point, and the regiment was formally disbanded. The only American officer remaining was a captain named Richard J. Kelly, who was 'authorized to raise a company from the disbanded volunteers', and led more than a hundred die-hards towards Bacalar, which was recaptured earlier in Cetina's absence when the commanding officer surrendered the fort to spare the lives of the garrison short of supplies. By 18 March, after four months, many mercenaries – all of whom had undoubtedly seen enough of the elephant – began arriving in New Orleans. One *New York Herald* article noted their 'pitiful' condition, 'their wo-begone [*sic*] countenances telling a tale of hardships, and hopes of golden expectations blasted … half starved, shoeless, and nearly naked', and bitter about Yucatan.[10]

The Cetina expedition to recapture Bacalar, consisting of around 800 soldiers with an auxiliary force of about 65 Americans, left Sisal in April. The period before their arrival saw uncommon public posturing by Mayan leaders such as Chi, who invoked Christian principles in a press release from Tepich claiming it was the whites who had plotted to exterminate the Indians. Chi also appealed to the British to send a commissioner to 'divide Yucatan under the head of the supreme government of Belize'. The expedition arrived near St. George's Caye, proceeded up the Rio Hondo in the direction of Bacalar, encountered some resistance along the way resulting in the death of Captain Kelly, and seized the Fortress of San Felipe from a garrison of about 500 Mayan soldiers. Once again, the Yucatecans were in charge of Bacalar, but how the British would respond was a matter of conjecture. The *Delta* contemplated British intervention and quoted a 29 August report from Campeche believing the Mexican government might 'concede to the Indians a portion of the territory of the peninsula … doubtless under the British protectorate, or as allies under the king of Mosquitia.' That result had been O'Reilly's fear as well, but in actuality, the consequences of the back-and-forth fighting between the two sides ultimately forced Fancourt to issue an order in the fall prohibiting the sale of weapons to either side, thus putting an end to speculation the British intended to enlarge Belizean territory by arbitrating a political solution.[11]

The threat of American reprisals and involvement in Yucatan may have played a small role in that decision, as US soldiers in Mexico City slated to be mustered out of the occupation army were being recruited to take part in a post-war expedition to the peninsula. On 30 May, the *American Star*, the US Army's newspaper in the capital, reported the expedition would be 'organized in this city, and not in Vera Cruz as had been the first intention'.

When officials under the command of General William O. Butler, who replaced Scott after his departure, heard of it, they promptly forced John H. Peoples, the *Star*'s publisher, to inform the soldiers that the US Army would 'discharge no man from the service until after their arrival in the United States'. Despite being discouraged from partaking in the campaign, proponents believed it would only delay it because 'it will be easy to sail from New Orleans to Campeachy [sic], as from Vera Cruz.' Apparently, there were at least a thousand US soldiers in Mexico City still eager for action. 'But very few of the thousand and more men,' the *Star* surmised, 'who have volunteered their services to the assistance to the whites of Yucatan, will draw off because they have to go to New Orleans first; and at that point treble the number can be raised after their final discharge from the services of Uncle Sam.' One important factor the *Star* obviously underestimated was the gold fever sweeping the United States, and the promise of riches in the hills surrounding Sacramento drew off thousands of young men who would have otherwise been inclined to further their adventures in Yucatan. The west, not the south, became the destination of choice.[12]

In September, Jacinto Pat, who was attempting to cement his position and expand his wealth amidst an 'ancient rivalry between the oriental warlords' of the east, was hunted down and killed by another faction of Mayans led by Venancio Pec. Ancono wrote that Pat fled to Bacalar 'to present himself to Cetina, as some suppose; either to look for a refuge within the English possessions, or perhaps finally to request the support of the rebels who besieged that town.' This was rumour, but there was no doubt his support had abandoned him and he 'was overtaken by his pursuers and sacrificed'. In December, Cecelio Chi learned that a lover of his who had 'followed him in all his campaigns, perhaps more out of fear than love' was now in love with his secretary Atanasio Flores. To pre-empt the inevitable retribution as a result of this betrayal, Flores decided to sneak up from behind Chi and land a machete blow on his skull – a not unpoetic reflection of the suffering the *batab* inflicted on Yucatan. Thus, the two most infamous instigators of the Caste War succumbed to the personal and factional divisions sundering the Mayans – contributing to the long-term impasse and racial violence between eastern and western Yucatan that persisted for another fifty years. The Caste War also proved to Americans that Yucatan was not Mexico's Mayan Texas, nor destined to become a part of the United States, and it would carry the distinction of being the longest war in the Gulf of Mexico – beating the Florida Wars against the Seminoles by ten years.[13]

Central America and the Monroe Doctrine

While American soldiers were coming home from Mexico, the situation in Yucatan was eclipsed by that in Central America. Essentially, the westward movement of people forced an Anglo-American contest over the isthmus – the region facilitating much of the expected migration. More precisely, the ratification of the Bidlack Treaty with New Granada granting the US certain rights to the Panamanian isthmus put pressure on the British to retain their possession of San Juan and protectorate over the Mosquito Kingdom on the east coast of Nicaragua. In an early 1849 article entitled 'Bridging the Continent,' the Baltimore *Sun* summed up the arrangement: 'This treaty, therefore, is but a simple advertisement to all the world that for the next twenty years, at least, we will, with the permission of New Granada, cross the Isthmus of Panama, and you must not interfere.'[14]

In his memoir of John M. Clayton, who was the Secretary of State under the incoming presidency of Zachary Taylor, Joseph P. Comegys wrote that among the 'first steps' and priorities of the new administration 'was the dislodgement of the British from Central America'. Clayton was a vocal opponent of the Mexican War and expansionist policies sponsored by his Senate rivals, but he understood the importance of the isthmus and British reluctance to negotiate, since it was 'the first power in the world, strong in wealth and in preparation for war by land and sea, and strong also in her determination to yield nothing which it was her interest to retain.' Thus going about it was a delicate matter, and Clayton quickly realized it was easier to criticize the administration as an observer of policy rather than guide it. The advantage of Polk, and by extension, Buchanan, in that regard was they were less predictable and willing to threaten war – which frustrated the British but made them more cautious. Clayton, however, was more passive, and when the issue of Central America intensified, Democrat opponents seized upon it with scorn by claiming the war hero Taylor was not upholding American honour. At the height of the crisis in late 1849, critics of the administration, such as the *New York Herald*, were denouncing Clayton and demanding accountability: 'In Central America, the United States flag has been insulted, torn down, trampled upon, and disgraced, by British agents, and British officers. Where is the spirit, the courage, and the determination which led on the American troops at Monterey and Buena Vista?'[15]

Fortunately for Clayton, Hise overcame the obstacles preventing his appearance in Guatemala, and notwithstanding his late arrival, laid the groundwork for his successor Ephraim George Squier, who was authorized to effect agreements with any Central American state willing to negotiate. By the time Squier arrived in Central America, Hise was discussing a treaty proposed by Buenaventura Selva, the Nicaraguan chargé d'affaires in Guatemala. Selva's idea was to grant the US 'exclusive privilege of opening the inter-oceanic canal through the isthmus' of that country – despite British control over the eastern outlet at San Juan. Article 5 of the proposed treaty stipulated Nicaragua would not 'enter into negotiation with any other government or private parties regarding the canal' (i.e. the British), and agreed that the US would 'forever or perpetually enjoy the privilege that its vessels or conveyances of any kind which might be in its service for the transportation of its troops, arms, employees etc.' More importantly, like the Bidlack Treaty concerning Panama, Article 9 obliged the US 'to protect the sovereignty, liberty and independence of the state of Nicaragua, and the dominion of all the coasts, ports, lakes, rivers and territories.' Article 9 detailed the potential US role in the treaty, and while it did not oblige the US 'to assist, sustain or defend Nicaragua in offensive wars or wars entered into by it with foreign powers', it did stipulate, 'for greater explanation and clarity', the requirement to come to Nicaragua's aid if attacked. Thus, the terms of the treaty enhanced the possibility of an Anglo-American conflict, since if Nicaragua became 'involved in a war with any foreign power or contiguous state within its own limits, in order to defend the territories which may legally belong to it, or to recover territories which may have been taken from it, the United States undertakes to defend and assist Nicaragua.'[16]

The proposal was an indication of the desperation the Nicaraguans felt vis-à-vis the British, but Hise was not officially authorized to make agreements with states other than Guatemala. However, he was keen to elaborate to Selva that if Nicaragua desired American safeguarding, a 'charter' granting 'favourable terms & privileges to a company' would facilitate 'the protection of my government and its interference to wrest from the English the port of San Juan, exclusively for the benefit of Nicaragua.' What Hise meant by 'wrest' was anyone's guess, and although he did not mention Cornelius Vanderbilt by name – a wealthy New Yorker interested in building a canal or railroad over the Nicaraguan isthmus – there was an obvious connection because his replacement (Squier) was also a New Yorker with ties to Vanderbilt's proposed American Atlantic and Pacific Ship Canal Company, later named the Accessory Transit Company.[17]

In April, before his departure to Guatemala via Nicaragua, Squier, while in New York City, informed Clayton that 'the company headed by C. Vanderbilt' was poised to pursue negotiations and that despite 'the jealousy of the Nicaraguans towards the English, the positive advantages of a canal ... are so obvious, that it is extremely likely they would make almost any arrangement, even with a people they hated, rather than forego a great benefit to themselves.' When Squier wrote to Clayton in September that he had completed 'A General Treaty of Amity, Navigation and Commerce' between the two states, the Vanderbilt enterprise was listed as the company under contract with 'exclusive right to the administration, management and control' of the canal project. Although the revised 'treaty and contract' with Nicaragua did not fully commit the parties – in that obligations extended only to 'jointly agree to protect and defend the above named company ... from its inception to its completion and after its completion, from any acts of invasion' – it predictably turned into a potential crisis due to British opposition to American encroachment on the Caribbean coast.[18]

Squier may have downplayed his predecessor's role in initiating negotiations with other Central American states but both diplomats shared a commitment to promote US interests at the expense of their rivals. Squier believed Nicaragua had been 'bullied by Great Britain, robbed of her territory, threatened with an extinguishment of her national independence,' and therefore it was 'not surprising that Nicaragua turned to the United States for countenance and protection'. He would make Central America, and especially Nicaragua, his mission (to the detriment of his marriage), later wrote several works about the region, and even after his diplomatic tenure believed the sleepy port of San Juan would become a global emporium of sorts. 'When the political questions connected with British aggressions in Nicaragua shall have been satisfactorily and permanently adjusted,' he wrote, 'and the projected canal really commenced, this port will become one of the first importance, if not the most important, on the continent.'[19]

Another aim of the American mission to Central America was to encourage the reunification of the small republics to enable them to act in unison. Guatemala and Costa Rica were more or less aligned with the British, but it was believed San Salvador, Honduras and Nicaragua were open to the American idea. Before leaving the US, Buchanan informed Hise that the Americans 'entertained the highest hopes' for the federation's success but that its dissolution 'encouraged Great Britain in her encroachments upon the territories of Honduras, Nicaragua, and Costa Rica, under the mask of protecting the so-called kingdom of the Mosquitos.' Squier was aware of Buchanan's instructions 'to promote the reunion of the states of the old confederation' and the New Yorker also devoted 'considerable attention upon this point'. When he arrived in Central America he discovered 'much cordiality' between the three states 'and that between Honduras and Nicaragua, a secret league, both defensive and offensive existed. Between the three also exist treaties, binding them together in very intimate relations.' In late 1852, when Squier published the second volume of his work, *Nicaragua: Its people, scenery, monuments and the proposed interoceanic canal*, he noted how the three states had recently 'agreed upon the basis of a union' – leaving an option for Guatemala and Costa Rica to join later. That effort, however, was thwarted by 'the old aristocratic or monarchical faction, or rather the remnants of it' who 'had the countenance and support of the British officials' who used their connections in Guatemala and Costa Rica to denounce 'the whole plan of federation, and what they called the "American Policy".'[20]

Squier also claimed he needed to employ 'private couriers' to conduct correspondence and official business because the seals on letters leaving the US legation were constantly broken and he suspected that they were being 'passed under the eyes of the British Consul General, or those of his subordinates or hirelings'. Some of his correspondence arrived as much as three months late, and his dismay was aggravated by British officials 'who took a malicious satisfaction in showing us how much more efficient, active, and intelligent is the British government, in the conduct of its foreign relations, than our own.' For a while, he received letters and other material from Washington as late as a year from the date in which they were sent – a testament to the distance and inability of the Americans to catch up with the British, whose documents were 'never thirty days behindhand'. In that regard, using private couriers was a sensible move that expedited his mission.[21]

Squier had plenty of reasons to be careful about the British discovering his activities. In addition to notifying the French consul in Leon of the contract between 'the largest capitalists of the continent' and the Nicaraguan government – an agreement backed by 'the faith of the US for the protection of this company in all its rights' – Squier took it upon himself to notify 'the Commander of the United States Squadron on the west coast of Central America' – ostensibly Robert F. Stockton, commander of the US naval forces in the Pacific. On 13 August from Leon, Squier wrote that he had completed a canal treaty claiming that the 'route, suffice it to say, is now in American hands, and as you have perhaps been already advised, it is the determination of the present administration to defend it from all encroachments and invasions from whatever quarter the same may proceed.' Squier suggested a larger US naval presence further north at the Nicaraguan port of Realejo, near present-day Corinto, would be received 'with open arms and with the greatest hospitality'. Indeed, if any British official had read Squier's despatch, it would have been prudently assumed the Americans were preparing for hostilities. 'The English will seize every opportunity to visit their vengeance upon the Republics and embarrass our relations with them.' Based on information he received, Squier believed the port of Realejo was in imminent danger of being blockaded, 'which have been of so frequent occurrence on this coast, and which have never been preceded by any declaration of war, or any other notice whatever.' To counter this aggression, the diplomat urged a more robust US naval presence:

> Now as this port is one at which our steamers on the Pacific propose soon to stop regularly, for their supply of provisions, and as American vessels often call there in the pursuit of their legitimate trade, we cannot allow it to be obstructed by any petty naval force which the caprice of the British officials in this quarter may choose to place before it.[22]

To observers, it appeared that an Anglo-American clash was developing. 'The British government and people want one route independent of Americans,' the editors of the *Delta* wrote of Nicaragua, 'and they are determined to have it.' The New Orleans newspaper believed that, since the route through Nicaragua would 'allow of a ship canal, it will be more valuable than our Panama route' – an effort that would be mitigated by the American construction of 'a railroad by the Tehuantepec route, and also one or two across the continent.' Furthermore, it appeared that 'English papers treat this question as decided ... we know here, in Washington, from other sources, that the British government will not yield a hair, on the question, except to superior and irresistible force.' The *Delta* may have been correct about the steadfast British position, but like other New Orleans pundits, the paper was overconfident about a Tehuantepec route, which was beginning to diminish in priority with the refocus on Nicaragua. There were still surveys to conduct, and a 'Great Tehuantepec Meeting' was even held in New Orleans on 5 October to make it the 'metropolis of the world' by placing it 'in the very centre' of world commercial activity. New York interests and resentful Mexican officials, however, would have their say in the matter.[23]

Back in Central America, Squier kept up the momentum at a pace nearly fatal to Anglo-American relations. By 10 October he confirmed a 'general convention of peace and friendship, commerce and navigation' had been consummated with an 'extremely anxious' Honduran commissioner. More importantly, embedded within the appendix of the treaty was a 'declaration' recognizing 'the principle put forward explicitly by Mr. Monroe' excluding 'monarchical powers from interference in the domestic affairs of the American States.' Squier, whose spelling seemed to deteriorate as his proficiency in Spanish improved, believed the declaration was 'harmeless' [sic] but admitted he did not 'know that there is any exact precedent for anything of the kind.' The problem was that the treaty appeared to be a bold affront to British claims on the east coast of the isthmus – particularly in the second article of the declaration mentioning 'the extension of monarchical institutions by conquest, colonization, or support of savage chiefs to sovreignty [sic] or savage tribes to national existance [sic], or by other means, upon the American continent.'[24]

The *New York Herald*, a pro-Democrat publication, reacted to news of the Nicaragua treaty with scepticism but was generally supportive of any initiative granting American rights to the isthmus. Squier's dealings with the French consul had also become public, and even the invocation of 'the policy which Mr. Monroe promulgated' – noting that the 'not yet known' treaty was under consideration in Washington. Because of this, the contents of the agreement with Honduras invoking Monroe, which became a part of the public discussion, was enveloped into the debate over Nicaragua. In other words, the Nicaragua treaty did not mention 'Monroe' specifically, but the issue was linked in the public debate in the United States – particularly in the aftermath of the contemplation of US intervention in Yucatan and British interference there. The Yucatan debate, despite being a failure for expansionists, opened up the utilization of the anti-monarchical policy initiated under Monroe. The *Herald*, and other Democrat organs, opposed the Whigs during the election, but when it came to undermining the British position in Central America, they 'were much pleased' and firmly supportive. Despite their limited approval, there was still doubt as to whether a 'blundering' Clayton would maintain the bold diplomatic work begun under Hise and brought to fruition by his successor. 'This is all very good as far as it goes, especially Mr. Squier's enunciation of the policy of Mr. Monroe ... The question arises, will the American Secretary of State uphold Mr. Squier in the course which he has taken? We fear not.'[25]

The *Republic*, a Whig mouthpiece in the capital, was eager to assert Whigs were more capable of obtaining strategic objectives without the bellicosity with which they accused their political opponents. 'When the history of the Mosquito question becomes more thoroughly understood,' the editors opined, 'the people of the United States will be convinced that the Polk dynasty came to an end none too soon.' They also stated that Americans would 'rejoice that an administration which vibrated between bravado and submission has been replaced by one which pursues an even, solid course between these extremes of weakness.' The *Republic* conveniently forgot that the British seized Nicaragua's eastern port of San Juan at the same time that Democrats were pushing to annex Mexico, and that the Yucatan debate centred around Polk's invocation of Monroe's 1823 policy to justify military intervention. Regardless, the *Republic* was among the first to coin the term 'Monroe Doctrine' – which henceforth was used to justify US involvement in Latin American affairs rather than its original application as a bulwark opposing Spanish counter-revolutionary efforts and the Holy Alliance, as Calhoun explained during the debate. In essence, a policy that was never intended to be directed towards the British was now squarely aimed at them for domestic political gain and geostrategic leverage. Nicaragua had thus become the lightning rod for protecting American continental interests:

> They will learn that a cabinet which claimed to be the special prop and pillar of the 'Monroe Doctrine,' abandoned, with heartless apathy, the republic of Nicaragua to usurpation and partition; and whilst boasting its vigilance over the integrity of the American soil, beheld, without a murmur, the forcible establishment of foreign-European jurisdiction upon the most important coast of the Gulf of Mexico, south of the boundaries of the United States.[26]

Claims of integrity over the Democrats would return to beset the Whigs because they were still unaware of the implications of the agreement and the 'declaration' Squier made with Honduras. Observers in London could see where the intransigence of both sides was headed. 'By making a concession of the passage to citizens of the United States,' *The Times* stated, 'they evidently hope to extort in the name of the cabinet of Washington what Lord Palmerston peremptorily refused to the ministers of Nicaragua.' Thus, the deadlock created by the treaty was potentially explosive. 'It is clear, however, that the strong measures and determined language of the British government admit of no qualification, and we are as much bound to defend Bluefields and San Juan as any part of the British empire.'[27]

Pacific 'Gibraltar': Tiger Island

Squier's treaty with Honduras was similar to the one with Nicaragua in that it granted Vanderbilt's company exclusive rights. The question arises, where did those interests converge geographically? The answer lies in the assumptions made regarding the potential outlet for a canal on the Pacific side of the isthmus. At the time, most people believed a canal could be cut north-west from Lake Managua to the Estero Real, where it would drain into the Gulf of Fonseca. 'This Estero is as broad as the East River at New York,' Squier wrote, 'and has, for most of its extent, an ample depth of water.' Most of the Gulf of Fonseca is situated within Honduran territory but it also includes El Salvador and Nicaragua. It was assumed Lake Nicaragua and Lake Managua would be connected, which in turn could be connected with the Atlantic through the outlet emanating from the San Juan River (present-day Rio Indio) ending at the British protectorate of Greytown (San Juan). Squier partly based this assumption on a survey conducted in the late 1830s by British explorer and hydrographer Sir Edward Belcher, who published some of his findings in an 1843 work, *Narrative of a Voyage Around the World*. Even though Belcher believed there was 'little feasibility in the scheme' he noted the Nicaraguans were employing 'every effort to connect these lakes of Nicaragua and Managua with either ocean; but I think the day of achievement is yet distant.' Nevertheless, he believed if such an effort could be achieved, it would go through the Estero Real.[28]

Another survey, which Squier quoted extensively in his work, was conducted by Englishman John Baily, who was commissioned by the Federal Republic of Central America in the late 1830s to examine the feasibility of a canal. Baily concurred about connecting the lakes through the Tipitapa River but also contemplated making a more direct cut from Lake Nicaragua west into the Pacific using the Rio Lajas. When *The Times* took up the subject in early 1849 and cited Baily's work, they concluded a canal might terminate in the estuary located in the Realejo area on the Pacific coast, which was one of the three options Squier included in a map of his findings. If the Realejo route was used, it would not touch upon Honduran territory, and in his drawing Squier 'proposed' three routes emanating from Lake Managua. The political benefit of the agreement with Honduras, in that regard, was that it brought the two states closer together because both would potentially benefit from a canal, and the Bay of Fonseca was much more conducive to navigation. Squier wrote that the bay 'completely commands the whole coast from Panama to San Diego, and in the hands of any maritime nation must control the transit across either isthmus, and with it the commerce of the world.' In his mind, it was the perfect strategic location for the United States to maximize its naval and commercial potential:

> The entrance may be effected with any wind, and the exit can always be made with the tide. Fresh water may be obtained in abundance on the islands and along the shores; the climate is delicious and healthy; the surrounding mountains furnish timber of superior quality, including pine, for ship building and repairs; in short, nature has here lavished every requisite to make the Bay of Fonseca the great naval centre of the globe.[29]

In the Honduran treaty, Squier negotiated concessions of large swathes of property on Tigre (Tiger) Island in the Gulf of Fonseca for the construction of 'warehouses, depots, shipyards, and other buildings or works' associated with the isthmian project. More importantly, the treaty granted the United States 'the right to establish a naval station, depot, and shipyard and to make such other establishments as may be of advantage to its National Marine, upon the aforesaid island of the Tigre or upon any other of the islands belonging to Honduras' in the Gulf. Squier believed that by possessing the volcanic island, the US would 'exercise a command over the commerce of the western part of the continent, like that which the possession of Gibraltar by the English, gives them to exercise over that of Europe.' In his 1852 publication, Squier asserted that the island had once served as the 'principal station on the South Sea' for English privateers (licensed pirates) such as Sir Francis Drake, and that the British Admiralty were aware of its 'importance, in a naval point of view' – a key reason it was 'carefully surveyed by Capt. Belcher, R.N., in 1839.' When Squier informed Clayton of the agreement, he stressed that the acquisition enabled the Americans 'to defeat the ambitious designs of the English by giving us rights there, which render it certain that the United States cannot regard with indifference any improper interference or encroachment on the part of nations more powerful than scrupulous.'[30]

Back in London, the British were still reacting to the American weaponization of 'Monroe's extravagant doctrine' employed against them. *The Times*, among many other publications, was advocating a demilitarization of the isthmian contest and 'perpetual neutrality' over any canal to ensure the issue remained 'beyond the hazards of war.' Palmerston was more or less in agreement with that sentiment, and word was sent to Sir Henry Bulwer, who was already in Washington on a mission to explain the terms of the evolving Canadian Reciprocity Treaty, which granted more economic freedom to that country (i.e. trade with the US) to prevent rebellion. It was hoped that the Taylor Administration and Clayton could come to an agreement to prevent 'a few wrong-headed individuals' from sparking 'a serious quarrel out of a matter in which the interests of England, of the United States, and of the world, are identically the same.' *The Times* addressed the Democrats' achievement in 'hurrying the nation into two great acts of violence and aggression, the seizure of Texas and the invasion of Mexico'. Thus, expansionists were seen as the obstacle to concluding a peaceful solution to the impasse: 'There is in the United States a small but active and noisy party ... who are eager to plunge into every tumult. They would wrest Cuba from Spain, they clamoured for the whole of Oregon ... [but] their policy did not raise General Taylor and his friends to power.'[31]

The *Daily Union*, the Democrat party organ in Washington, was perhaps the noisiest critic of all. The sentiment among their pro-war readership was that the British implemented their mid-war policy to thwart American expansion by limiting US options in each of the three potential transit points across the isthmus. To them, the pattern of events confirmed these beliefs: 'she set on foot intrigues to prevent the United States from inducing Mexico to grant the right of way ... across the isthmus of Tehuantepec ... Her intrigues in relation to the Panama route, and to prevent this country from acquiring control of it, have been manifest to all who have watched her course.' In addition, the Democrats had long memories when it came to Texas, and the 'balance-of-power' policy employed before the conflict was still resented. 'Who does not remember her conduct with respect to Texas prior to its annexation to the United States, adopted to defeat that measure?'[32]

The issue of Belize was also raised, which the Democrats believed was effected 'under the pretext of protecting the whites against the insurrectionary savages commanded by Jacinto Pat ... to get a foothold in the country.' However, among the litany of perceived grievances alleged against the British, the most bitter was the spoil of war wrested from the hands of victory: 'There are those who believe that her successful intrigues with respect to Tehuantepec are of much deeper injury to this country in their results than if she succeeds in the accomplishment of her designs as to Panama and Nicaragua.' Thus, extreme measures, including hostilities initiated by invoking the Monroe Doctrine, were advocated to counter the 'sinister designs' of the rival preventing total continental domination. Just as the Spanish and Portuguese in the fifteenth and sixteenth centuries had once declared the oceans theirs, the United States and Mexico should do the same with the gulf and Tehuantepec:

> It is more defensible by the United States than either of the other routes, and that in times of war the exclusive use of it by us as a channel of communication could readily be secured. It is urged that the United States and Mexico, being together possessed of the entire country surrounding the Gulf of Mexico, could jointly ... declare that gulf a *mare clausum* as to the whole world ... we have no dread of the power of England or France on land or on sea.[33]

Despite the combative hyperbole, Americans still had plenty to be concerned about when it came to British naval capabilities. In the absence of knowledge of Bulwer's assignment, British authorities in Central America under the direction of Frederick Chatfield reacted to news of Squier's treaty. Around 2.00 pm on 16 October, Vicente Lechuga, the commander of the port of Amapala on the Island of Tigre, observed five boats loaded with cannons and eighty soldiers approaching the waterfront. Lechuga had just enough time to have his men take up arms and the Honduran flag hoisted to meet the first boat as it landed. British officers, led by Commander James Aylmer

Paynter, of HMS *Gorgon*, approached Lechuga with an interpreter and informed him – as 'the boats turned their cannon against the town and the troops landed under their cover' – that he needed 'to lower the colors of the republic so that the English flag might be raised.' Lechuga reluctantly acceded, and after this was done, the British soldiers saluted the flag and hailed Queen Victoria for their bloodless victory. Tigre Island was under British control.[34]

As early as August, Squier knew the British might attempt to seize Honduran territory under the pretext of securing outstanding debts, and following the seizure Chatfield and Squier exchanged letters in which neither conceded the other's arguments. At that point, Squier was acting as a one-man state department, and issuing threats in the absence of a formidable naval force to back up his bravado. 'The subsequent occupation ... under your orders,' he wrote to Chatfield on 23 October, 'is therefore an invasion of the rights of the United States.' He also warned that 'It now becomes my duty to apprise you that unless the island of the Tigre is evacuated within six days from the receipt of this communication, the persistance [sic] in occupation will be considered an act of aggression and hostility against the United States.' The British also seized a number of other islands in the Gulf that day.[35]

'The British have been committing some new outrages in this part of the world,' a correspondent from the *New York Express* reported, citing Chatfield as the chief instigator among a 'catalogue of abuses' committed by the British. One letter from a minister in the Honduran government was quoted as saying that the actions amounted to 'piracy' and that their flag had been 'forcibly taken down' under protest, 'making an exhibition of power, trampling under foot the most sacred rights of a free people, profiting of our weakness and of our inability to meet face to face the tyrant of the ocean'. The *Daily Union* quoted the more circumspect *Boston Courier* regarding 'imperfect accounts hastily dispatched' from a region Americans knew little about. Moreover, it was noted that acquiring 'new territory by the United States, at a distance from home, and lying in close connection with a foreign nation, is an entirely novel phase' of US foreign policy. 'Before we spy a speck of war in this business, we deem it necessary to know first that Tiger island is actually ours.' For the most part, Americans had no idea what Squier had done in Central America, and 'the public have hitherto been kept quite in ignorance of the designs of our cabinet.'[36]

Clayton-Bulwer Treaty

Throughout the winter, Clayton and Bulwer met to settle the matter amicably, despite detractors critical of the US deferring to Great Britain when it came to matters they believed were at issue only between the US and the respective states of Central America. In that regard, there was little Clayton could do to mitigate the scorn directed at him other than endure it. Even officials from the former administration, particularly Buchanan, were sensitive to the 'assailings' of critics claiming they did not uphold the 'Monroe Doctrine against European colonization on this continent' – a doctrine that by 1850 had acquired new meaning. On 13 April, a few days before the Clayton-Bulwer Treaty was signed, Buchanan wrote to journalist Francis J. Grund, addressing public complaints from Horace Greely in the *New-York Tribune*:

> The last administration have given so many proofs of their devotion to the Monroe doctrine that it is now too late in the day to dispute it: & they were never afraid, upon any proper occasion, to avow it to the world. They twice did so, in the face of Great Britain, whilst the Mexican war was raging; although they well knew how hostile the government of that country was to us in this war & how friendly to Mexico.[37]

The Clayton-Bulwer Treaty was an imperfect arrangement that continued to be scrutinized long after its ratification. It was successful, however, in that it served as a legal mechanism designed to prevent war, and it calmed the passions of those who might otherwise act precipitately without consulting the government. In other words, it served as a means to de-escalate tensions arising from the isthmian frenzy that occupied the naval powers of the North Atlantic as a result of the Mexican War. It pledged cooperation in the construction of a canal (which did not materialize until the twentieth century), urged neutrality for shipping and commerce, and halted the tendency to establish colonies or protectorates to further the geostrategic objectives of the two states. On 7 May 1850, Clayton wrote to Squier: 'Your conduct in the negotiation of the treaty with Nicaragua, which was the great business of your mission, has been highly approved by your government', but that the 'treaty with Honduras for a grant in Tigre Island, having been made without instructions, though with the best intentions on your part has been disapproved.' Chatfield received similar reprimands, although he had also served his country admirably and faithfully. Thus, the Union Jack only flew over Tigre Island briefly, and the Stars and Stripes did not meet the occasion.[38]

The treaty would be violated, expeditions to Latin America continued, the Caste War remained, and despite all the evidence to the contrary, some still believed the American sphere could be enlarged beyond the Gulf. In late 1850, President Millard P. Fillmore, who replaced Zachary Taylor after his sudden death, stated in a presidential message to Congress that he hoped the treaty would serve as a 'harmonizing' force for 'conflicting claims to territory' and that 'the two governments will come to an understanding.' More importantly, he stated that it was 'an imperative duty not to interfere in the government or internal policy of other nations … in their struggle for freedom, our principles forbid us from taking any part in such foreign contests.' That sentiment, more aspirational than practical, reflected the way in which that president may have looked upon his nation, and his desire to put the war in the past and begin anew in the spirit of traditional foreign policy. The war was over, the soldiers and sailors had come home, and therefore it was easier to invoke a more cordial and accommodating atmosphere reflective of the Civil War which he and others were working to prevent:

> We make no wars to promote or to prevent successions to thrones; to maintain any theory of a balance of power; or to suppress the actual government which any country chooses to establish for itself. We instigate no revolutions, nor suffer any hostile expeditions to be fitted out in the United States to invade the territory or provinces of a friendly nation. We should act towards other nations as we wish them to act towards us; and justice and conscience should form the rule of conduct between governments, instead of mere power, self-interest, or the desire of aggrandizement. To maintain a strict neutrality in foreign wars, to cultivate friendly relations, to reciprocate every noble and generous act, and to perform punctually and scrupulously every treaty obligation – these are the duties which we owe other states.[39]

In his informative 2002 work, *Manifest Destiny's Underworld: Filibustering in Antebellum America*, historian Robert E. May notes that presidents during the pre-Civil War era, including Fillmore and Buchanan, 'used their annual messages and other communications to Congress as further opportunities for discrediting filibustering.' The idea was that such adventurism was not only detrimental to the American image, but that it ultimately hurt US commercial interests. Aware of the contradictions implicit in Fillmore's message, May aptly writes that 'Words come cheaply.'[40] Nevertheless, official remonstrances against filibustering were less of a deterrent to those who might otherwise engage in military expeditions and more of an admission of the limitations of American power. If American statesmen truly believed continental expansion might eventually encompass, and even overwhelm, the small states of Central America (or even Cuba) they would not have made such pronouncements. In the end, they opposed filibusterism because they understood that the US Army and Navy were in no position to support militarily what could not be expropriated politically. Yucatan proved it, but the allure of empire was a powerful elixir to those who failed to understand the enormous and practical distinctions between 'annexation' and 'manifest destiny'. In short, military planners, and the statesmen who heeded their advice, understood what provocative poets and pundits did not.[41]

Lessons and Legacy

For much of the 1850s, with the expansionist war fading into the background, and conflict with Great Britain avoided, Americans looked inward as the debate over slavery intensified. For ten years the word 'annexation' was on the lips of Americans. From New England to New Mexico, debates ensued as to whether the United States should absorb the breakaway Republic of Texas and go to war with Mexico to conquer the coveted lands of the Pacific. Some believed the war could have been avoided, but the more realistic understood the inevitable consequences of the seemingly endless tides of immigrants pouring into the United States, natural growth, and the desire to aggrandize at the expense of a neighbour that had once been a partner in the effort to liberate a continent from the monarchies of the Old World.

'Annexation' was not only an expression of politicians and newspaper editors employing popular persuasion, but reflected the general sentiment of those who lived in the Mississippi Valley, beyond the old colonies, who would soon outnumber the population on the Atlantic coast and began demanding the United States extend itself for the sake of their enrichment, and thus the inheritances of their progeny. In essence, the war was sanctioned by the people, and the politicians reflected that desire. For this reason, the conflict was initially popular but became less so when a growing body of sceptics believed it might last forever – while overzealous expansionists who advocated annexing everything began exceeding their mandates. Ultimately, 'annexation' outlived its purpose, but ensuring a transit route connecting the two oceans was always viewed as the job of the US government. However, that dream, and the transcontinental railroad, would wait until after the Civil War.

The Mexicans, for their part, understood the overwhelming odds they faced, which were exacerbated by the internal divisions that for a generation had troubled their polity. They saw it happening over many years, and those who visited the United States, like Lorenzo de Zavala and General Antonio Lopez de Santa Anna, understood it better. Despite intimate connections among elites, the Republic of Yucatan, and even Tabasco to a certain extent, were states on the periphery – a reflection of the geography that made them islands in a sea shared by their northern neighbours. Ultimately, the attempt by Mexican authorities to arrest Yucatecan independence undermined their efforts to regain Texas, and further weakened them when war with the United States came to their doorsteps. Disunity, then, in the face of a formidable opponent, sapped much of the Mexican spirit when they began losing battles that numerically favoured them, and their divisions were exploited by opponents who for years had contemplated the requirements of an invasion. Indeed, Texans fought with vengeance on the battlefields, but more notably, the US Navy was eager to prove itself and demonstrate that it had a role to play to ensure the United States became a two-ocean power. Preparations for that role, carried out by ambitious officers such as Matthew Perry (the son of a captain), were set in motion long before the phrase 'manifest destiny' was coined. Dry docks, naval stations, the construction of large vessels, financing and educating a new generation of officers took years of careful planning and preparation. Indeed, for many, the war was underway long before American cannons were aimed at the walls of Veracruz's castle of San Juan de Ulúa.

The American landing at Veracruz proved beyond all doubt that the United States dominated the Gulf, but it also demonstrated the limits within which it could operate. These were expressed in a number of ways. One represented the physical limitation in projecting power, its ability to expand southward at the expense of Mexico, and the limitations manifested by the complicated political and ethnic terrain of Yucatan and beyond. All of these considerations were underpinned by military and naval capabilities, logistics, and even the draught of older vessels and thus technological innovations rapidly changing methods and ways of war. The US may have owned the Gulf of Mexico, but its officers were limited to sympathetic coastal enclaves culturally removed from the less cosmopolitan regions of the interior – just as it took Americans decades to subdue the Seminoles of Florida. Nor could the Navy dictate terms when Great Britain still commanded the greatest fleet in the world and was master of the Caribbean and the east coast of Central America. Nevertheless, for the Americans, the Mexican War was a demonstration of the efficacy of expeditionary warfare – a first glimpse into the future of joint forces operations in a region the United States claimed as its own.

Another limitation for the would-be empire arose from its longstanding tradition of non-intervention. The war was inherited from the annexation of Texas and given approval by vote and popular consent, but Yucatan, and the contemplated military adventure under the auspices of humanitarian assistance and preoccupation with potential European involvement using the thereunto unnamed 'Monroe Doctrine' represented a Rubicon the young and growing nation was not ready to cross. In that regard, Justo Sierra O'Reilly's mission was not only undermined by the chaotic and unfortunate events of the Caste War, but by American reluctance to abandon its former identity as a non-interventionist republic. Annexation of sparsely settled Mexican territory, conquered in battle, was one matter, but employing a doctrine originally intended to safeguard independence in the Americas as a pretence for military involvement was entirely different. In other words, it was a war of conquest, and the concept of the spoils of war were understood by all, but developing a rationale for creating new conflicts to enlarge itself was still too abstract for America's political digestion in an era with few rivals apart from Great Britain.

These limitations thus resulted in the United States becoming a different type of empire, which first manifested itself during the Mexican War. For most of its early history as a nominal power it based its enlargement along traditional methods of accumulating lands once the domain of formidable tribes, but it became something more novel in the modern era – a power with strategic enclaves and outposts suited to maintaining the security of the core of its continental conquests and overseas commercial endeavours. America's leadership realized it could not sweep Latin America or the Gulf in the same manner that it had swept the plains and the west, and that compromise with Great Britain was prudent to avoid a third Anglo-American war and ensure an isthmian route connecting the two oceans was accessible to both peoples. After the war, the increasing usage of the term 'strategic points' became more applicable as the US recognized the long-term efficacy of the age-old policy employed by Great Britain to maintain dominance of the seas. For their part, the British shelved the 'balance of power' approach to North American affairs until the Civil War opened up old wounds, and monarchy was reintroduced in Mexico while Americans slaughtered each other over slavery and states' rights. In the 1850s, and especially after the failed 1851 Lopez Expedition to seize Cuba, annexation was abandoned as a tool for expansion in favour of the policy of intervention – which was more flexible and legalistically palatable to the European powers who originally inspired it. This is one of the legacies of the Mexican War and a reason why Fillmore's words in 1850 appear idealistic and even quaint.

Later on, as the United States grew in prestige and power, the interventionist Rubicon would be crossed so many times that the original warnings of the 1848 Yucatan debate were all but forgotten. Intervention became the norm, and the ideals and sage advice of the Founders were dismissed. Filibustering, beginning in early nineteenth-century Florida, Sentmanat, mercenaries in Yucatan, Cuba in 1851, and later a man named William Walker in Nicaragua; all were tolerated somewhat but officially disavowed until the federal government began using 'intervention' as a mechanism for leveraging weaker states and perceived enemies when diplomacy failed to provide the expected results.

In 1913, before the Great War and one year before the opening of the long-anticipated Panama Canal, George Lockhart Rives wrote in the preface of his work covering relations between Mexico and the United States between 1821 and 1848, that 'it is not doubtful that some lessons of extreme importance may be drawn from a study of our dealings with the nearest of our Latin-American neighbors. We have not always been fortunate in our conduct toward the other nations of this hemisphere, and our failures have, as I think, been chiefly due to our ignorance.'[42] That is not to say the US was not admired by its neighbours, many of whom, such as Zavala and later O'Reilly, both Yucatecans, wished to emulate aspects in which the US was successful but were entirely aware of its shortcomings – especially slavery. They, like many Mexicans, saw the United States during its ascendant era and were simultaneously awed and frightened by its potential. The drama beginning in Texas in 1835 was merely the opening act of that long war ending in 1848 when the last American soldier left Veracruz. The Americans, however, would return.

And so, when Raphael Semmes sat down sometime before 1851 to write his story, *Service afloat and ashore during the Mexican War*, he harboured 'not a doubt' that Yucatecans would have willingly acceded to annexation and incorporation into the United States. That belief, which in retrospect appears overconfident, or perhaps naïve, was based on his time in the Gulf and interaction with Mexicans during the war. Moreover, his words encapsulated a zeitgeist that existed for a brief period when it seemed the nation which he served was unstoppable and without limitations. Semmes, who during the Civil War so tenaciously and successfully fought against many whom he had served honourably with in the Home Squadron, was therefore the personification of the sea change that America underwent before and after the war. The talented captain, who became the bane of the US Navy, retrospectively pondered what would have occurred had the United States squandered its potential early on, as he believed Mexico did in its formative years, in the absence of less noble and disinterested statesmen who advised their countrymen to avoid entangling alliances, divisive and caustic party politics and destructive self-interest undermining unity and prosperity. His words in 1851 serve as both providential history and allegory:

> It required all the energy and decision of Washington, aided by his great weight of character, to prevent our army, at the close of our revolutionary war, from throwing away the laurels it had so gloriously won, and entering upon a sanguinary struggle with the civil power of the government. Who can calculate the misery and wretchedness which would probably have been entailed upon the country, if the place had been occupied by an ambitious and unscrupulous chief? We of the present generation might, in that event, possibly have read our own history in that of unfortunate Mexico. If then, our law-loving and law-abiding people, who were nearly all republicans and among whom there were none of those elements of discord, growing out of the unequal distribution of property and of privileges, which we have seen in Mexico, were so near shipwreck in the very hour of making their port.[43]

Thus, it came to be that the latecomers to the continent and travellers to the lands of the Mississippi Valley and Gulf of Mexico, those who arrived hundreds of years after Juan de Grijalva plied the coast of Yucatan and the Gulf in the early sixteenth century, and toppled the ancient states and civilizations of the New World, were the ones who would seize and settle the frontiers of North America, and not the Mexicans who had long been there. For whatever reason, it was their time, and certainly nothing manifest that propelled their destiny, but rather the result of a process inherent in empires that flow and ebb most certainly over time, as naturally as the tide.

Notes

Introduction

1. *Congressional Globe*, 29th Congress, 1st Session (Washington, DC: Library of Congress, 1846), 798. 12 May 1846.
2. *Mexican Affairs and War, 1825-1848*, vol. 2, 30th Congress, 1st Session, *Executive Document No. 69. House of Representatives. Treaty with Mexico. Message from the President of the United States, transmitting A copy of the treaty of peace, friendship, limits, and settlement, between the United States and republic of Mexico, ratifications of which were exchanged in the city of Queretaro, in Mexico, on the 30th of May, 1848.* 22 July 1848 (Washington DC, 1848), 14. Article V of the treaty notes 'Map of the United Mexican States, as organized and defined by various acts of the Congress of said republic, and constructed according to the best authorities. Revised edition. Published at New York, in 1847, by J. Disturnell.'; Jack Jackson, 'General Taylor's 'Astonishing' Map of Northeastern Mexico,' *The Southwestern Historical Quarterly* 101, no. 2 (1997): 143–73. See: Jorge L. Tamayo, 'Contenido de La Geografía.' *Investigación Económica* 8, no. 1 (1948): 1–28. Delineations on Mexico's southern borders were equally obscure.
3. José de Garay, *Survey of the Isthmus of Tehuantepec, Executed in the Years 1842 and 1843 with the Intent of establishing a communication between the Atlantic and Pacific Oceans* (London: Ackermann and Company, 1844), 130–4. See: Edmund Otis Hovey, 'The Isthmus of Tehuantepec and the Tehuantepec National Railway,' *Bulletin of the American Geographical Society* 39 (1907), 80. Three years after the US government formally took over the Panama Canal zone, and seven years before the great canal was completed, Edmund Otis Hovey confirmed Garay's assertions when he wrote that the Tehuantepec route for US ports on Atlantic and gulf was about '1,000 to 1,900 miles shorter' than that of Panama – saving roughly five days for the average steamer.
4. William Davis Robinson, *Memoirs of the Mexican Revolution: including a narrative of the expedition of General Xavier Mina: with some observations on the practicability of opening a commerce between the Pacific and Atlantic Oceans, through the Mexican Isthmus in the Province of Oaxaca, and at the Lake of Nicaragua, and on the future importance of such commerce to the civilized world, and more especially to the United States* (Philadelphia: Lydia R. Bailey, 1820), 350–9; William D. Robinson, *Memoirs of the Mexican Revolution*, vol. 1 (London: Lackington, et al, 1821), viii.
5. Ibid.
6. Major John G. Barnard, *The Isthmus of Tehuantepec* (New York: D. Appleton and Company, 1852).
7. 'Nicaragua' *The Republic*, Washington DC, 22 Oct. 1849; 'The Bungling Cabinet' *Richmond Enquirer*, 26 Oct. 1849; 'The Opposition Press on the Mosquito Question' *Daily Richmond Times*, 3 Nov. 1849.
8. 'Annexation of Texas!!!' *Morning Courier*, Louisville, 22 May 1844; 'Married' *Daily American Star*, Mexico City, 11 Feb.1848. (No. 113, 2). Nettie Lee Benson Latin American Collection (subsequently BLAC), University of Texas, Austin.

9. 'Tobasco in Mexico.' *Charleston Mercury*, 4 Feb. 1832. (via *Boston Gazette*). For Yucatán, see: María Cecilia Zuleta Miranda, 'El federalismo en Yucatán: Política y militarización (1840-1946),' *Secuencia, Nueva época* 31 (1995): 23–50.
10. See: Terry Rugeley, 'The Outsider' in *The River People in Flood Time: The Civil Wars in Tabasco, Spoiler of Empires* (Redwood City: Stanford University Press, 2014): 109–148.
11. George P. Garrison, ed. *Diplomatic Correspondence of the Republic of Texas* (*Annual Report of the American Historical Association for the Year 1908*), vol. 2 (Washington Government Printing Office, 1911), 610–12. (Subsequently: DCRT) Colonel Barnard Elliot Bee Sr. (Mexico City) to Secretary of State of Texas Abner Smith Lipscomb, 5 Feb. 1840.
12. Valladolid pronouncement', 12 Feb. 1840; 'Act of the garrison of Mérida,' Feb. 18, 1840. University of St. Andrews Pronunciamiento Project (subsequently referred to as USAPP), Mexican War Pronunciamientos; The Pronunciamiento in Independent Mexico 1821–1876. See: Will Fowler, *Malcontents, Rebels, and Pronunciados: The Politics of Insurrection in Nineteenth-Century Mexico* (Lincoln: University of Nebraska Press, 2012).
13. DCRT, vol. 2, 579. James Treat (Mexico City) to MB Lamar (Austin), 29 Feb 1840; 'Decree of the Yucatan Congress,' Merida, 4 March 1840 (USAPP).
14. DCRT, vol. 2, 581–5. Burnet (Austin) to Richard Pakenham (Mexico), 12 March 1840; Burnet to Treat, 12 March 1840; Treat to Lamar, 25 March 1840. See: Justin H. Smith, 'The Mexican Recognition of Texas,' *The American Historical Review* 16, no. 1 (Oct. 1910): 36–55.
15. 'Government preventions for the restoration of order,' San Juan Bautista (Villahermosa) 31 May 1840 (USAPP).
16. Alex Dienst, *The Navy of the Republic of Texas* (Temple, TX, 1909), 82–3. See: Tom Henderson Wells, *Commodore Moore and the Texas Navy* (Austin: University of Texas Press, 1960).
17. DCRT, vol. 2, 652. Lamar (Galveston) to Commodore E. W. Moore, 20 June 1840.
18. Alex Dienst, *The Navy of the Republic of Texas* (Temple, TX, 1909), 84–5; Moore (at sea aboard sloop-of-war *Austin*) to Texas Secretary of Navy Louis P. Cooke (Austin, TX) 24 Aug. 1840; 'Conquest of Texas' *Carlisle Herald and Expositor*, PA, 25 Nov. 1840.
19. DCRT, vol. 2, 616–17. Bee (Veracruz) to Lipscomb, 29 August 1840; 'Tobasco Taken' *The National Gazette* (Philadelphia), 26 Dec. 1840 (via *New Orleans Bulletin*, Dec. 14.)
20. *The Times*, London. 31 July, 17 Aug. 1840; *Morning Post*, London, 6 Oct 1840.
21. William Kennedy, *Texas: The Rise, Progress, and Prospects of the Republic of Texas* [1841] (Reprint: Fort Worth, TX: The Molyneaux Craftsmen, 1925); David Pletcher, *The Diplomacy of Annexation: Texas, Oregon, and the Mexican War* (Columbia, University of Missouri Press, 1973).
22. *Daily Herald*, New York, 5 January 1838. Letter from Marcy (Albany) dated 2 January 1838.
23. *The Sun*, Baltimore, 8 January 1838.
24. *Observer*, London, 4 February 1838.
25. Andrew Bonthius, 'The Patriot War of 1837–1838: Locofocoism with a Gun?' *Labour/Le Travail* 52 (2003), 10. See: Oscar A. Kinchen, *The Rise and Fall of the Patriot Hunters* (New York: Bookman Associates, 1956), 37. 'One of the most active in the organization of lodges along the lake frontier was Orrin Scott, a nephew of General Winfield Scott.'
26. J. C. Carter, 'One Way Ticket to a Penal Colony: North American Political Prisoners in Van Diemen's Land,' *Ontario History* 101, No. 2 (Autumn 2009), 191–2.

27. Kennedy, *Texas: The Rise, Progress, and Prospects of the Republic of Texas*, intro. 44 (xliv), 9 (ix), 525. See: David Montejano, *Anglos and Mexicans in the Making of Texas, 1836-1986* (Austin: University of Texas Press, 1987).
28. Kennedy, *Texas: The Rise, Progress, and Prospects*, 661–7. Hunt to Forsyth, 6 July 1837; Forsyth to Hunt, 25 Aug. 1837.
29. Ephraim Douglas Adams, ed., *British Diplomatic Correspondence Concerning the Republic of Texas – 1838-1846* (Austin: Texas State Historical Association, 1918), 45–6. Kennedy to Aberdeen, 20 Oct. 1841.
30. *Diario del Gobierno de la Republica Mexicana*, Mexico City, 7 Jan. (vol. 19, no. 2062); 8 Jan. (vol. 19, no. 2063) via Veracruz. 29 Dec. 1840 (Texas, 14 Nov. 1840); Jan. 27 (vol. 19 no. 2082); 16 Feb. 1841 (vol. 19 no. 2101, via *Conciliador* Xalapa, Veracruz. 5 Feb.); 26 Feb1841 (vol. 19, no. 2111). Biblioteca Nacional de España, subsequently: BNE.
31. Ibid. 8 March 1841 (vol. 19, no. 2121); 4 April 1841 (vol. 19, no . 2146). BNE. For Sonora, see: Bill Hoy, 'War in Papaguería: Manuel Gándara's 1840-41 Papago Expedition,' *The Journal of Arizona History* 35, no. 2 (1994): 141–62.
32. 'Manifesto of Francisco de Sentmanat' San Juan Bautista, 25 May 1841. (USAPP)
33. Rugeley, 'The Outsider,' *The River People in Flood Time*, 126–8.
34. DCRT, vol. 2, 761–3. James Webb to Lamar, Galveston, 29 June 1841.
35. DCRT, vol. 2, 792–4. Lamar to Barbachano, 20 July 1841; Barbachano to Lamar, 24 Aug. 1841
36. John L. Stephens, *Incidents of Travel in Yucatan*, vol. 1 (New York: Harper and Brothers, 1843), 81; Dienst, *The Navy of the Republic of Texas*, 94–7.
37. Eligio Ancono, *Historia de Yucatán, desde la época más remota hasta nuestros días*, vol.3 (Mérida: M. Heredia Argüelles, 1879), 398.
38. Rugeley, 'The Outsider', 130–1.
39. William Fowler, *Santa Anna of Mexico* (Lincoln: University of Nebraska Press, 2007), 216; José María Roa Bárcena, *Recuerdos de la invasiónnorte-americana, 1846-1848* (Mexico: Librería Madrileña de San Buxó, 1883), 15. See: Will Fowler, *Tornel and Santa Anna: The Writer and the Caudillo* (Westport, Conn: Greenwood Press, 2000); Michael P. Costeloe, 'The Triangular Revolt in Mexico and the Fall of Anastasio Bustamante, August-October 1841,' *Journal of Latin American Studies* 20, no. 2 (1988): 337–60.
40. José María Tornel y Mendívil, *Discurso pronunciado por el exmo. sr. general ministro de guerra y marina don José Maria Tornel en la sesión del 12 de octubre de 1842 del Congreso constituyente. en apoyo del dictamen de la mayorá de la comisión de constitución del mismo* (México [DF]: José M. Lara, 1842), 33–5. See: Ted Schwarz, Robert H. Thonhoff, ed., *Forgotten Battlefield of the First Texas Revolution: The Battle of Medina, August 18, 1813* (Fort Worth: Eakin Press, 1985).
41. Ibid. 35–40.
42. Mariano Otero, *Ensayo sobre el verdadero estado de la cuestion social y politica que se agita en la República Mexicana* (México [DF]: Ignacio Cumplido, 1842), 94–5. 1 June 1842.
43. *Picayune*, 27 Nov. 1841; Rugeley, 'The Outsider,' 130. Rugeley notes that on 19 December 1841, Sentmanat 'held a ball celebrating Yucatecan indepedendence.'
44. Ancono, *Historia de Yucatán*, vol.3, 398–401.
45. Ibid. 402–3. 'Quoted from the pamphlet Quintana published in Mexico in 1842 and which bears the title: 'Manifesto of Mr. Quintana Roo to the provisional government of Mexico, on his commission to Yucatan'. This document was reprinted in Mérida.'
46. Ibid. 403–5.

47. DCRT, vol. 2, 800, 804. Joaquin G. Rejon (Merida) to Acting Texas Secretary of State Waples, 18 Jan. 1842; Rejon to Texas President, 9 April 1842; Ancono, *Historia de Yucatán*, vol.3, 405.
48. John L. Stephens, *Incidents of Travel in Yucatan*, vol. 1 (New York: Harper and Brothers, 1843), 461; Eligio Ancono, *Historia de Yucatán*, vol.3, 411–13.
49. Ancono, *Historia de Yucatán*, vol. 3, 415–16.
50. Ibid. 417–19.
51. 'From Campeachy' *Picayune*, 8 Feb. 1843; Ancono, *Historia de Yucatán*, vol. 3, 419–26.
52. 'From Havana' *New-York Daily Tribune*, 26 April 1843. (via *New Orleans Bulletin*, report from Mexico dated 18 March); Ancono, *Historia de Yucatán*, vol. 3, 431–6. See: *Richmond Enquirer*, 20 June 1843 (via *New Orleans Herald*, 20 June), reports of Mexican complaints 'that the Yucatecos have armed the Indians, and availed themselves of the services of savages.'
53. Ancono, *Historia de Yucatán*, vol. 3, 437–41; 'Later from Yucatan,' *Picayune*, 6 July 1843.
54. 'From Campeachy' *Picayune*, 16 Aug. 1843; 'From Vera Cruz' *New York Herald*, 10 Aug. 1833 (via *New Orleans Tropic* and *New Orleans Bulletin*).
55. Dienst, *The Navy of the Republic of Texas*, 128–30.
56. Ibid. 130–2.
57. 'Late from Campeachy' *Charleston Courier*, 2 June 1843; 'Important from Campeachy' *New York Herald*, 6 June 1843 (via *New Orleans Republican*, 27 May); Amelia W. Williams and Eugene C. Barker, ed., *The Writings of Sam Houston, 1821-1847*, vol. 4 (Austin: University of Texas Press, 1941), 204–6. 13 May 1834.
58. Dienst, *The Navy of the Republic of Texas*, 132–3, 140.
59. Thomas J. Green, *Journal of the Texian expedition against Mier; subsequent imprisonment of the author; his sufferings, and the final escape from castle of Perote* (New York: Harpers, 1845), 127.
60. William Preston Stapp, *The prisoners of Perote: containing a journal kept by the author, who was captured by the Mexicans at Mier, December 25, 1842, and released from Perote, May 16, 1844* (Philadelphia, G. B. Zieber and Company, 1845), 58–68.
61. Green, *Journal of the Texian expedition*, 170.
62. Williams and Barker, ed., *The Writings of Sam Houston, 1821–1847*, vol. 4, 197. 7 May 1843.
63. Adams, ed., *British Diplomatic Correspondence Concerning the Republic of Texas*, 143-4. Elliot (Galveston) to Henry Unwin Addington, 16 Dec. 1842.

Chapter 1
1. *Congressional Globe*, 28th Congress, 1st Session (Washington, DC: Library of Congress, 1844), 655. 10 June 1844.
2. Benjamin Lundy, *The War in Texas; a review of the facts and circumstances showing that this contest is a crusade against Mexico, set on foot and supported by slaveholders, land-speculators, &c. in order to re-establish, extend, and perpetuate the system of slavery and the slave trade.* (Philadelphia: Merrihew and Gunn, 1837), 3, 35. Adams' speech, House of Representatives, 25 May 1835.
3. Henry Stuart Foote, *Texas and the Texans: or, advance of the Anglo-Americans to the south-west; including a history of leading events in Mexico, from the conquest by Fernando Cortes to the termination of the Texan revolution*, vol. 2 (Philadelphia: Thomas, Cowperthwait & Co., 1841), 391, 399.
4. Ibid., 71.

5. *Diario del Gobierno*, 16 Aug. 1843. vol. 26 no. 2976. BNE (Excerpt from Massachusetts Legislature)
6. José María RoaBárcena, *Recuerdos de la invasiónnorte-americana, 1846-1848* (Mexico: Librería Madrileña de San Buxó, 1883), 16; Upshur quoted in: George Lockhart Rives, *The United States and Mexico, 1821-1848*, vol. 1 (New York: Charles Scribner's Sons, 1913), 588-90; Almonte to Upshur, 3 Nov. 1843; Upshur to Almonte, 8 Nov. 1843.See: See: John Hays Hammond, 'José María Roa Bárcena: Mexican Writer and Champion of Catholicism,' *The Americas* 6, no. 1 (1949): 45-55;Earl R. McClendon, 'Daniel Webster and Mexican Relations: The Santa Fe Prisoners,' *The Southwestern Historical Quarterly* 36, no. 4 (1933): 288-311.
7. 'Later from Mexico' *Public Ledger*, Philadelphia, 20 June 1844; 'No Compromise' *Public Ledger*, Philadelphia 1 May 1844. For Benton, see: *Congressional Globe*, 28th Congress, 1st Session (Washington, DC: Library of Congress, 1844), 655. 10 June 1844.
8. *Republican Banner*, Nashville, 6 May 1844 (citing Raleigh letter); 'Texas Opinions of the Press' *Nashville Union*, 11 May 1844 (citing Van Buren's letter); 'The Great Mass Meeting of the Whigs' *New York Herald*, 30 Aug. 1844 (Ashland letter, 27 July); 'The Issue.' *The Ohio Democrat*, New Philadelphia, 4 July 1844. For an account of Raleigh, see: Henry Thomas Shanks, ed., *The Papers of Willie Person Mangum*, vol. 4, 103 (Raleigh: State Department of Archives and History, 1955), 103.
9. 'From Texas' *Morning Courier*, Louisville, 22 May 1844 (via *Picayune*); 'Mexico and Texas' *Picayune*, 27 July 1844.
10. Joseph Milton Nance, 'Adrian Woll: Frenchman in the Mexican Military Service,' *New Mexico Historical Review* 33, 3 (1958), 177; Williams and Barker, ed., *The Writings of Sam Houston, 1821-1847*, vol. 4, 242. Houston to George W. Hockley and Samuel M. Williams, 3 Feb. 1844.
11. Rugeley, 'The Outsider,' 133-9; 'Sentmanat and his Expedition' *Picayune*, 5 June 1844.
12. 'Tobasco, Mexico' *New York Herald*, 21 July 1844 (Report from Frontera, 10 June); US Consul John F. McGregor (Campeche) to US Secretary of State John C. Calhoun 3 July 1844. Despatches from US Consuls in Campeche, Mexico, 1820-1880, National Archives and Records at College Park, MD (subsequently: NACP), M286 (nos. 494-7). *Voz de la Naturaleza* (authored by 'Los hombres sensibles') dated 3 July 1844; 'Mexico' *Star of Freedom*, Leeds, 3 Aug. 1844 (via *Picayune*). Mexico's Minister of Foreign Relation, Manuel Crecencio Rejon, accused the US of being involved in the Sentmanat expedition, which was denied. See: *Mexican Affairs and War, 1825-1848*, vol. 1, 28th Congress, 2nd Session, *House Executive Document 19: Message from the President of the United States, Transmitting the correspondence between Mr. Shannon, American Minister to Mexico, and Señor Rejon*. 19 Dec. 1844. (Washington DC, 1844), 32. E. Porter (Tabasco) to Benjamin E. Green, Secretary of the US Legation (Mexico City) 6 Sept. 1844.
13. 'Later From Mexico' *Picayune*, 18 Aug. 1844; 'The Tabasco Expedition' *Morning Courier*, Louisville, 12 July 1844. (via *New Orleans Tropic*, 4 July).
14. 'The Mexican Frigates' *The Evening Post*, New York City, 6 Sept. 1844; 'The Mexican War Steamers' *New York Herald*, 25 June 1844; 'Mexican War Steamers' *Buffalo Daily Gazette*, 13 June 1844.
15. *Congressional Globe*, 28th Congress, 2nd Session, 4, 16, 50 (LOC).
16. Fowler, *Santa Anna of Mexico*, 234-7.
17. Adams, ed., *British Diplomatic Correspondence Concerning the Republic of Texas*, 428. Aberdeen to Elliot, 23 Jan. 1845; Cuevas quoted in: Justin H. Smith, 'The Mexican

Recognition of Texas,' *The American Historical Review* 16, no. 1 (Oct. 1910), 45. F. O. Mexico, 192, Dom. Van, Captain George Elliot to Sir Charles Adam, 4 April 1845, explaining the plan.
18. Ephraim Douglas Adams, *British Interests and Activities in Texas, 1838-1846* (Baltimore: Johns Hopkins Press, 1910), 206–12. For the plan, see: 'F. O. Mexico, 192, Dom. Van, Captain George Elliot to Sir Charles Adam, 4 April 1845'.
19. Ephraim Douglas Adams, *British Interests and Activities in Texas, 1838-1846* (Baltimore: Johns Hopkins Press, 1910), 212–20.
20. 'Important from Mexico' *New York Herald*, 29 May 1845 (via *Picayune* May 20); 'Relations with Mexico' *Niles' National Register*, Baltimore, 31 May 1845. (via *Picayune*).
21. 'The Spleen of the English Press' *Daily Union*, Washington DC, 7 Oct. 1845. See: Allan Nevins, Frémont, Pathmarker of the West (New York: D. Appleton-Century Company, 1939), 201. 'In these years men like Calhoun were almost hypnotized by a belief that England would at any favorable moment turn aggressor in the western hemisphere.'
22. Ibid.
23. 'Territorial Aggrandizement' *Daily Union*, Washington DC, 7 Oct. 1845; Benjamin J. Swenson, *The Dawn of Guerrilla Warfare: Why the Tactics of Insurgents against Napoleon failed in the US Mexican War* (Barnsley, UK: Pen and Sword, 2023), 119–20. For Guizot, see: Frederick Merk, *The Monroe Doctrine and American Expansionism, 1843-1849* (New York: Alfred A. Knopf, 1966), 50–7. See also: David M. Pletcher, *The Diplomacy of Annexation: Texas, Oregon, and the Mexican War* (Columbia: University of Missouri Press, 1973).
24. Merk, *The Monroe Doctrine and American Expansionism, 1843-1849*, 60–1; *Congressional Globe*, 29th Congress, 1st Session (Washington, DC: Library of Congress, 1846), 5–7. 2 Dec 1845.
25. Decree of the Yucatan Assembly, 1 Jan. 1846 (USAPP); 'Another Revolution in Mexico' *American Republican and Baltimore Daily Clipper*, 9 Feb. 1846.
26. Williams and Barker, ed., *The Writings of Sam Houston, 1821-1847*, vol. 5, 48–50. 8 May 1848.
27. Foote, *Texas and the Texans*, 10; *House Executive Document No. 60. Mexican War Correspondence* (Washington DC, 30th Congress, 1st Session, 28 April 1848), 576. Stanton to Thomas, 17 Aug. 1845. (Subsequently HED NO. 60). See: Daniel J. Burge, *A Failed Vision of Empire: The Collapse of Manifest Destiny, 1845-1872* (Lincoln: University of Nebraska Press, 2022).

Chapter 2

1. Frederick W. Seward, *William H. Seward: an autobiography from 1801 to 1834, with a Memoirs of his Life and Selections of His Letters, 1831-1846* (1877: Reprint: New York: Derby and Miller, 1891), 755.
2. *Congressional Globe*, 783. 11 May 1846
3. M.A. De Wolfe Howe, ed., *The Life and Letters of George Bancroft*, vol. 1 (New York: Charles Scribner's Sons, 1908), 282. Bancroft to Louis McLane, 29 Mar. 1846; Karl Jack Bauer, *The Mexican War, 1846-1848* (1974: Reprint: Lincoln and London: University of Nebraska Press, 1992), 18–19; Linda Arnold, 'Too Few Ships, Too Few Guns, and Not Enough Money: The Mexican Navy, 1846-1848,' *The Northern Mariner/Le Marin du nord* 9, no. 2 (April 1999), 2.
4. *Congressional Globe*, 29th Congress, 1st Session (Washington, DC: Library of Congress, 1846), 798. 12 May 1846. For a look at the war's popularity, Robert W. Johannsen, *To*

the Halls of the Montezumas: The Mexican War in the American Imagination (New York: Oxford University Press, 1985).

5. Quaife, (ed.), *The Diary of James J. Polk During his Presidency, 1845-1849*, vol. 1 (Chicago: A.C. McClurg & Co., 1910), 35 (17 Sept.) 93 (10 Nov.), 83-4 (30 Oct.). Slidell left New Orleans 17 Nov. to Pensacola (to receive his naval escort), before going to Mexico. See: *Diary of James J. Polk*, vol. 1, 101. 23 Nov. 1845.

6. Allan Nevins, *Frémont, Pathmarker of the West* (New York: D. Appleton-Century Company, 1939), 200; Seward, *William H. Seward: an autobiography*, 756; John Charles Frémont, *Memoirs of My Life*, vol. 1 (Chicago and New York: Belford, Clarke & Company, 1887), 488–9. See: John Bassett Moore, ed. *The Works of James Buchanan, comprising his speeches, state papers, and private correspondence*; vol. 6 (Philadelphia, London, J.B. Lippincott Company, 1909), 275. Secretary of State James Buchanan to Thomas O. Larkin, Consul of the United States at Monterey, Oct. 17, 1845: 'should California assert and maintain her independence, we shall render her all the kind offices in our power, as a sister Republic.' See also: Justin H. Smith, *The War with Mexico*, vol. 1(New York: Macmillan, 1919), 325-6, 530; Richard R. Stenberg, 'Polk and Frémont, 1845-1846.' *Pacific Historical Review* 7, no. 3 (Sept. 1938): 211–27.

7. Charles Francis Adams (ed.), *Memoirs of John Quincy Adams, Comprising Portions of His Diary from 1795 to 1848*, vol. 11 (Philadelphia: J.B. Lippincott & Co., 1876), 156–7, 277–8, 18 May, 10 Dec. 1842 (respectively). See: Claude H. Hall, 'Abel P. Upshur and the Navy as an Instrument of Foreign Policy,' *The Virginian Magazine of History and Biography* 69, no. 3 (1961): 290–99; Edward P. Crapol, 'John Tyler and the Pursuit of National Destiny' *Journal of the Early Republic* 17, no. 3 (1997): 467–91; Maria Angela Diaz, 'To Conquer the Coast: Pensacola, the Gulf of Mexico, and the Construction of American Imperialism, 1820-1848,' *The Florida Historical Quarterly* 95, no. 1 (2016): 1–25.

8. Philip Syng Physick Conner, *The Home squadron under Commodore Conner in the war with Mexico, being a synopsis of its services* (Philadelphia, 1896), 14–15.

9. Henry Halleck, *Military Art and Science; or Course of Instruction in Strategy, Fortification, Tactics of Battles, &c; Embracing the Duties of Staff Infantry, Cavalry, Artillery, and Engineers, Adapted to the Use of Volunteers and Militia* (New York: D. Appleton & Company, 1846), 202. Halleck's report submitted to the Senate October 20, 1843, was entitled: *Report on the Means of National Defence*. See: S.J. Watson, 'Knowledge, Interest and the Limits of Military Professionalism: The Discourse on American Coastal Defence, 1815-1860,' *War in History* 5, no. 3 (1998): 280–307.

10. Raphael Semmes, *Service afloat and ashore during the Mexican War* (Cincinnati: WM. H. Moore & Co., 1851), 78.

11. 'The Navy' *The Sun*, Baltimore, 1 July 1846; 'Commodore Stockton's Proclamation' *Richmond Daily Whig*, 31 Oct. 1846.

12. Semmes, *Service afloat and ashore during the Mexican War*, 80–1; Bauer, *The Mexican War, 1846-1848*, 112.

13. 'The Mexican Steamers and Privateers' *Picayune*, 4 June 1846.

14. Campbell (Havana) to Buchanan, 3 June, 10 Nov. 1847. Despatches from US Consuls in Havana, Cuba, 1783-1906. NACP, M899 (no. 180, 189, 193-4, 207); *Congressional Globe*, 29th Congress, 2nd Session, 9. 8 Dec. 1848.

15. Andrés Reséndez Fuentes, 'Guerra e Identidad Nacional,' *Historia Mexicana* 47, no. 2 (1997), 427, 433; Bárcena, *Recuerdos de la invasiónnorte-americana, 1846-1848*, 484. See: 'Pronunciation of Traconis with the garrison of San Juan Bautista', 12 August

1846. (USAPP) Article 6: 'The Hon. Mr. Division General Don Antonio López de Santa Anna as General in Chief of the Liberation Army, and consequently he will take command of it immediately when he appears in the territory of the Republic.' On neutrality, see: Smith, *The War with Mexico*, vol. 2, 443. Smith cites a letter of 19 May 1846 from Bancroft to Conner. For Alvarado: Semmes, *Service afloat and ashore during the Mexican War*, 88–9; William Elliot Griffis, *Matthew Calbraith Perry: a typical American naval officer* (Boston: Cupples and Hurd, 1887), 199: 'Owing to lack of ships of light draught, Conner had been able to accomplish little. The splendid opportunities of the first year were lost, and naval expeditions, even when attempted, proved failures. The most notorious of these was the second unsuccessful demonstration at Alvarado, October 16, which shook the faith of the strongest believers in the abilities and resolution of Commodore Conner.'
16. Griffis, *Matthew Calbraith Perry: a typical American naval officer*, 198–9. In defending his father, Philip S. P. Conner disputed Griffis' assertions. See: Philip S.P. Conner, *Commodore Conner*: note on 'Maclay's History of the United States navy,' Mexican War (Philadelphia, United Service Review, 1895), 33–5.
17. E. Porter (Frontera, Tabasco) to Secretary of State Buchanan, 12 July 1846. Despatches From US Consuls in Tabasco, Mexico, 1832-1874. NACP, M303 (no. 283).
18. Bauer, *The Mexican War, 1846-1848*, 125 (footnote 38), 118; Griffis, *Matthew Calbraith Perry*, 201. *The Evening Post*, New York, 7 March 1842: 'Late from Mexico' *Picayune*, 11 June 1844. 'The Petrita brought over Señor J. Gonzalez, bearer of despatches for Gen. Almonte, the Mexican Minister, who is now on his way to Washington post haste.'
19. 'Manifesto and measures adopted by the governor and commander of Tabasco when the state was invaded by United States forces, 23 October 1846', 26 October 1846. (USAPP), See: *Diaro*, 11 Nov. 1846. BNE; Smith, *The War with Mexico*, vol. 1, 200; Griffis, *Matthew Calbraith Perry*, 202; 'General headquarters in San Juan Bautista, at twelve o'clock.' 26 October 1846. (USAPP); Bauer, *The Mexican War, 1846-1848*, 118. See: Gabrielle M. Neufeld Santelli, *Marines in the Mexican War* (Washington DC: History and Museums Division Headquarters, US Marines Corps, 1991), 30.
20. 'Pronouncement of the Tabasco garrison', 19 November 1846; 'Act signed in San Juan Bautista', 20 November 1846. (USAPP); House Executive Document No. 60, US Congressional Documents: Library of Congress, (US Serial Set No. 520), 782. Address of General Antonio Lopez de Santa Anna. 16 Aug 1846. Subsequently referred to as HED No. 60. (LOC); 'Decree of the extraordinary congress of Yucatan', 25 August 1846. (USAPP).
21. Pedro de Regil y Estrada (Merida) to Secretary of State Buchanan, 25 Oct. 1846. English version (nos. 198–9) translated at 'Consulate of Sisal.' NACP, M287 (nos. 203–9).
22. Semmes, *Service afloat and ashore during the Mexican War*, 83–5. Eneas M. McFaul to Buchanan, 14 May (New York), 22 Sept. (Laguna), 1846. Despatches from US Consuls in Ciudad del Carmen, Mexico, 1830–1872. NACP, M308 (no. 264, 268). See; *Picayune*, 5 June: McFaul went missing in April 1847.
23. Philip S.P. Conner, *The Home squadron under Commodore Conner*, 53, 13–14.
24. María Cecilia Zuleta Miranda, 'Yucatán y la guerra con estados unidos: ¿Una neutralidad anunciada?' in *México al tiempo de su guerra con Estados Unidos(1846-1848)* (El Colegio de México, 1997), 582. Zuleta Miranda cites: Eneas M. Faul Jr, Consul US at Laguna,

to James Buchanan Secretary of State (6 Jan. 1846, and 25 July 1846); Conner, *The Home Squadron*, 39-40. Perry (Mississippi) to Mason (Washington DC), 16 Nov. 1846.
25. Semmes, *Service afloat and ashore during the Mexican War*, 84–5; William Elliot Griffis, *Matthew Calbraith Perry: a typical American naval officer* (Boston: Cupples and Hurd, 1887), 209.
26. Benjamin Franklin Sands, *From Reefer to Rear-Admiral* (New York: Frederick A. Stokes, 1899), 181–2.
27. Semmes, *Service afloat*, 112; George Meade, *The Life and Letters of George Gordon Meade*, vol. 1 (New York: Charles Scribner's Sons, 1913), 169. Monterrey, 8 Dec. 1846.
28. HED No. 60, 1270. 'Vera Cruz and its castle, New line of operations, thence upon the capital', 12 Nov. 1846; John Reese Kenly, *Memoirs of a Maryland volunteer. War with Mexico, in the years 1846-8* (Philadelphia: J.B. Lippincott, 1872), 232–4; For Scott's explanation see: Lieutenant General Winfield Scott, *Memoirs* (New York: Sheldon & Co., 1864), 402–8. For Scott's original 'Vera Cruz and its Castle', 27 Oct. 1846, see: HED No. 60, 1268–70. The updated version of Scott's plan is also found at *House Executive Document No. 59. Correspondence between the Secretary of War and General Scott* (Washington DC, 30th Congress, 1st Session, 26 April 1848), 56–9. Subsequently HED No. 59.
29. Kenly, *Memoirs*, 175, 190–1, 226.
30. Kenly, *Memoirs*, 227–8.
31. Kenly, *Memoirs of a Maryland volunteer*, 229–30; Santelli, *Marines in the Mexican War*, 31.
32. George Ballentine, *The Mexican War, By an English Soldier. Comprising incidents and adventures in the United States and Mexico with the American army* (New York: W.A. Townsend & Company, 1860), 121–3.
33. Ballentine, *The Mexican War, By an English Soldier*, 123–4.
34. Ibid. 124–7.
35. Ibid. 127–35.
36. Ibid. 138–9.
37. Robert W. Johannsen, *To the Halls of the Montezumas: The Mexican War in the American Imagination* (New York: Oxford University Press, 1985), 87; Jacob J. Oswandel, *Notes of the Mexican war 1846-47-48. Comprising incidents, adventures and everyday proceedings and letters while with the United States army in the Mexican war* (Philadelphia, 1885), 443. San Angel, Mexico. 7 Jan. 1848; Albert G. Brackett, *General Lane's Brigade in Central Mexico* (Cincinnati: H.W. Derby & Company, 1854), 314. See: Timothy D. Johnson and Nathanial Cheairs Hughes Jr., eds. *Notes of the Mexican War, 1846–1848, J. Jacob Oswandel* (Knoxville: University of Tennessee Press, 2010).
38. Ballentine, *The Mexican War, By an English Soldier*, 139–40.
39. Kenly, *Memoirs*, 238–9.
40. Kenly, *Memoirs*, 239; Scott, *Memoirs*, 540. Scott's martial laws were implemented on his arrival on 19 February. See: Benjamin J. Swenson, '"Measures of Conciliation": Winfield Scott, Henry Halleck, and the Origins of US Army Counterinsurgency Doctrine,' *Journal of Military History* 86, no. 4 (Oct. 2022): 859–81.
41. *The Liberator*, Boston, 25 Dec. 1846.
42. HED No. 60, 1175–78. LOC. Taylor (Monterrey) to Adjutant General (Washington DC), 8, 16 June 1847. See: HED No. 60, 1178–80. LOC. Taylor (Monterrey) to Adjutant General (Washington DC), 23, 30 June 1847.
43. HED No. 60, 1191-2. LOC. *Marcy* (Washington DC) to Taylor (Monterrey), 26 June 1847. 'They have come out as militia, as distinguished from volunteers …'

44. Lucas Alamán, *Historia de Méjico desde los primeros movimientos que prepararon su independencia en el año de 1808, hasta la época presente*, vol.5 (Méjico: J.M. Lara, 1852), 846–7.
45. HED No. 60, 568, 892, 896; Jesup to Marcy, 27 Dec. 1846, Conner (Anton Lizardo) to Scott, 18 Jan 1847, Scott to Marcy, 28 Feb. 1847; Edmund March Blunt and G.W. Blunt, *The American Coast Pilot: containing directions for the principal harbors, capes and headlands, on the coasts of North and South America* (New York: Edmund and George W. Blunt, 1847), 10, 290. Letter dated 31 Dec. 1846.
46. Bauer, *The Mexican War*, 239; HED No. 60, 568, Jesup to Marcy, 27 Dec. 1846. See also: Bauer, *Surfboats and Horse Marines: US Naval Operations in the Mexican War, 1846-48* (Annapolis: US Naval Institute, 1969).
47. Potter Woodburne, *The war in Florida: being an exposition of its causes, and an accurate history of the campaigns of Generals Clinch, Gaines, and Scott* (Baltimore: Lewis and Coleman, 1836), viii, 166.
48. Myer M. Cohen, *Notices of Florida and the Campaigns* (Charleston: Burger &Honour, 1836), 223–4.
49. HED No. 60, 896. Scott to Marcy, 28 Feb. 1847.
50. Ibid. See: Ulysses S. Grant, *Personal Memoirs of US Grant*, vol. 1 (New York: Charles L. Webster & Company, 1885), 124–5. 'The passage was a tedious one, and many of the troops were on shipboard over thirty days from the embarkation at the mouth of the Rio Grande to the time of debarkation south of Vera Cruz.'
51. Ethan Allen Hitchcock, *Fifty Years in Camp and Field* (New York: Ed. W.A. Croffut. G.P. Putnam's Sons, 1909), 237; Conner, *Home Squadron*, 19.
52. Scott, *Memoirs*, 422, 427; Semmes, *Service afloat*, 77. For Scott's plan titled, 'Vera Cruz and its castle,' see: HED No. 60, 1268–70. (LOC) 27 Oct. 1846.
53. Scott, *Memoirs*, 419; Conner, *Home Squadron*, 19, 46; Charles Colcock Jones, The *Life and services of Commodore Tattnall* (Savanna: Morning News Steam Printing, 1878), 55–6.
54. Oswandel, *Notes of the Mexican war*, 70–2.
55. Oswandel, *Notes of the Mexican war*, 73–6.
56. James Fenimore Cooper, *History of the Navy of the United States of America* (New York: G.P. Putnam, 1853), 83; Conner (Temple, *Memoir of the Landing of United States Troops at Vera Cruz in 1847*), 69–70. See: Paul C. Clark Jr. and Edward H. Moseley, 'D-Day Veracruz, 1847 – A Grand Design,' *Joint Forces Quarterly* (Winter 1995-96), 108-110; See also: Karl Jack Bauer, 'The Veracruz Expedition of 1847,' *Military Affairs* 20, no. 3 (1956): 162–9.
57. Hitchcock, *Fifty Years in Camp and Field*, 243-4.
58. Kenly, *Memoirs of a Maryland volunteer*, 254; Griffis, *Matthew Calbraith Perry*, 150; Scott, *Memoirs*, 425. See: Conner, *The Home Squadron*, 5: 'Thus it is seen that the relief of Commodore Conner, in the middle of a siege, was not an intentional rebuke on the part of the government, but arose from chance, the accidental arrival of Commodore Perry at that particular time.'
59. Scott, *Memoirs*, 421.
60. Scott, *Memoirs*, 423–5; 'The Progress of the War' *The Somerset Herald* (PA), 20 April 1847. Quoting from New Orleans *Delta*, 31 March 1847.
61. 'The Progress of the War' *The Somerset Herald* (PA), 20 April 1847. Quoting from aNew Orleans *Delta*, 31 March 1847; 'Vera Cruz' *Daily Union*, Washington DC, 21 July 1847.

62. Robert A. Law and A. M. Manigault. 'A Letter from Vera Cruz in 1847,' *The Southwestern Historical Quarterly* 18, no. 2 (1914), 216-17.
63. Halleck, *Military Art and Science*, 202, 159; HED No. 60, 1268-70; Swenson, "Measures of Conciliation': Winfield Scott, Henry Halleck, and the Origins of US Army Counterinsurgency Doctrine,' JMH, 860-8; Swenson, *The Dawn of Guerrilla Warfare*, 85-7. The term 'expeditionary warfare' seems to be an English invention from the late 1860s, it did not come into modern usage until the turn of the century. See: 'Fudge About Invasion', *The Examiner*, London, 1 Dec. 1866.
64. Halleck, *Military Art and Science*, 158-68.
65. Ibid. 164-9.
66. Bruce A. Elleman, S.C.M. Paine, eds., *Naval Power and Expeditionary Wars: Peripheral Campaigns and New Theatres of naval warfare* (New York: Routledge, 2011), 17. Duffy's essay is entitled 'Festering the Spanish ulcer: The Royal Navy and the Peninsular War, 1808-1814'.
67. Robert K. Sutcliffe, *British Expeditionary Warfare and the Defeat of Napoleon, 1793-1815* (Woodbridge, UK: The Boydell Press, 2016), xiii-xiv, 2; HED No. 60, 588. Jesup to Asst. Quartermaster Captain M.M. Clark, Columbus, GA, 12 June 1846. For a good example of a 'purchase or charter' report see, HED No. 60, pp. 694-5: Deputy Quartermaster Thomas F. Hunt (New Orleans) to Acting Quartermaster General Colonel Henry Stanton (Washington DC), 26 Oct. 1846.
68. Scott, *Memoirs*, 404; HED No. 60, 568. (LOC) 27 Dec. 1846. Jesup to Marcy.
69. Cited in: Antonio Lopez de Santa-Anna, *Apelación al buen criterio de los nacionales y estraneros* (Mexico City: Imprenta Cumplido, 1849), 175.
70. 'Later from Tampico'/'Later from Mexico' *The Sun*, 17 March 1847.
71. Ramón Gamboa, *Impugnación al informe del señor General Antonio Lopez de Santa-Anna, y constancias en que se apoyan las ampliaciones de la acusación del señor diputado Don Ramón Gamboa* (Mexico City: Vicente García Torres, 1849), 3, 22-30.
72. Santa-Anna, *Apelación al buen criterio de los nacionales y estraneros*, 5, 30-1.
73. Ibid. 33-6.
74. Ibid. 5, 8-9.
75. Ancono, *Historia de Yucatán*, vol. 3, 475.
76. Moore, ed. *The Works of James Buchanan*, vol. 7, 222-3. Buchanan to Mason, 22 Feb 1847; Zuleta Miranda, 'Yucatán y la guerra con estados unidos,' 611; 'From Yucatan' *Picayune*, 13 Feb. 1847; 'Affairs in Yucatan' *New York Herald*, 19 March 1847. See: Mary Wilhelmine Williams, 'Secessionist Diplomacy of Yucatan,' *The Hispanic American Historical Review* 9, no. 2 (1929): 132-43.
77. *Diary of James J. Polk*, vol. 2, 392-3, 424-5, 465-7 (26 Feb., 10 March, 10 Apr. respectively)
78. *Diary of James J. Polk*, vol. 2, 471-8. Evidence suggests Polk did not believe in the success of Trist's mission. On 14 April he wrote, 'It will be a good joke if he should assume the authority and take the whole country by surprise & make a Treaty. Mr. Buchanan's strong impression is that he may do so.' (Ibid. 477).
79. *Diary of James J. Polk*, vol. 2, 263. 30 Jan. 1847; Moore, ed. *The Works of James Buchanan*, vol. 7, 212-14. 'Message of President Polk on a Treaty with New Granada' 10 Feb. 1847. Senate Executive Journal, VII. 19,1-193; reprinted in S.Doc. 16,58 Cong. 1 Sess. 13-16. See: 'By the President of the United States of American. A Proclamation.' *Daily Union 16 June 1848*. The Bidlack Treaty laid the diplomatic groundwork for the Panama Canal. See also: John Haskell Kemble, 'The Panamá Route to the Pacific Coast, 1848-1869,' *Pacific Historical Review* 7, no. 1 (1938): 1-13.

80. Moore, ed. *The Works of James Buchanan*, vol. 7, 286–7. 23 April 1847; Bauer, *The Mexican War, 1846-1848*, 338. (Perry seized Lagune on 16/17 May).
81. Griffis, *Matthew Calbraith Perry*, 255–6.
82. Sands, *From Reefer to Rear-Admiral*, 180–2; 'Canal of the Isthmus of Tehuantepec' *Daily Union*, Washington DC, 25 June 1847.
83. Major John G. Barnard, *The Isthmus of Tehuantepec* (New York: D. Appleton and Company, 1852), 167, 11; *Sketch from the mouth of the Coatzacoalcos River to the town of Mina-Titlan; made by order of Commodore M.C. Perry. Comdg. Home Squadron. 1847.* By Lieuts. Alden, Blunt & [William] May. (inset) View of the entrance of the Coatzacoalcos River. (to accompany) *Maps Illustrating The Isthmus of Tehuantepec.* (New York: D. Appleton & Co., 1847). '...pursuant to Major Barnard's instructions, a party under Mr. W. [William] G. Temple, USN., commenced a survey of the Coatzacoalcos River, at Mina-titlan; and another under J.C. Avery was directed to make a reconnaissance at Mt. Encantada, situated on the west bank of the Coatzacoalcos, about 40 miles southwesterly from Mina-titlan, on the route of the proposed survey.' (Barnard, 11) See: *Mouth of the Coatzacoalcos River surveyed Jan. 1848 by order of Com. M.C. Perry. By officers of the US Brig Stromboli.* Engraved by Sherman & Smith, N.Y. (to accompany) *Maps Illustrating The Isthmus of Tehuantepec.* (New York: D. Appleton & Co., 1848); *Map of the Isthmus of Tehuantepec, embracing all the surveys of the engineering & hydrographic parties, and shewing the proposed route of the Tehuantepec Rail Road; surveyed under the direction of Maj. J.G. Barnard US Engrs. Chief Engineer 1851.* (New York: D. Appleton & Co., 1852). Gershom J. Van Brunt was appointed governor of Frontera.
84. 'Canal of the Isthmus of Tehuantepec' *Daily Union*, Washington DC, 25 June 1847.
85. Griffis, *Matthew Calbraith Perry*, 242; Bauer, *The Mexican War*, 342. Griffis counted eleven vessels and 1,084 men, Smith counted nine and 'more than 1,100 men' (vol. 2, 204).
86. Sands, *From Reefer to Rear-Admiral*, 181, 184–5; Bauer, 342.
87. 'The Isthmus of Tehuantepec' *Diario*, 3 June 1847 (vol. 4 no. 83) BNE; 'Isthmus of Tehuantepec' *Weekly National Intelligencer*, Washington DC, 1 May 1847. (Quoting from *Spirit of the Times*)
88. *Diario*, 8 July 1847 (vol. 4 no. 117) BNE; 'Things in Washington' *National Whig*, Washington DC, 17 May 1847.
89. *Diary of James J. Polk*, vol. 3, 23–4. 13 1847; Santelli, *Marines in the Mexican War*, 34–7.
90. 'State of Oaxaca' *Diario*, 20 1847 (vol. 4, no. 129) BNE. *Nueva Era constitucional* article dated 6 July 1847.
91. 'Francisco Ortiz de Zárate, Governor of Oaxaca announces that the news was false concerning the invasion of Tehuantepec by 500 Americans,' (1847): pp. 239–44. *Archivo Historico De La Secretaria De Relaciones Exteriores. Guerra de Texas y La Guerra Mexico - Estados Unidos* (1849) The University of Texas – Rio Grande Valley (UTRGV) Digital Library.
92. 'The Isthmus of Tehuantepec' *Diario*, 28 July 1847 (vol. 4, no. 137) BNE; 'Hands off.' *National Whig*, Washington DC, 12 May 1847. See also: 'Isthmus of Tehuantepec' *Alexandria Gazette*, 13 May 1847; 'Isthmus of Tehuantepec' *Brooklyn Evening Star*, 13 May 1847.
93. Bauer, *The Mexican War, 1846-1848*, 342.
94. Thomas J. Green, *Journal of the Texian expedition against Mier; subsequent imprisonment of the author; his sufferings, and the final escape from castle of Perote* (New York: Harpers, 1845), 142.

95. Ibid., 143
96. Garrison, *Diplomatic Correspondence of the Republic of Texas*, vol. 2, 461–2. Bee to James Webb, 9 July 1839.
97. Scott, *Memoirs*, 413.
98. J.J. McGrath and Walace Hawkins, 'Perote Fort: Where Texans Were Imprisoned,' *The Southwestern Historical Quarterly* 48, no. 3 (Jan. 1945): 344–5.
99. George Wilkins Kendall, *Narrative of the Texan Santa Fé Expedition*, vol. 2 (New York: Harper and Brothers, 1844), 17. See also: See: Ralph A. Wooster, 'Texas Military Operations against Mexico, 1842-1843.' *The Southwestern Historical Quarterly* 67, no. 4 (April 1964): 465-84.
100. Thomas J. Green, *Journal of the Texian expedition against Mier; subsequent imprisonment of the author; his sufferings, and the final escape from castle of Perote* (New York: Harpers, 1845), 373-4.
101. Ibid. 364.
102. Hitchcock, *Fifty Years in Camp and Field*, 263, 339, 342; See: A. Brooke Caruso, *The Mexican Spy Company: United States Covert Operations in Mexico, 1845-48* (Jefferson, NC: McFarland and Company, 1991).

Chapter 3

1. John L. Stephens, *Incidents of Travel in Yucatan*, vol. 1 (New York: Harper and Brothers, 1843), 206–8.
2. Stephens, *Incidents of Travel in Yucatan*, vol. 1, 207. See: Robert Patch, *Maya and Spaniard in Yucatan, 1648–1812* (Stanford: Stanford University Press, 1995); Terry Rugeley, 'The Maya Elites of Nineteenth-Century Yucatán,' *Ethnohistory* 42, no. 3 (1995): 477–93.
3. Nelson Reed, *The Caste War of Yucatan* (1964: Reprint: Stanford University Press, 2001), 68, 5, 107, 141–2. See: Serapio Baqueiro, *Ensayo histórico sobre las revoluciones de Yucatán desde el año 1840 hasta 1864*. 5 vols (Mérida: Manuel Heredia Argüelles, 1878). Baqueiro's seminal work is cited often by Caste War historians.
4. John L. Stephens, *Incidents of travel in Central America, Chiapas, and Yucatan*, 2 vols. (London: John Murray, 1841). See: Gilmar Visoni-Alonzo, *The Carrera Revolt and 'Hybrid Warfare' in Nineteenth-Century Central America* (London: Palgrave Macmillan, 2017).
5. Stephens, *Incidents of Travel in Yucatan*, vol. 2, 191–2.
6. Stephens, *Incidents of travel in Central America*, vol. 2, 377, 72.
7. Ancono, *Historia de Yucatán*, vol.4, 10–11. See: Terry Rugeley, *Yucatan's Maya Peasantry and the Origins of the Caste War, 1800–1847* (Austin: University of Texas Press, 1996), 23.
8. Reed, *The Caste War of Yucatan*, 66–7.
9. 'Yucatan Act' Campeche, 8 December 1846 (USAPP); Ancono, *Historia de Yucatán*, vol.3, 337.
10. Ancono, *Historia de Yucatán*, vol.3, 467–71.
11. Moore, ed. *The Works of James Buchanan*, vol. 7, 222. Buchanan to Mason; Ancono, *Historia de Yucatán*, vol.3, 474. See: Louis De Armond, 'Justo Sierra O'Reilly and Yucatecan-United States Relations, 1847-1848,' *The Hispanic American Historical Review* 31, no. 3 (1951): 420–36.
12. Ancono, *Historia de Yucatán*, vol.4, 13; Terry Rugeley, *Rebellion Now and Forever: Mayas, Hispanics, and Caste War Violence in Yucatán, 1800-1880* (Stanford University Press, 2009), 56.

13. Reed, *The Caste War of Yucatan*, 63–6; Ancono, *Historia de Yucatán*, vol.4, 18–19; Rugeley, *Rebellion Now and Forever*, 58–9.
14. Ancono, *Historia de Yucatán*, vol.4, 18–19; Reed, *The Caste War of Yucatan*, 62–3, 72.
15. Rajeshwari Dutt, 'Business As Usual: Maya and Merchants on Yucatán-Belize border at the Onset of the Caste War,' *The Americas* 74, no. 2 (2017): 201–26; Wayne Clegern, 'British Honduras and the Pacification of Yucatan,' *The Americas* 18, no. 3 (Jan. 1962): 243–54; Richard W. Van Alstyne, 'The Central American Policy of Lord Palmerston, 1846-1848,' *The Hispanic American Historical Review* 16, no. 3 (1936): 339–59.
16. Thomas Young, *Narrative of a Residence on the Mosquito Shore, During the Years 1839, 1840, & 1841: With an Account of Truxillo* [Trujillo] (London: Smith, Elder & Co., 1842), 78.
17. Archibald Robertson Gibbs, *British Honduras: An Historical and Descriptive Account of the Colony from its Settlement, 1670* (London: Sampson Low, Marston, Searle, & Rivingson, 1883), 104–5, 107.
18. Ancono, *Historia de Yucatán*, vol.4, 233; Rugeley, *Rebellion Now and Forever*, 32–3.
19. Rugeley, *Rebellion Now and Forever*, 39–42.
20. Thomas Kanon, '"A slow, Laborious Slaughter": The Battle of Horseshoe Bend,' *Tennessee Historical Quarterly* 58, no. 1 (1999), 12; John K Mahon, 'British Strategy and Southern Indians: War of 1812.' *The Florida Historical Quarterly* 44, no. 4 (1966), 286–88; John Spencer Bassett, ed.' Correspondence of Andrew Jackson, vol. 1 (Washington DC: Carnegie Institute, 1926: Reprint: New York: Kraus Co., 1969), 250. Jackson to Willie Blount (Nashville), 21 Dec. 1812.
21. Conner, *The Home Squadron*, 40; Semmes, *Service afloat*, 84.
22. 'West Indies' *Niles' National Register*, Baltimore, 14 Sept. 1844.
23. *British and Foreign State Papers*, vol. 38, 1849-1850 (London: Harrison and Sons, 1862), 73–6. Viscount Palmerston to Frederick Chatfield (Leon), 29 Feb 1848; 'Proclamation of the Supreme Director of the State of Nicaragua' Leon, 12 Nov. 1847.

Chapter 4

1. SED No.40, 11. Sierra to Buchanan, 7 March 1848.
2. Some of his works, generally published after his death in 1861, include: *Algunas leyendas* (Mérida: La Revista de Mérida, 1892); *Un año en el hospital de San Lazaro* (México: V. Agüeros, 1905); *La hija del judío (novela yucateca)*. (Mérida: Gamboa Guzmán, 1926).
3. Ty West, 'Justo Sierra O'Reilly and John L. Stephens: Translation, History, and Transnational Romanticisms in the Americas,' *Journal of Latin American Cultural Studies* 28, no. 1 (2019), 89.
4. Margaret Swett Henson, *Lorenzo de Zavala: The Pragmatic Idealist* (Fort Worth: Texas University Christian Press, 1996), 17, 102–3; W. S. Cleaves, 'Lorenzo de Zavala in Texas,' *The Southwestern Historical Quarterly* 36, no. 1 (1932), 30–3; Margaret Swett Henson, 'Understanding Lorenzo de Zavala, Signer of the Texas Declaration of Independence,' *The Southwestern Historical Quarterly* 102, no. 1 (1998), 1–5. For Zavala's background, Henson uses: Raymond Estep, *The Life of Lorenzo de Zavala* (Austin: University of Texas, 1942). See: Lorenzo de Zavala, *Viaje a los Estados-Unidos del Norte de America* (Paris: Decourchant, 1834). Zavala's most important work is: *Ensayo histórico de las revoluciones de México, desde 1808 hasta 1830* (Paris: P. Dupont et G.-Languionie, 1831 [vol. 1], Nueva York: Elliot y Palmer, 1832 [vol. 2]).

5. Lorenzo de Zavala, Justo Sierra O'Reilly, *Viaje a los Estados-Unidos del Norte de America* (Merida: Castillo y Compañía, 1846), 3, 10.
6. Ibid. 53–4.
7. Ibid., 190. 'All those who try to make social improvements in the towns that march towards progress, cast their eyes on Great Britain, or on the United States of the North; true and original types of solid and progressive social organizations. But the first, great nation, mistress of the Ocean, depository of immense wealth, fertile in eminent and profound men, still has many steps to take towards a more liberal, more economical order, in short, more independent of the old fetters.' (Ibid., 372)
8. Ibid. 56–7.
9. Héctor Pérez Martínez, ed., Sierra O'Reilly, *Diario de nuestro viaje a los Estados Unidos: la pretendida anexión de Yucatán* (México: Biblioteca Histórica Mexicana de Obras Inéditas, Antigua Librería Robredo, de José Porrúa e Hijos, 1938), 5–8.
10. Ibid., 9, 61–2.
11. O'Reilly, *Diario de nuestro viaje a los Estados Unidos*, 9–11; 'From Yucatan' *American Star*, Mexico City, 25 Sept. 1847 (BLAC). Report from *La Patria*.
12. O'Reilly, *Diario de nuestro viaje a los Estados Unidos*, 12; *Senate Executive Document 40: Message from the President of the United States with communications From the government of Yucatan, representing the state of suffering to which that country is reduced by an insurrection of the Indians, imploring the protection of the United States, and offering, in case it may be granted, to transfer the dominion and sovereignty of the peninsula to the United States* (Washington DC, 30th Congress, 1st Session, 29 April 1848. LOC), 7. (Hereafter: SED No. 40) O'Reilly to Buchanan, 24 Nov. 1847.
13. President Polk's 3rd Annual Message to Congress, 7 Dec. 1847. *Congressional Globe*, 30th Congress, 1st Session, Washington DC (LOC), 6.
14. Ibid., 7. See: John Douglas Pitts Fuller, *The Movement for the Acquisition of All Mexico, 1846-1848* (Baltimore: John Hopkins Press, 1936), 158–9; Swenson, *The Dawn of Guerrilla Warfare*, 152–65; Wallace L. Ohrt, *Defiant Peacemaker: Nicholas Trist and the Mexican War* (College Station: Texas A&M University Press, 1997).
15. Moore, ed. *The Works of James Buchanan*, vol. 7, 485. 24 Dec. 1847.
16. 'Later from Yucatan' *Daily American Star*, Mexico City, 20 Jan. 1848 (BLAC); Reed, *The Caste War*, 83.
17. *Senate Executive Document 43: Message from the President of the United States with Information in Relation to Yucatan, called for by a resolution of the Senate of the 8th* [of May] *Instant.* (Washington DC, 30th Congress, 1st Session, 9 May 1848. LOC) (Hereafter: SED No. 43), 2. Perry to Mason, 30 Jan. 1848; 'Decree of Governor Santiago Méndez,' Maxcanú, 6 February 1848 (USAPP).
18. *Senate Executive Document 42: Message from the President of the United States, With the Correspondence with the Secretary of State, with Don Justo Sierra, representative of Yucatan, called for by a resolution of the Senate.* 5 May 1848 (Washington DC, 30th Congress, 1st Session, 5 May 1848. LOC), 5-7. (Hereafter SED No. 42) See: O'Reilly, *Diario de nuestro viaje a los Estados Unidos*, 81–8. For some reason, O'Reilly's opinion of Perry had considerably soured.
19. SED No. 43, 2–3. Perry to Mason, 15 Feb. 1848 (LOC); 'Guatemala and Honduras' *Daily American Star*, Mexico City, 24 Feb. 1848 (BLAC).
20. SED No. 43, 3–7. Bigelow to Perry, 29 Feb., Perry to Mason, 29 Feb., 1848 (LOC). *Union* article dated 8 Feb.
21. SED No. 43, 4. Bigelow to Perry, 29 Feb.1848 (LOC).

22. *Congressional Globe*, 415 (30th Congress, 1st Session) 4 March 1848 (LOC).
23. O'Reilly, *Diario de nuestro viaje a los Estados Unidos*, 21–2. 1, 2, 6 March; SED No. 40, O'Reilly to Buchanan, 7 March 1848 (LOC). See: Richard K. Crallé, ed., *The Works of John C. Calhoun*, vol. 4 (New York: D. Appleton and Company, 1855), 478. John C. Calhoun, US Senate speech, 15 May 1848. 'Yucatan does not look to Mexico for protection. On the contrary, they are more alarmed at the danger they have to fear from Mexico than from the Indians. Unfortunately for themselves, they assumed a position of neutrality, or, as they say, of independence. They thereby became traitors in the eyes of Mexico; and, no doubt, they will be held responsible as such. Hence we see Mr. Sierra makes a strong remonstrance against the treaty with Mexico.'
24. *Diary of James J. Polk*, vol. 3, 372–4. 7 March 1848. See SED No. 42, 16–17. Mason to Perry, 8 March 1848. (LOC).
25. SED No. 43, 7–9. Perry to Mason, 13 March 1848 (LOC). See: SED No. 43, 22–3. Perry to Mason, 29 March 1848. 'Corporation of the town of Carmen', 13 March 1848. '… soliciting that meanwhile the Indian war continues, the forces of the United States occupying this island may not be withdrawn, but remain for the object in view.'
26. Ancono, *Historia de Yucatán*, vol.4, 96–9; Reed, *The Caste War*, 92.
27. Ancono, *Historia de Yucatán*, vol.4, 99–101; Reed, *The Caste War*, 93.
28. SED No. 43, 19, 26. M. Mason to Perry, 18 March 1848; Bigelow to Perry, 26 March 1848 (LOC).
29. SED No. 43, 27–9. McGregor to Bigelow, 22 March, M. Mason to Bigelow, 22 March, Glasson to M. Mason, 2 April, M. Mason to John Y. Mason, 2 April, 1848 (LOC).
30. SED No. 40, 16–18. O'Reilly to Buchanan, 18 April 1848 (LOC).
31. SED No. 43, 30. Perry to J. Y. Mason, 15 April 1848 (LOC); Ancono, *Historia de Yucatán*, vol. 4, 232.
32. 'Difficulties with England' *The Sun*, Baltimore, 19 April 1848. *The Sun* quoting New York *Star*.
33. SED No. 40, 13. O'Reilly to Buchanan, 3 April 1848 (LOC). See: Frank Lawrence Owsley, 'The Role of the South in the British Grand Strategy in the War of 1812,' *Tennessee Historical Quarterly* 31, no. 1 (1972): 22–38. See also: 'Affairs in Yucatan' *Brooklyn Evening Star*, 11 April 1848. Excerpts of O'Reilly's 3 April letter were made public.
34. SED No. 40, 14–15. O'Reilly to Buchanan, 3 April 1848 (LOC); O'Reilly, *Diario de nuestro viaje a los Estados Unidos*, 23–6.
35. 'California Claims' *National Intelligencer*, Washington DC, 1 April 1848. Dix's senate speech 29 March 1848. For Dix on Guizot, see: *Congressional Globe, 30th Congress*, 252–3. 26 Jan. 1848. See also: Frederick Merk, *The Monroe Doctrine and American Expansionism, 1843-1849* (New York: Alfred A. Knopf, 1966), 50–4.
36. O'Reilly, *Diario de nuestro viaje a los Estados Unidos*, 30. 19 April 1848.

Chapter 5

1. SED No. 40, *Message from the President of the United States with communications From the government of Yucatan*, 2 (LOC).
2. *Diary of James J. Polk*, vol. 3, 430–2. 22 April 1848; O'Reilly, *Diario de nuestro viaje a los Estados Unidos*, 32. 'I informed Mr. Polk of some particularities that he was unaware of, despite having made them known to the Minister in advance, because it is fatal to have powerful people as enemies who can one day serve us in such critical circumstances.'

3. *Diary of James J. Polk*, vol. 3, 433–8, 444–5. 25–29 April 1848; *Congressional Globe*, 712. 29 April 1848 (LOC); O'Reilly, *Diario de nuestro viaje a los Estados Unidos*, 36. Walker expressed interest in annexing Yucatan in a 6 May cabinet meeting.
4. SED No. 40, *Message from the President of the United States with communications From the government of Yucatan*, 2-3; *Congressional Globe*, 709. 29 April 1848 (LOC); 'From Washington' *Public Ledger*, Philadelphia, 2 May 1848.
5. 'Proposed Occupation of Yucatan' *Weekly National Intelligencer*, Washington DC, 13 May 1848.
6. Ibid.
7. Ibid. See: *Diary of James K. Polk*, vol 3., 444. 10 May: 'Senator Douglass of Illinois called with John O'Sullivan, Esqr., of New York. Their business with me was to urge that I would take early measures with a view to the purchase of the Island of Cuba from Spain. I heard their views, but deemed it prudent to express no opinion on the subject … Though I expressed no opinion to them I am decidedly in favour of purchasing Cuba & making it one of the States of the Union.'
8. 'Speech of Mr. Cass' *The Daily Union*, Washington DC, 14 May 1848 (Speech 10 May).
9. *Diary of James K. Polk*, vol. 3, 447. 12 May; 'Speech of Mr. Miller of New Jersey, on the proposed occupation of Yucatan', *Weekly National Intelligencer*, Washington DC, 10 June 1848 (*Congressional Globe* accurately dates Miller's speech to 13 May. pp. 765–6).
10. O'Reilly, *Diario de nuestro viaje a los Estados Unidos*, 42–5. 8–13 May.
11. Crallé, *The Works of John C. Calhoun*, vol. 4 (New York: D. Appleton and Company, 1855), 455–7; *Congressional Globe*, 770 (LOC). 'This [Monroe] declaration, also, belongs to the history of that day.' See: *The Works of John C. Calhoun*, vol. 4, 1174. Former President John Tyler (Sherwood Forest) to Calhoun, 5 June 1848. 'Your explanation of Mr. Monroe's declaration is exceedingly valuable. It was necessary to the truth of history. I confess I never before fully understood it. The measures set forth in your speech for your advocacy of Texas annexation are fully sufficient to justify the adoption of that measure.'
12. Ibid. 458–70.
13. O'Reilly, *Diario de nuestro viaje a los Estados Unidos*, 45–7. 15, 16 May.
14. O'Reilly, *Diario de nuestro viaje a los Estados Unidos*, 47. 17 May.
15. *Congressional Globe*, 777–8. 17 May (LOC); SED No. 45, 4. Mason to Perry, 12 May 1848.
16. O'Reilly, *Diario de nuestro viaje a los Estados Unidos*, 50–3. 19–29 May; 'Affairs in Washington' *New York Herald*, 5 June 1848.
17. Serapio Baqueiro, *Ensayo histórico sobre las revoluciones de Yucatán desde el año 1840 hasta 1864*, vol. 1 (Mérida: Manuel Heredia Argüelles, 1878), 420; 'Important from Yucatan', Correspondence of the Vera Cruz Arco Iris', 'The Yucatan Question' *National Intelligencer*, 20 May 1848; Reed, *The Caste War*, 98–9.
18. Marte R. Gomez, 'Sobre Justo Sierra O'Reilly,' *Historia Mexicana* 3, no. 3 (1954): 320–1.
19. Ancono, *Historia de Yucatán*, vol. 4, 237–46. For Yucatecans selling Mayans as slaves, see: *British and Foreign State Papers*, vol. 37, 1848–1849, 313–16. James Kennedy, British Commissioner at Havana, 18 May, 18 Oct. 1848.
20. Serapio Baqueiro, *Ensayo histórico sobre las revoluciones de Yucatán desde el año 1840 hasta 1864*, vol. 2 (1879), 170–7.
21. Baqueiro, *Ensayo histórico sobre las revoluciones de Yucatán*, 177; 'Later from Honduras and Yucatan' *Daily Union*, Washington DC, 14 May 1848 (via *Picayune* 6 May).

22. US Consul Christopher Hempstead to James Buchanan, 26 May 1848. Despatches From US Consuls in Belize, British Honduras, 1847–1906. NACP, T334 (nos. 11–12); 'Affairs in Yucatan' *The Examiner*, London, 24 June 1848.
23. 'Central America and Yucatan' *New Orleans Weekly Delta*, 22 May, 1848.
24. 'Philadelphia, 16 May' *Morning Chronicle*, London, 31 May 1848.
25. Moore, *The Works of James Buchanan*, vol. 8, 90. 17 June 1848.
26. Ibid., 90–4.
27. Ibid., 99–100.
28. US Consul Christopher Hempstead to James Buchanan, 23 Aug. 1848. Despatches From US Consuls in Belize, British Honduras, 1847–1906. NACP, T334 (nos. 17–22). For Hempstead on arms trade, see: Hempstead to Buchanan, 29 July 1848, T334 (nos. 13–15). For Hempstead with US merchants, see: Hempstead to Buchanan, 20 Jan. 1849. NACP, T334 (no. 27).
29. Moore, *The Works of James Buchanan*, vol. 8, 155–6. 7 Aug. 1848.
30. Irving W. Levinson, *Wars within War: Mexican Guerrillas, Domestic Elites, and the United States of American, 1846-1848* (Fort Worth: TCU Press, 2005), xv.
31. 'Decree of reincorporation of Yucatan to the other states of the Mexican confederation,' Merida, 17 Aug. 1848 (USAPP); Ancono, *Historia de Yucatán*, vol. 4, 247, 276–81.
32. Ancono, *Historia de Yucatán*, vol. 4, 276–84; Rugeley, *Rebellion Now and Forever*, 59.
33. 'Expedition to Yucatan' *Picayune*, New Orleans, 1 Dec. 1848.

Chapter 6

1. 'Yucatan' *The Republic*, Washington DC, Oct. 3, 1849 (via *Picayune*).
2. 'Loss of the United States Schooner On-KA-HY-E' *Daily Evening Transcript*, Boston, 12 July 1848; Sketches of the Island of Jamaica' *Daily Union*, Washington, 12 Dec. 1848.
3. Moore, *The Works of James Buchanan*, vol. 8, 78–84, 380–1; William R. Manning, *Diplomatic Correspondence of The United States, Inter-American Affairs, Vol. 3, Central America, 1831-1850* (Washington DC: Government Printing Office, 1933), 36–7. John M. Clayton, Secretary of State of the US, to Ephraim George Squier, US chargé d'affaires in Guatemala. 1 May 1849.
4. Manning, *Diplomatic Correspondence of The United States, Inter-American Affairs, Vol. 3*, 294–5. Hise to Buchanan, 20 Dec.1848.
5. Manning, *Diplomatic Correspondence*, vol. 3, 295–7. Hise to Buchanan, 20 Dec. 1848, Salinas to Hise, 22, 24 Dec. 1848. Manning notes 'Mr. Henry Savage … does not appear to have been a commissioned consul either, at least within the period covered by this publication [1831–1850], though he is several times referred to as consul, and communications from him are included in the bound volumes of Consular Letters, Guatemala. The only entry regarding him, in the records of the Bureau of Appointments of the Department of State, indicates that he was appointed consul, at Guatemala City, on March 13, 1863, by a recess appointment, which was rejected by the Senate on May 29, 1865.' (Ibid. 193) Although Savage was mentioned in numerous reports in the early 1830s, his first letter as 'charge of the Legation of the United States' was to Daniel Webster, 18 June 1842.
6. *British and Foreign State Papers*, vol. 38, 1849-1850 (London: Harrison and Sons, 1862), 774, 749; Salinas to Viscount Palmerston, 13 March 1848, Vice Admiral Sir F. Austen to Sec. of Admiralty, Jamaica, 5 March 1848; Manning, *Diplomatic Correspondence*, vol. 3, 296. Hise to Buchanan, 20 Dec. 1848.'Important from Central America, Open

Hostilities' *New York Herald*, 23 Feb. 1848. For Salinas to Chatfield, 14 Oct. 1847, see *British and Foreign State Papers*, vol. 38, 771–7.

7. 'Important from Yucatan' *New Orleans Delta*, 22 Jan. 1849; Reed, *The Caste War*, 122–4.
8. Reed, *The Caste War*, 124; Edward H. Thompson, 'A Page of History' *Paper Read Before the American Antiquarian Society*, 12. Worcester, Mass., 21 October 1905.
9. Thompson, 'A Page of History' *Paper Read Before the American Antiquarian Society*, 12–13.
10. 'Our Volunteers in Yucatan' / 'From Yucatan' *New Orleans Delta*, 19 March 1849. First article reported by Captain Tobin, Valladolid, 18 Jan. 1849; 'Interesting from Yucacan' *New York Herald*, 19 April 1849.
11. 'Late From Yucatan – Capture of Bacalar' *Charleston Courier*, 26 May 1849. (*Picayune*, 30 May); 'Later from Yucatan and Central America' *New Orleans Delta*, 1 Oct. 1849; *Daily News*, London, 19 Dec. 1849.
12. 'Intelligence from Mexico' *New York Herald*, 23 June 1849 (via *American Star*, 30 May).
13. Ancono, *Historia de Yucatán*, vol. 4, 260–4.
14. 'Bridging the Continent' *The Sun*, Baltimore, 20 Jan. 1849. See: H. W. Brands, *The Age of Gold: The California Gold Rush and the New American Dream* (New York: Anchor Books, 2002).
15. Joseph P. Comegys, *Memoir of John M. Clayton* (Wilmington: Historical Society of Delaware, 1882), 190; 'Important from Central America – Aggressions of the British' *New York Herald*, 27 Dec. 1849.
16. *Diplomatic Correspondence*, vol. 3, 324–5. Buenaventura Selva, Nicaraguan chargé d'affaires in Guatemala to Hise (Guatemala City), 5 June 1849.
17. *Diplomatic Correspondence*, vol. 3, 328–31; Hise (Guatemala City) to Selva, 6 June 1849.
18. *Diplomatic Correspondence*, vol. 3, 316, 360–1; Squier (New York) to Clayton, 16 April 1849, Squier (Leon, Nicaragua) to Clayton, 10 Sept. 1849. See: Mario Rodríguez, 'The 'Prometheus' and the Clayton-Bulwer Treaty,' *The Journal of Modern History* 36, no. 3 (1964): 260–78.
19. *Diplomatic Correspondence*, vol. 3, 335. Squier (Guatemala) to Clayton, 23 June 1849; Ephraim G. Squier, *Nicaragua; Its people, scenery, monuments and the proposed interoceanic canal*, vol. 1 (New York: D. Appleton & Co., 1852), 78.
20. Moore, *The Works of James Buchanan*, vol. 8, 78–9. Buchanan's instructions to Hise, 3 June 1848; *Diplomatic Correspondence*, vol. 3, 352. Squier (Leon) to Clayton, 20 Aug. 1849; Ephraim G. Squier, *Nicaragua; Its people, scenery, monuments and the proposed interoceanic canal*, vol. 2 (New York: D. Appleton & Co., 1852), 135.
21. *Diplomatic Correspondence*, vol. 3, 352. Squier (Leon) to Clayton, 20 Aug. 1849; Squier, *Nicaragua; Its people*, 99.
22. *Diplomatic Correspondence*, vol. 3, 353–5. Squier (Leon) to French Consul General in Central America, 12 Aug. 1848, Squier (Leon) to the Commander of the United States Squadron on the west coast of Central America, 13 Aug. 1849.
23. 'Washington, Oct. 9' *New Orleans Delta*, 22 Oct. 1849; 'Mr. Benjamin's Speech' *New Orleans Delta*, 8 Oct. 1849.
24. *Diplomatic Correspondence*, vol. 3, 393, 403–4. Squier to Clayton, 10 Oct. 1849.
25. 'Our relations with Nicaragua – Queer Doings of the Secretary of State' *New York Herald*. 17 Oct. 1849.
26. 'Nicaragua' *The Republic*, Washington DC, 22 Oct. 1849.
27. *The Times*, London, 13 October 1849.

28. Squier, *Nicaragua; Its people, scenery, monuments and the proposed interoceanic canal*, vol. 2, 168, 244; Edward Belcher, *Narrative of a Voyage Around the World* (London: Henry Colburn, 1843), 306–7.
29. Squier, *Nicaragua*, vol. 2, 234–8, 168; *The Times*, London, 13 Feb. 1849.
30. *Diplomatic Correspondence*, vol. 3, 399–402. Squier (Leon) to Clayton, 10 Oct. 1849; Squier, *Nicaragua*, vol. 2, 244, 168.
31. *The Times*, London, 21 Nov. 1849. Hickson, G. F. 'Palmerston and the Clayton-Bulwer Treaty,' *Cambridge Historical Journal* 3, no. 3 (1931): 295–303.
32. 'Annexation of Tigre Island, in the Gulf of Fonseca, to the United States' *Daily Union*, Washington, 20 Nov. 1849.
33. Ibid.
34. *Diplomatic Correspondence*, vol. 3, 418. Vicente Lechuga, Comandante of the port of Amapala, Tigre Island, Honduras, to the General-in-chief, 16 Oct. 1849 (attached in report from Squier to Clayton, 25 Oct. 1849).
35. *Diplomatic Correspondence*, vol. 3, 416, 427. Squier (Leon) to Chatfield, 23 Oct. 1849; Chatfield (*Gorgon*) to Squier, 25 Oct. 1849. See (Ibid. 344): Squier to Francisco Ferrer, Director of Honduras, 16 Aug. 1849: 'Great Britain has determined, in pursuance of the policy which led her to seize upon the Island of Roatan, and the Port of San Juan – to take possession of the island of Tigre in the gulf of Fonseca. The pretext for this extraordinary proceeding is the alleged indebtedness of Honduras to England or British subjects.'
36. 'Highly Important from Honduras' *The Republic*, Washington DC, 14 Dec. 1849. J. Maria Monada, Tegucigalpa, 21 Oct. 1849; 'The Tiger Island Affair' *Daily Union*, Washington DC. Quoting *Boston Courier*, 13 Dec.
37. Moore, *The Works of James Buchanan*, vol. 8, 377–81. Buchanan to Francis J. Grund, 13 April 1850.
38. *Diplomatic Correspondence*, vol. 3, 61. Clayton to Squier, 7 May 1850.
39. *Congressional Globe*, 31st Congress, 2nd Session, 2. 2 Dec 1850.
40. Robert E. May, *Manifest Destiny's Underworld: Filibustering in Antebellum America* (Chapel Hill: University of North Carolina Press, 2002), 124.
41. See: Daniel J. Burge, *A Failed Vision of Empire: The Collapse of Manifest Destiny, 1845-1872*, 2. 'These conflicting takes [on meaning of the term] demonstrate the wide divergence between those who wrote about manifest destiny in the nineteenth century and those who have examined it in the early twenty-first. But what explains these vastly different interpretations? The simple answer is that the definition of manifest destiny changed over time.'
42. Rives, *The United States and Mexico, 1821-1848*, vol. 1 (New York: Charles Scribner's Sons, 1913), vi.
43. Semmes, *Service afloat and ashore during the Mexican War*, 22.

Bibliography

Abbreviations
BLAC: Nettie Lee Benson Latin American Collection, University of Texas, Austin
BNE: Biblioteca Nacional de España (Madrid)
DCRT: Diplomatic Correspondence of the Republic of Texas
JMH: Journal of Military History
LOC: Library of Congress
NACP: National Archives College Park
USAPP: University of St. Andrews Pronunciamiento Project
UTRGV: The University of Texas, Rio Grande Valley

Newspapers
American
Alexandria Gazette
American Republican and Baltimore Daily Clipper
Brooklyn Evening Star
Carlisle Herald and Expositor, PA
Charleston Mercury
Daily American Star, Mexico City
Daily Evening Transcript, Boston
Daily Richmond Times
Morning Courier, Louisville
Nashville Union
National Whig, Washington DC
New Orleans Bulletin
New Orleans Weekly Delta
New York Herald
Niles' National Register, Baltimore
Picayune, New Orleans
Public Ledger, Philadelphia
Republican Banner, Nashville
Richmond Daily Whig
Richmond Enquirer
The Evening Post, New York City
The Daily Union, Washington
The Liberator, Boston
The National Gazette, Philadelphia
The Republic, Washington DC
The Somerset Herald (PA)
The Sun, Baltimore

Washington Globe
Weekly National Intelligencer, Washington DC

British
Daily News, London
Morning Chronicle, London
The Examiner, London
The Observer, London
The Times, London

Mexican
Conciliador, Xalapa
Diario del Gobierno de la República Mexicana, Mexico City
El Arco Iris, Veracruz

Primary Sources
Adams, Charles Francis, ed. *Memoirs of John Quincy Adams, Comprising Portions of His Diary from 1795 to 1848*, vol. 11. Philadelphia: J.B. Lippincott & Co., 1876.
Adams, Ephraim Douglas, ed. *British Interests and Activities in Texas, 1836–1846*. Baltimore: The Johns Hopkins Press, 1910.
—— ed., *British Diplomatic Correspondence Concerning the Republic of Texas – 1838–1846*. Austin: Texas State Historical Association, 1918.
Alamán, Lucas. *Historia de Méjico desde los primeros movimientos que prepararon su independencia en el año de 1808, hasta la época presente*, vol. 5. Méjico: J.M. Lara, 1852.
Ancono, Eligio. *Historia de Yucatán, desde la época más remota hasta nuestros días*, vols. 3–4. Merida: M. Heredia Argüelles, 1879.
Archivo Historico De La Secretaria De Relaciones Exteriores. Guerra de Texas y La Guerra Mexico - Estados Unidos(1849), 'Francisco Ortiz de Zárate, Governor of Oaxaca announces that the news was false concerning the invasión of Tehuantepec by 500 Americans,' (1847): pp.239–244. UTRGV Digital Library, The University of Texas – Rio Grande Valley. BD0025-L-E-1090. Accessed:https://scholarworks.utrgv.edu/guerra/March 4, 2023.
Ballentine, George. *The Mexican War, By an English Soldier. Comprising incidents and adventures in the United States and Mexico with the American army.* New York: W.A. Townsend & Company, 1860.
Baqueiro, Serapio. *Ensayo histórico sobre las revoluciones de Yucatán desde el año 1840 hasta 1864*.Vols. 1–2. Mérida: Manuel Heredia Argüelles, 1878–9.
Barnard, Major John G. *The Isthmus of Tehuantepec*. New York: D. Appleton and Company, 1852.
Bassett, John Spencer, ed. Correspondence of Andrew Jackson, Vol. 1. Washington DC: Carnegie Institute, 1926: Reprint: New York: Kraus Co., 1969.
Belcher, Edward. *Narrative of a Voyage around the World*. London: Henry Colburn, 1843.
Biblioteca Nacional de España: Hemeroteca Digital (BNE). Accessed: 28 Jan.–5 Oct. 2023. http://www.bne.es/es/Catalogos/HemerotecaDigital/
Blunt, Edmund March and G.W. Blunt. *The American Coast Pilot: containing directions for the principal harbors, capes and headlands, on the coasts of North and South America*. New York: Edmund and George W. Blunt, 1847.
Brackett, Albert G. *General Lane's Brigade in Central Mexico*. Cincinnati: H.W. Derby & Company, 1854.

British and Foreign State Papers, vols. 37–38, 1848–1850. London: Harrison and Sons, 1862.

Cohen, Myer M. *Notices of Florida and the Campaigns*. Charleston, SC: Burger & Honour, Charleston, 1836.

Congressional Globe, Library of Congress (LOC), 28th–31st Congress, Washington DC, 1844–1850.

Comegys, Joseph P. *Memoir of John M. Clayton*. Wilmington: Historical Society of Delaware, 1882.

Cooper, James Fenimore. *History of the Navy of the United States of America*. New York: G.P. Putnam, 1853.

Crallé, Richard K., ed. *The Works of John C. Calhoun*, vol. 4. New York: D. Appleton and Company, 1855.

Foote, Henry Stuart. *Texas and the Texans: or, advance of the Anglo-Americans to the southwest; including a history of leading events in Mexico, from the conquest by Fernando Cortes to the termination of the Texan revolution*, vol. 2. Philadelphia: Thomas, Cowperthwait & Co., 1841.

Gamboa, Ramón. *Impugnación al informe del señor General Antonio Lopez de Santa-Anna, y constancias en que se apoyan las ampliaciones de la acusación del señor diputado Don Ramón Gamboa*. Mexico: Vicente García Torres, 1849.

Garay, José de. *Survey of the Isthmus of Tehuantepec, Executed in the Years 1842 and 1843 with the Intent of establishing a communication between the Atlantic and Pacific Oceans*. London: Ackermann and Company, 1844.

Garrison, George P., ed. *Diplomatic Correspondence of the Republic of Texas (Annual Report of the American Historical Association for the Year 1908)*, vol. 2. Washington Government Printing Office, 1911.

Grant, Ulysses S. *Personal Memoirs of US Grant*, vol. 1. New York: Charles L. Webster & Company, 1885.

Green, Thomas J. *Journal of the Texian expedition against Mier; subsequent imprisonment of the author; his sufferings, and the final escape from castle of Perote*. New York: Harpers, 1845.

Griffis, William Elliot. *Matthew Calbraith Perry: a typical American naval officer*. Boston: Cupples and Hurd, 1887.

Halleck, Henry. *Military Art and Science; or Course of Instruction in Strategy, Fortification, Tactics of Battles, &c; Embracing the Duties of Staff Infantry, Cavalry, Artillery, and Engineers, Adapted to the Use of Volunteers and Militia*. New York: D. Appleton & Company, 1846.

Hitchcock, Ethan Allen. *Fifty Years in Camp and Field*. New York: Ed. W.A. Croffut. G.P. Putnam's Sons, 1909.

House Executive Document No. 59. Correspondence between the Secretary of War and General Scott. Washington DC, 30th Congress, 1st Session, 26 April 1848.

House Executive Document No. 60. Mexican War Correspondence. Washington DC, 30th Congress, 1st Session, 28 April 1848.

Howe, M.A. De Wolfe, ed., *The Life and Letters of George Bancroft*, vol. 1. New York: Charles Scribner's Sons, 1908.

Johnson, Timothy D., and Nathanial Cheairs Hughes Jr., eds. *Notes of the Mexican War, 1846–1848, J. Jacob Oswandel*. Knoxville: University of Tennessee Press, 2010.

Jones, Charles Colcock. The *Life and services of Commodore Tattnall*. Savanna: Morning News Steam Printing, 1878.

Kenly, John Reese. *Memoirs of a Maryland volunteer. War with Mexico, in the years 1846–8*. Philadelphia: J.B. Lippincott, 1872.

Kennedy, William. *Texas: The Rise, Progress, and Prospects of the Republic of Texas*, 1841. Reprint: Fort Worth, TX: The Molyneaux Craftsmen, 1925.

Law, Robert A., and A. M. Manigault. 'A Letter from Vera Cruz in 1847.' *The Southwestern Historical Quarterly* 18, no. 2 (1914): 215–18.

Lundy, Benjamin. *The War in Texas; a review of the facts and circumstances showing that this contest is a crusade against Mexico, set on foot and supported by slaveholders, land-speculators, &c. in order to re-establish, extend, and perpetuate the system of slavery and the slave trade.* Philadelphia: Merrihew and Gunn, 1837.

Manning, William R. ed. *Diplomatic Correspondence of The United States, Inter-American Affairs, Vol. 3, Central America, 1831–1850.* Washington DC: Government Printing Office, 1933.

Maps Illustrating The Isthmus of Tehuantepec. New York: D. Appleton & Co., 1847.

Martínez, Héctor Pérez, ed., Sierra O'Reilly, *Diario de nuestro viaje a los Estados Unidos: la pretendida anexión de Yucatán.* México: Biblioteca Histórica Mexicana de Obras Inéditas, Antigua Librería Robredo, de José Porrúa e Hijos, 1938.

Meade, George. *The Life and Letters of George Gordon Meade*, vol. 1. New York: Charles Scribner's Sons, 1913.

Mendívil, José María Tornel. *Discurso pronunciado por el exmo. sr. general ministro de guerra y marina don José Maria Tornel en la sesión del 12 de octubre de 1842 del Congreso constituyente. en apoyo del dictamen de la mayorá de la comisión de constitucioń del mismo.* México [DF]: José M. Lara, 1842.

National Archives and Records Administration (NACP), College Park, MD. https://catalog.archives.gov/ accessed 1 Feb.– 30 May 2023:

    Despatches From US Consuls in Belize, British Honduras, 1847–1906. (T334, National Archives Identifier, Control No. 212003133), National Archives and Records at College Park, MD.

    Despatches from US Consuls in Campeche, Mexico, 1820–1880 (M286, National Archives Identifier, Control No. 211163371).

    Despatches From US Consuls in Ciudad del Carmen, Mexico, 1830–1872. (M308, National Archives Identifier, Control No. 211205113), National Archives and Records at College Park, MD.

    Despatches from US Consuls in Havana, Cuba, 1783–1906. (M899, National Archives Identifier, Control No. 211325581), National Archives and Records at College Park, MD.

    Despatches From US Consuls in Merida, 1843–1897, and Progreso, Mexico, 1897–1906, 1843–1906. (M287, National Archives Identifier, Control No. 211164220).

Oswandel, J[ohn]. Jacob. *Notes of the Mexican war 1846–47–48. Comprising incidents, adventures and everyday proceedings and letters while with the United States army in the Mexican war.* Philadelphia, 1885.

Otero, Mariano. *Ensayo sobre el verdadero estado de la cuestion social y politica que se agita en la República Mexicana.* México [DF]: Ignacio Cumplido, 1842.

Quaife, Milo (ed.). *The Diary of James J. Polk during his Presidency, 1845–1849. 4 Vols.* Chicago: A.C. McClurg & Co., 1910.

Robinson, William Davis. *Memoirs of the Mexican Revolution: including a narrative of the expedition of General Xavier Mina: with some observations on the practicability of opening a commerce between the Pacific and Atlantic Oceans, through the Mexican Isthmus in the Province of Oaxaca, and at the Lake of Nicaragua, and on the future importance of such commerce to the civilized world, and more especially to the United States.* Philadelphia: Lydia R. Bailey, 1820.

Sands, Benjamin Franklin. *From Reefer to Rear-Admiral.* New York: Frederick A. Stokes, 1899.

Santa-Anna, Antonio Lopez de. *Apelación al buen criterio de los nacionales y estraneros*. Mexico: Imprenta Cumplido, 1849.

Scott, Lieutenant General Winfield. *Memoirs*. New York: Sheldon, 1864.

Semmes, Raphael. *Service afloat and ashore during the Mexican War*. Cincinnati: WM. H. Moore & Co., 1851.

Senate Executive Document 40: Message from the President of the United States with communications From the government of Yucatan, representing the state of suffering to which that country is reduced by an insurrection of the Indians, imploring the protection of the United States, and offering, in case it may be granted, to transfer the dominion and sovereignty of the peninsula to the United States. Washington DC, 30th Congress, 1st Session, 29 April 1848.

Senate Executive Document 42: Message from the President of the United States, With the Correspondence with the Secretary of State, with Don Justo Sierra, representative of Yucatan, called for by a resolution of the Senate. 5 May 1848. Washington DC, 30th Congress, 1st Session, 5 May 1848.

Senate Executive Document 43: Message from the President of the United States with Information in Relation to Yucatan, called for by a resolution of the Senate of the 8th [of May] *Instant*. Washington DC, 30th Congress, 1st Session, 9 May 1848.

Seward, Frederick W. *William H. Seward: an autobiography from 1801 to 1834, with a Memoir of his Life and Selections of His Letters, 1831–1846*. (1877) Reprint: New York: Derby and Miller, 1891.

Shanks, Henry Thomas, ed. *The Papers of Willie Person Mangum*, vol. 4. Raleigh: State Department of Archives and History, 1955.

Squier, Ephraim G. *Nicaragua; Its people, scenery, monuments and the proposed interoceanic canal*, 2 Vols. New York: D. Appleton & Co., 1852.

Stapp, William Preston. *The prisoners of Perote: containing a journal kept by the author, who was captured by the Mexicans at Mier, December 25, 1842, and released from Perote, May 16, 1844*. Philadelphia, G. B. Zieber and Company, 1845.

Stephens, John L. *Incidents of travel in Central America, Chiapas, and Yucatan*, 2 vols. London: John Murray, 1841.

——— *Incidents of Travel in Yucatan*, 2 vols. New York: Harper and Brothers, 1843.

Thompson, Edward H. 'A Page of History'. *Paper Read Before the American Antiquarian Society*. Worcester, Mass., 21 October 1905: 1–14.

University of St. Andrews Pronunciamiento Project (USAPP), Mexican War Pronunciamientos. Arts and Humanities Council (AHRC), 2007–2010. Accessed Dec. 24, 2022-Feb. 20, 2023. https://arts.st-andrews.ac.uk/pronunciamientos.

Williams, Amelia W., and Eugene C. Barker, ed. *The Writings of Sam Houston, 1821–1847*, vol. 4. Austin: University of Texas Press, 1941.

Woodburne, Potter. *The war in Florida: being an exposition of its causes, and an accurate history of the campaigns of Generals Clinch, Gaines, and Scott*. Baltimore: Lewis and Coleman, 1836.

Young, Thomas. *Narrative of a Residence on the Mosquito Shore, During the Years 1839, 1840, & 1841: With an Account of Truxillo* [Trujillo]. London: Smith, Elder & Co., 1842.

Zavala, Lorenzo de. *Viaje a los Estados-Unidos del Norte de America*. Paris: Decourchant, 1834.

Zavala, Lorenzo de, Justo Sierra O'Reilly. *Viaje a los Estados-Unidos del Norte de America*. Merida: Castillo y Compañía, 1846.

Secondary Sources

Bauer, Karl Jack. *The Mexican War, 1846–1848* (1974): Reprint: Lincoln and London: University of Nebraska Press, 1992.

―― *Surfboats and Horse Marines: US Naval Operations in the Mexican War, 1846–48.* Annapolis: US Naval Institute, 1969.

Bárcena, José María Roa. *Recuerdos de la invasión norte-americana, 1846–1848.* Mexico: Librería Madrileña de San Buxó, 1883.

Brands, H.W. *The Age of Gold: The California Gold Rush and the New American Dream.* New York: Anchor Books, 2002.

Burge, Daniel J. *A Failed Vision of Empire: The Collapse of Manifest Destiny, 1845–1872.* Lincoln: University of Nebraska Press, 2022.

Caruso, A. Brooke. *The Mexican Spy Company: United States Covert Operations in Mexico, 1845–48.* Jefferson, NC: McFarland and Company, 1991.

Conner, Philip S. *The Home Squadron under Commodore Conner in the War with Mexico.* Philadelphia: 1896.

Dienst, Alex. *The Navy of the Republic of Texas.* Temple, TX, 1909.

Elleman, Bruce A., S.C.M. Paine, eds. *Naval Power and Expeditionary Wars: Peripheral Campaigns and New Theatres of naval warfare.* New York: Routledge, 2011.

Estep, Raymond. *The Life of Lorenzo de Zavala.* Austin: University of Texas, 1942.

Fowler, William. *Malcontents, Rebels, and Pronunciados: The Politics of Insurrection in Nineteenth-Century Mexico.* Lincoln: University of Nebraska Press, 2012.

―― *Santa Anna of Mexico.* Lincoln: University of Nebraska Press, 2007.

―― *Tornel and Santa Anna: The Writer and the Caudillo.* Westport, Conn: Greenwood Press, 2000.

Fuller, John Douglas Pitts. *The Movement for the Acquisition of All Mexico, 1846–1848.* Baltimore: John Hopkins Press, 1936.

Gibbs, Archibald Robertson. *British Honduras: An Historical and Descriptive Account of the Colony from its Settlement, 1670.* London: Sampson Low, Marston, Searle, & Rivingson, 1883.

Johannsen, Robert W. *To the Halls of the Montezumas: The Mexican War in the American Imagination.* New York: Oxford University Press, 1985.

Kinchen, Oscar A. *The Rise and Fall of the Patriot Hunters.* New York: Bookman Associates, 1956.

Levinson, Irving W. *Wars within War: Mexican Guerrillas, Domestic Elites, and the United States of American, 1846–1848.* Fort Worth: TCU Press, 2005.

May, Robert E. *Manifest Destiny's Underworld: Filibustering in Antebellum America.* Chapel Hill: University of North Carolina Press, 2002.

Merk, Frederick. *The Monroe Doctrine and American Expansionism, 1843–1849.* New York: Alfred A. Knopf, 1966.

Nevins, Allan. *Frémont, Pathmarker of the West.* New York: D. Appleton-Century Company, 1939.

Ohrt, Wallace L. *Defiant Peacemaker: Nicholas Trist and the Mexican War.* College Station: Texas A&M University Press, 1997.

Patch, Robert. *Maya and Spaniard in Yucatan, 1648–1812.* Stanford: Stanford University Press, 1995.

Pletcher, David M. *The Diplomacy of Annexation: Texas, Oregon, and the Mexican War.* Columbia: University of Missouri Press, 1973.

Reed, Nelson. *The Caste War of Yucatan.* (1964) Reprint: Stanford University Press, 2001.

Rives, George Lockhart. *The United States and Mexico, 1821–1848.* 2 Vols. New York: Charles Scribner's Sons, 1913.

Rugeley, Terry. *Rebellion Now and Forever: Mayas, Hispanics, and Caste War Violence in Yucatán, 1800–1880.* Stanford University Press, 2009.
—— *Yucatan's Maya Peasantry and the Origins of the Caste War, 1800–1847.*
—— Austin: University of Texas Press, 1996.
Santelli, Gabrielle M. Neufeld. *Marines in the Mexican War.* Washington DC: History and Museums Division Headquarters, US Marines Corps, 1991.
Schwarz, Ted, Robert H. Thonhoff, ed., *Forgotten Battlefield of the First Texas Revolution: The Battle of Medina, August 18, 1813.* Fort Worth: Eakin Press, 1985.
Smith, Justin H. *The War with Mexico*, 2 vols. New York: Macmillan, 1919.
Sutcliffe, Robert K. *British Expeditionary Warfare and the Defeat of Napoleon, 1793–1815.* Woodbridge, UK: The Boydell Press, 2016.
Swenson, Benjamin J. *The Dawn of Guerrilla Warfare: Why the Tactics of Insurgents against Napoleon failed in the US Mexican War.* Barnsley, UK: Pen and Sword, 2023.
Visoni-Alonzo, Gilmar. *The Carrera Revolt and 'Hybrid Warfare' in Nineteenth-Century Central America.* London: Palgrave Macmillan, 2017.
Wells, Tom Henderson. *Commodore Moore and the Texas Navy.* Austin: University of Texas Press, 1960.

Articles

Alstyne, Richard W. van. 'The Central American Policy of Lord Palmerston, 1846–1848.' *The Hispanic American Historical Review* 16, no. 3 (1936): 339–59.
Arnold, Linda. 'Too Few Ships, Too Few Guns, and Not Enough Money: The Mexican Navy, 1846–1848.' *The Northern Mariner/Le Marin du nord* 9, no. 2 (April 1999): 1–10.
Bauer, Karl Jack. 'The Veracruz Expedition of 1847.' *Military Affairs* 20, no. 3 (1956): 162–9.
Bonthius, Andrew. 'The Patriot War of 1837–1838: Locofocoism with a Gun?' *Labour/Le Travail* 52 (2003): 9–43
Carter, J. C. 'One Way Ticket to a Penal Colony: North American Political Prisoners in Van Diemen's Land.' *Ontario History* 101, No. 2 (Autumn 2009), 188–221.
Clark, Paul C., and Edward H. Moseley. 'D-Day Veracruz, 1847 – A Grand Design.' *Joint Forces Quarterly* (Winter 1995–96): 103–15.
Cleaves, W. S. 'Lorenzo de Zavala in Texas.' *The Southwestern Historical Quarterly* 36, no. 1 (1932): 29–40.
Clegern, Wayne M. 'British Honduras and the Pacification of Yucatan.' *The Americas* 18, no. 3 (1962): 243–54.
Costeloe, Michael P. 'The Mexican Press of 1836 and the Battle of the Alamo.' *The Southwestern Historical Quarterly* 91, no. 4 (1988): 533–43.
—— 'The Triangular Revolt in Mexico and the Fall of Anastasio Bustamante, August-October 1841.' *Journal of Latin American Studies* 20, no. 2 (1988): 337–60.
Crapol, Edward P. 'John Tyler and the Pursuit of National Destiny.' *Journal of the Early Republic* 17, no. 3 (1997): 467–91.
De Armond, Louis. 'Justo Sierra O'Reilly and Yucatecan-United States Relations, 1847–1848.' *The Hispanic American Historical Review* 31, no. 3 (1951): 420–36.
Diaz, Maria Angela. 'To Conquer the Coast: Pensacola, the Gulf of Mexico, and the Construction of American Imperialism, 1820–1848.' *The Florida Historical Quarterly* 95, no. 1 (2016): 1–25.
Dutt, Rajeshwari. 'Business As Usual: Maya and Merchants on Yucatán-Belize Border at the Onset of the Caste War.' *The Americas* 74, no. 2 (2017): 201–26
Fuentes, Andrés Reséndez. 'Guerra e Identidad Nacional.' *Historia Mexicana* 47, no. 2 (1997): 411–39.

Gomez, Marte R. 'Sobre Justo Sierra O'Reilly.' *Historia Mexicana* 3, no. 3 (1954): 309–27.
Hall, Claude H. 'Abel P. Upshur and the Navy as an Instrument of Foreign Policy.' *The Virginian Magazine of History and Biography* 69, no. 3 (1961): 290–9.
Hammond, John Hays. 'José María Roa Bárcena: Mexican Writer and Champion of Catholicism.' *The Americas* 6, no. 1 (1949): 45–55.
Henson, Margaret Swett. 'Understanding Lorenzo de Zavala, Signer of the Texas Declaration of Independence.' *The Southwestern Historical Quarterly* 102, no. 1 (1998): 1–17
Hickson, G. F. 'Palmerston and the Clayton-Bulwer Treaty.' *Cambridge Historical Journal* 3, no. 3 (1931): 295–303.
Hovey, Edmund Otis. 'The Isthmus of Tehuantepec and the Tehuantepec National Railway.' *Bulletin of the American Geographical Society* 39 (1907): 78–91.
Hoy, Bill. 'War in Papaguería: Manuel Gándara's 1840–41 Papago Expedition.' *The Journal of Arizona History* 35, no. 2 (1994): 141–62.
Jackson, Jack. 'General Taylor's "Astonishing" Map of Northeastern Mexico,' *The Southwestern Historical Quarterly* 101, no. 2 (1997): 143–73.
Kanon, Thomas. '"A slow, Laborious Slaughter": The Battle of Horseshoe Bend.' *Tennessee Historical Quarterly* 58, no. 1 (1999): 2–15.
Kemble, John Haskell. 'The Panamá Route to the Pacific Coast, 1848–1869.' *Pacific Historical Review* 7, no. 1 (1938): 1–13.
Mahon, John K. 'British Strategy and Southern Indians: War of 1812.' *The Florida Historical Quarterly* 44, no. 4 (1966): 285–302.
McClendon, Earl R. McClendon, 'Daniel Webster and Mexican Relations: The Santa Fe Prisoners.' *The Southwestern Historical Quarterly* 36, no. 4 (1933): 288–311.
McGrath, J.J and Walace Hawkins, 'Perote Fort: Where Texans Were Imprisoned.' *The Southwestern Historical Quarterly* 48, no. 3 (Jan. 1945): 344–5.
Nance, Joseph Milton. 'Adrian Woll: Frenchman in the Mexican Military Service.' *New Mexico Historical Review* 33, 3 (1958): 177–86.
Owsley, Frank Lawrence. 'The Role of the South in the British Grand Strategy in the War of 1812.' *Tennessee Historical Quarterly* 31, no. 1 (1972): 22–38.
Rodríguez, Mario. 'The 'Prometheus' and the Clayton-Bulwer Treaty.' *The Journal of Modern History* 36, no. 3 (1964): 260–78.
Rugeley, Terry. 'The Maya Elites of Nineteenth-Century Yucatán.' *Ethnohistory* 42, no. 3 (1995): 477–93.
—— 'The Outsider' in *The River People in Flood Time: The Civil Wars in Tabasco, Spoiler of Empires*. Redwood City: Stanford University Press, 2014: 109–48.
Smith, Justin H. 'The Mexican Recognition of Texas.' *The American Historical Review* 16, no. 1 (Oct. 1910): 36–55.
Stenberg, Richard R., and Archibald H. Gillespie. 'Further Letters of Archibald H. Gillespie: October 20, 1845, to January 16, 1846, to the Secretary of the Navy.' *California Historical Society Quarterly* 18, no. 3 (1939): 217–28.
—— 'Polk and Frémont, 1845–1846.' *Pacific Historical Review* 7, no. 3 (Sept. 1938): 211–27.
—— 'The Failure of Polk's Mexican War Intrigue.' *Pacific Historical Review* 4, no. 1 (Mar. 1935): 39–68.
—— Swenson, Benjamin J. '"Measures of Conciliation": Winfield Scott, Henry Halleck, and the Origins of US Army Counterinsurgency Doctrine.' *Journal of Military History* 86, no. 4 (Oct. 2022): 859–81.
Tamayo, Jorge L. 'Contenido de La Geografía.' *Investigación Económica* 8, no. 1 (1948): 1–28.

Watson, S.J. 'Knowledge, Interest and the Limits of Military Professionalism: The Discourse on American Coastal Defence, 1815–1860.' *War in History* 5, no. 3 (1998): 280–307.

West, Ty. 'Justo Sierra O'Reilly and John L. Stephens: Translation, History, and Transnational Romanticisms in the Americas.' *Journal of Latin American Cultural Studies* 28, no. 1 (2019):83–96.

Williams, Mary Wilhelmine. 'Secessionist Diplomacy of Yucatan.' *The Hispanic American Historical Review* 9, no. 2 (1929): 132–43.

Zuleta Miranda, María Cecilia. 'El federalismo en Yucatán: Política y militarización (1840–1946).' *Secuencia, Nueva época* 31 (1995): 23–50.

—— 'Yucatán y la guerra con estados unidos: ¿Una neutralidad anunciada?' in *México al tiempo de su guerra con Estados Unidos(1846–1848)* (El Colegio de México, 1997): 578–615.

Index

Aberdeen, Lord (George Hamilton-Gordon), xxii, xxv, 10–11
Acayucan, xxviii
Adams, John Quincy, 1–2, 19
Alabama, xxv, 85,
Alabama (ship), 96
Alamo (Siege of), 15
Algiers (French invasion of), 50–3
All-Mexico movement, 102, 109–10, 119
Alvarado, 23–4, 117
Amazon, 25
Ampudia, Pedro, xxxviii, xxxix, 6–8, 16, 24, 31
Anaya, Juan Pablo de, xvii, xxi, xxvii–xxviii, xxx, xxxiv
Anglophobia, xxii, 11
Anglo-Saxon, xxvii, 2–3
annexation of Mexico, 61, 102, 109–10, 113, 119
 (*see also* All-Mexico movement)
 of Hawaii (by British), 12, 19
 of Texas, x–xi, xiv–xvi, xix, xxii, xxv, xlii–xliii, 1–11, 13–8, 87, 112, 114, 116, 118, 146, 152
 of Yucatan, xi, 58, 88–9, 110, 113, 116, 119, 154
 of Yucatan (by British), 106
Anton Lizardo, 21, 42, 45–6
Arrangoiz, Francisco de Paula de, 125–6
artillery, 31, 39, 48–9, 56–7, 120
 flying, 49
Ascension Bay, 120, 126
Asia, xiii
Atlantic (ocean), xi–xiii, xvii, 22, 93, 107, 121, 123–4, 130, 143, 148, 150
Atocha, Alejandro, 61
Austin (city), 6, 40
Austin (ship), xx, xxxv–xxxvi, xl–xli,
Ay, Manuel Antonio, 81–2
Aztecs, 71

Bacalar, 84–5, 106–7, 119–20, 126
Bahamas, 112
Baily, John, 143–4
Baja California, 125
balance-of-power (policy), xxii, xxv, xliii, 10, 12–3, 146, 149, 153
Ballentine, George, 34–8
Bancroft, George, 17
Baqueiro, Serapio, 120
Barbachano, Miguel, xxix–xxx, xxxv–xxxvi, xxxviii, 27, 80, 82–3, 98–9, 106, 116–8, 126–7
Barnard, John G., 63
Barradas, Isidro, 41
Barret, Domingo, 81
batab, xxxviii, 78, 81–3, 85, 126, 135
Bee, Barnard Elliot, xvii–xviii, xxi, 70
Belcher, Edward, 143, 145
Belize (British Honduras), xiv, 76–7, 83–4, 86–7, 97, 100, 104, 106–9, 113, 116, 119–24, 126, 129, 132, 134, 146
Benton, Thomas Hart, 1, 4, 108
Bermuda, 42, 53
Bidlack, Benjamin A., 60
 (*see also* treaty, Bidlack)
Bigelow, Abraham, 29–30, 101, 105
blockade (of Mexico), xvi, xxxvii, 20–3, 27, 29–30, 58–9, 62, 66, 81, 86, 95, 97
 paper blockade, 22
Bluefields, 87, 131, 143
Blunt, Edmund March (Blunt's Coast Pilot), 42
Bocanegra, Jose Maria, 3–4
Bogota, 60
Bolonchén, 127
Boston, 40, 124, 147
Boulogne, 52–3
Bourmont, Louis, 50
Brackett, Albert Gallatin, 37
Brazos Santiago, 36, 42, 55

Breese, Samuel L., 63
British, xi, xiii–xiv, xix, xxii–xxvi, xli–xliii, 3, 8, 10–13, 18–20, 48, 52–4, 60, 68, 78, 83–8, 100, 106–9, 111–18, 120–4, 126, 128–30, 134, 136–43, 145–8
   Columbia, xxiv
   Honduras (*see* Belize)
   influence on Veracruz landing, 52–4
Buchanan, James, xiv, 23, 25, 27, 28, 58–61, 81, 89, 97–8, 100, 102–3, 106–8, 110, 116–17, 121–6, 129, 136, 139, 148–9
Buena Vista (Battle of), 32, 38, 55, 137
Buffalo (city), xxiii
Bulwer, Henry, xv, 123, 128, 145–6, 148
Burnet, David G., xix
Bustamante, Anastasio, 9, 18, 58
Butler, William, 135

cacique, 78
Calhoun, John C., 4, 17, 108, 110, 115–16, 119, 142
California, xv, xvii, xxv, 4, 12–3, 16, 18–9, 52, 59, 129–30
Campeche, xviii, xxi, xxviii, xxxiv, xxxvi–xl, xlii, 7–8, 15, 28, 58, 63, 71, 77–82, 85, 88–90, 95–6, 99–100, 103, 105, 134
   Battle of, xl, xlii
   Siege of, xxxvii–xxxix
Canada, xxii–xxiii
Canalizo, Valentin, 9
Canning, George, 115
Cape Horn, 12, 16
Cape Licosa, 53
Cape of Good Hope, xiii
Caribbean, xxii, 22, 83, 87, 116, 122–4, 129, 138, 152
Carlist, 13, 107
Carmen (*see* Laguna del Carmen)
Caroline (ship), xxiii–xxiv
Carrera, Rafael, 77–8, 101
Cass, Lewis, 61, 108, 113–14, 124
Caste War, xiv, 13, 74–88
   influence of Texas on, 85
Catholic, 69
Caudillo, xxviii, xxxiv, xxxix, 56
Central America, xiv–xv, xxvii, 60, 78, 87–8, 101, 121–4, 127–30, 136–42, 144, 146–8, 150, 152

Centralists (Mexico), xi, xvi–xvii, xxi, xxvii–xxx, xxxvii–xl
Cerro Gordo (Battle of), 57, 66
Cetina, José Dolores, 82, 119–20, 126, 134–5
Chagres, 128–9
Chalco, 73
Champion (ship) (*see Petrita*)
Chapultepec (Battle of), 24, 95
Charleston, xvi, 10, 35, 40, 51
Chatfield, Frederick, 130, 146–8
Chi, Cecilio, 78–9, 82–4, 104, 118, 134–5
Chiapas, xi–xii, xxvii–xxviii, 68–9, 77, 86, 94, 100, 125
Chichén Itzá, 132
Chihuahua, 13
Chiltepec, 7
China (Yucatan), xxxviii
Churroa (ship), 101
Churubusco (Battle of), 35, 95
Ciudad del Carmen (*see* Laguna de Carmen)
Ciudad Mier, xli, 6, 15, 70, 72
   (*see also* expedition)
Civil War (US), 19, 21–2, 31, 37, 49, 149, 151, 153–4
Clay, Henry, 4–5
Clayton-Bulwer Treaty, xv, 128, 148–9
Clayton, John M., 112, 136–8, 142, 145, 148
Clifford, Nathan, 125
Coatzacoalcos (river), xii, 63–4, 66–7
   (*see also* expedition)
Cohen, Myer M., 44
collaborators, xxxvii, 71, 102
Collado beach, 45–6, 50
Colombia, xiv
   (*see also* New Granada)
Comitán, xxviii
Congress (US), x, xv, 4, 9, 13–14, 16–17, 19, 21, 23, 97–8, 107, 109–10, 129, 149
Congress (Yucatecan), xviii–xix, xxix
   Mexican, xxvi, xxxii–xxxiii, 9
Conner, David, 20, 23–5, 28–9, 31, 34, 42, 45, 49, 58–9, 61
Constantinople, 53
constitution (1824, Mexico), xvii–xix, xxii, 91, 94
   US, 1, 16–7, 92, 110

Cooper, James Fenimore, 48
Cordillera mountains, xii
Córdoba, Francisco Hernández de, 41
Corpus Christi, 16
Costa Rica, xiii, 87, 129, 138–9
counter-insurgency, 51, 73, 126
Cozumel, 71, 105, 121
Creek War, 85, 107
Criollos, x, xxxiii, 76, 78, 82, 90, 99
Cuba, xiv–xv, xvii, xxv, xxviii, 22–3, 27, 62, 77, 101, 103, 105–6, 109, 111–13, 116, 118–19, 122–4, 150, 153
   US pivot towards, 122–4, 153
Cuevas, Luis Gonzaga, 10–1
Culumpich, 83

Dallas, George M., 61, 65–8, 81
Dampier, William, 84
Davis, Jefferson, 113
declaration of war, x, xv–xvi, 4–5, 9, 14, 16–17, 130, 140
Democrat, xxiv, xlii, 3–5, 11–15, 40, 61, 66, 86, 88, 110–11, 113–15, 124, 136, 141–3, 145–6
Dios Cosgaya, Juan de, xxxv
Disturnell Map, xi–xii
Dix, John, 108, 117, 125, 141
Dominguez, Manuel, 73
Drake, Sir Francis, 145
draught (of ships), 25, 34, 63–4
Duperré, Guy Victor, 50
Durfee, Amos, xxiii

Edson, Alvin, 34, 46
Electra (ship), 10
elephant (see the), 37–8, 47, 131, 134
Elliot, Charles, xliii, 10–11
El Salvador (San Salvador), 78, 129, 139, 143
Entente Cordiale, 12
Espita, 105
expedition, 6, 29, 41
   Anaya (Chiapas), xxviii
   Bacalar, 119–20, 126, 134
   centralist (Campeche), xxxvii
   Coatzacoalcos (survey), xv, 63–4, 66
   Frémont, 18
   Lopez (Cuba), 153

Mier, xli–xlii, 15
Perry (Japan), 24, 62
Perry (Tabasco) (*see* Tabasco)
Santa Fe, 4, 15
Sentmanat, 6–8, 15, 23
Texas Navy, xx
Veracruz (*see* Veracruz)
expeditionary (warfare), 20, 51–4
Eurydice (ship), 10

Falconer, Thomas, 84
Fancourt, Charles St John, 84, 87–8, 121, 124, 126, 134
fandango, 24, 30, 62, 74
Fannin, James Walker, 9
Farías, Valentine Gómez, 91
Federal Republic of Central America, xiv, xxvii, xxx, 78, 129
federalists (Mexico), xvi–xvii, xx, xxii, xxvii–xxix, xxxi, xxxiii–xxxiv, xl
filibusterism, xv, xxiii, xxviii, 7, 23, 149–50
Fillmore, Millard P., 149–50, 153
Fisher, William S., xli
Florida, xxv, 34, 43–4, 65, 76, 85, 109, 111, 136, 152–3
Florida (ship), 127, 133
Florida Wars (Seminole Wars), 43–5, 76, 85, 133, 136, 152
Foote, Henry S., 2–3, 15
Fonseca (Gulf of), 143–4
Forsyth, John, xxv
fortifications, 19, 42, 52–4, 101, 104, 119
Fort Jesup, 6
France, xiv, xxvii, xxxii, 12–13, 52, 58, 91, 107, 115, 146
Frémont, John C., 18
French, xvi, xxii, xxvii, xxxix, 8, 10, 12–3, 18, 21–2, 24, 49–54, 57, 60, 81, 83, 91, 104, 108, 139, 141
   and Indian War, 83
   Revolution, 52
Frobisher, Martin, 84
Frontera, 25–6, 63–4, 71, 86

Gamboa, Pastor, xxxvii, xxxix, 104
Gamboa, Ramón, 56–7
Galveston, xx, xxv, xl–xli, 11, 74
Garay, José de, xii, xiv, 63, 65, 67–8

Germantown (ship), 95
Gibbs, Archibald Robertson, 84
Gibraltar, 113, 143–4
Goliad, 9
Gorgon (ship), 147
Granja, Juan de la, 8
Greely, Horace, 148
Green, Thomas J., xli–xlii, 69–70, 72–3
Griffis, William Elliot, 24–6, 30, 49, 62, 64
Grijalva, Juan de, 25, 41, 155
Grijalva River, xii, 25, 62, 73, 86
Grund, Francis J., 148
Guanajuato, 125
Guadalajara (Mexico), 9
Guadalupe (ship), xl, 8, 23
Guadalupe Hidalgo (Treaty of), xii, xv, xxxiii, 89, 109, 122, 128
Guatemala, xiv, xxvii, 69, 76–8, 86, 90, 97, 100–1, 122, 128–31, 137–9
  City, 129–31
Guerrero, Jose, 88
guerrilla(s), xxxviii–xxxix, 13, 41, 65–6, 74, 76, 78–9, 82, 95, 107, 120, 131–2
  warfare/tactics, 76, 78–9, 131–2
Guichicovi, 67
Guizot, François, 12, 108
Gulf Squadron, 16, 19–21, 24, 28, 48–9, 59, 66, 100, 102
  (*see also* Home Squadron)
Gutierrez, José Ignacio, xvii, xix–xx, xxviii, 58

Haiti, 81
Halleck, Henry, 19–21, 51–4 (*see also* expeditionary warfare)
Hannegan, Edward, 110–13, 116–17, 130
Havana, xxxix, 22–4, 41, 74, 81–2, 90, 101, 129
Hawaii, 12, 19
Hays, Jack, 40
Hempstead, Christopher, 121, 124
Henderson, Archibald, 66
Herrera, Jose Joaquin de, 9, 18, 125
Hise, Elija, 128–31, 137, 139, 142
Hitchcock, Ethan A., 45, 49, 73
Hockley, George W., xli
Holland, xii, 52–3
Holy Alliance, 115, 142

Honduras, 7, 87, 122, 129, 139, 141, 143–4, 148
  Bay (Gulf) of, 83, 99, 104–6
  British Honduras (*see* Belize)
Home Squadron, 16, 19–21, 24, 28, 48–9, 59, 66, 100, 102
Horseshoe Bend, Battle of, 85
Houston, Sam, x, xli–xlii, 6, 14, 17
Hunters' Lodges, xxiii, xxv
Hunt, Memucan, xxv
Hunt, William, 28

Iberia, 54
Îles Saint-Marcouf, 53
Imán, Santiago, xviii
Ingraham, Duncan N., 28
isthmus
  of Nicaragua, 78, 87, 137–8, 141, 143–4, 148
  of Panama, xiv, 60–1, 128–9, 136, 140, 148
  of Tehuantepec, xii, xxx, 24–5, 29, 59, 61–3, 65–8, 122–3, 140, 145, 148

Jacinto (Battle of), x, 57
Jackson, Andrew, xix, 57, 85–6
Jalisco, xxxiii
Jamaica, 56, 83, 106, 116, 121, 129, 131
Japan (*see* expeditions, Perry)
John Potter (ship), 35–6
Jomini, Henri, 51
Jones, Anson, 11
Jonuta, 86
junta (Mexico), xxxi, xxxiii–xxxvii, 3, 9, 94

Kelly, Richard J., 134
Kendall, George Wilkens, 72
Kenly, John Reese, 31–4, 37–9
Kennedy, William, xxii, xxiv–xxv
Key West, 62
Kingston, 56, 129

La Balize (Louisiana), xxxix
Laguna (de Carmen), xxxvii, 28–30, 39, 58–9, 61–3, 71, 79, 81, 86, 92, 95–8, 100, 101–3, 105, 117
Lane, Joseph, 95
Latin America, xiv, 75, 142, 149, 152

laws of war, 41
Lee, Robert E., 49
Lerma, xxxvii, xl
Lipscomb, Abner S., xvii
Lobos, 41–2, 44–5, 55, 71
logistics, 13, 20, 41–5, 54, 61, 73, 107, 151
London, xiii, xix, xxii–xxiii, 18, 68, 100, 122, 143, 145
López de Llergo, Sebastian, xxxvii
Louisiana, 65
Lundy, Benjamin, 1–2

MacDonald, Alexander, 87
Mackenzie, William Lyon, xxii–xxiv
Madrid, 91, 123
Magruder, George A., 62
mahogany, xvii, 83–4, 87, 124
Maine, xxiv
Maldonado, Nicolas, xxvii–xxviii
Mallarino, Manuel Maria, 60
Manifest Destiny, xvi, 13, 15, 149–51, 155
Manigault, Arthur Middleton, 51
Marcy, William, xxiii, 42–5, 54
Marín, Francisco, xxxiv
mariners, 42
Marines, 24, 26, 34, 41, 43, 62, 64, 66–7, 117
Martello Bay (Corsica), 53
martial law, 39–41, 79
Mason, John Y., 29, 58, 62, 81, 99–100, 103–6, 117
Massachusetts (ship), 44–5
Matamoros, 40, 42, 55
Maya, x, xxxiii, xxxviii, 74, 76–9, 81–6, 89–91, 99–100, 102–4, 106–7, 109, 112–13, 116–21, 124, 126–7, 130–5
McFaul Jr., Eneas, 28–9
McGregor, John F., 7, 105
Meade, George, 31
Medina, Battle of, xxxii
Mejia, Francisco, xlii
Mendez, Santiago, xxx, xxxiv, xxxvi, 88, 90, 99, 103–4, 106–7, 114
Merida, xviii, xxix, xxxiv, xxxvi, xxxviii–xl, 27–8, 58, 77, 79–81, 85, 90, 92, 99, 101, 104–5, 111, 120, 126, 132–3
Mexico City, xi, xvi–xix, xxi, xxviii, xxx–xxxi, xxxv–xxxvi, xxxviii–xxxix, 3, 10 –11,
13, 24, 27, 29, 31, 37, 39–41, 49, 56, 65, 67–74, 85, 88, 90, 94–6, 99, 102, 107, 125, 134–5
occupation of, 67, 69, 88, 95, 102, 125, 134–5
Michoacán, 58
Mier (Ciudad), xli, 6, 15, 70, 72
Miller, Jacob W., 114
Minatitlan, 63–4
Miñón, Vicente, xxxvii–xxxviii
Mississippi River/Valley, xxxix, 1, 37, 61, 85–6, 123–4, 150, 155
Mississippi (ship), 42, 64, 103
Mobile (Alabama), xxv, 72
monarchists, xiii, xviii, 12, 68, 93, 97
Monroe 'Doctrine', xiv, 13, 93, 103, 107–10, 112, 115, 128, 136, 141–2, 145–6, 148, 152
Monroe, James, 107–8, 110, 112, 115, 128, 141–2, 145
Monterrey, 19, 27, 32, 37
Battle of, 19, 24, 30–1, 40
Montezuma, 34
Montezuma (ship), xl, 8, 23
Moore, Edwin Ward, xx–xxi, xxix, xxxv–xxxvi, xxxix–xlii
Mosquito Kingdom, xiv, 87, 107–8, 121, 123–4, 126, 130–1, 136, 139

Napoleon Bonaparte, xvii, xxxii, xxxvii, 19–21, 50, 51–5
Napoleonic Wars, 21, 40, 50, 52–4, 115
Nelson, Horatio, 52–3, 93
New Brunswick, xxiv
New England, 3, 17, 150
New Granada (*see also* Colombia), xiv, 60, 124, 128, 136
New Mexico, 13, 59, 72, 150
New Orleans, xvii, xxi–xxii, xxv, xxxiv–xxxv, xxxix–xl, 6–8, 15–17, 23, 26, 29, 33, 37, 41–3, 50, 54–5, 58, 61, 63, 69, 71–4, 85–6, 90, 95–6, 101, 109, 116–7, 121, 124–5, 127, 130–2, 134–5, 140–1
New Spain (*see also* Mexico), 71, 90
New World, xxxiv, 122, 155
New York City, xi, xxiii –xxiv, xl, 7–8, 13, 15, 18–19, 24–6, 28, 68, 108, 117, 124, 128–9, 134, 137–9, 141, 143, 147

Niagara River, xxiii
Nicaragua, xii–xiv, xxvii, 61, 65, 83, 87–8, 121, 124, 129, 130–1, 136–44, 146, 148, 153
  Lake, 123, 143–4
  (*see also* isthmus of)
North America, x, xii–xv, xix, xxv, xliii, 2–4, 10, 55, 74–5, 77, 82–3, 91, 108–9, 111, 113, 115, 121
northers, 35, 42, 46, 48, 71
North Carolina, 5, 70
Novelo, Bonifacio, 83
Nueces River, 16

Oaxaca, xi, xiii–xiv, 67–8
Old World, xiii, 12, 76, 150
Onkahye (ship), 128–9
Oregon (territory), xxiv, 4, 15, 145
O'Reilly, Justo Sierra, xxx, 88–104, 106–8, 110, 114–19, 128, 134, 152–3
O'Sullivan, John Louis, 13–15
Oswandel, J. Jacob, 37, 47
Otero, Mariano, xxxiii

Pacific (Ocean), xi–xiv, xvii, 2, 4, 12, 61, 121, 123–4, 128, 130, 140, 143–4, 150
  Squadron, 16, 140
Paixhans, xl, 48
Pakenham, Richard, xix
Palizada, 86
  River, 86, 97
Palo Alto (Battle of), 19, 49
Palmerston, Henry, 88, 122, 130, 143, 145
Panama, xii–xiv, 2, 60–2, 65, 87, 123, 128 136–7, 140, 144–6
  Canal, xi–xii, 153
  (*see also* isthmus of)
Panuco, 34
  River, 34, 36, 39
Paredes, Mariano, xxxi, xxxiii, 9, 22
Paris, 18, 83, 91
Pastry War, xvi, xxvii, 21, 46, 52, 57
Pat, Jacinto, 78–9, 82–3, 116–8, 120, 122, 126, 131, 135, 146
Pec, Venancio, 135
Peninsular War, 50, 54
Pensacola, 19, 59, 66, 85–6
Peraza, Martin Francisco, xxx

Perote (prison), 71–4
Perry, Matthew, xv, 25–31, 42, 49, 59–67, 69, 73, 86, 95–7, 99–103, 105–6, 107, 126, 151
Petén, 77, 97
Peto, 127
Petrel (ship), 34
Petrita (ship), 25–6, 45–8, 72–3
Pigot, Hugh, 86
Pillow, Gideon J., 45
pirate, xii, xxxvi, xli, 41, 120, 145
Polk, James K., xi, xiv, xvii, 1–5, 8–9, 13, 16–19, 23, 41, 59–62, 66, 68, 88, 97–8, 103, 107–14, 119, 121 123–5, 128–9, 131, 136, 142
Princeton (ship) 19
prisoners, xxiv, xxviii, xxxv–xxxvi, xxxviii, xli–xlii, 4, 26, 71–3, 79, 104
privateers, 22–3, 145
pronouncement(s) (Mexican), 18–19, xxvii, xxxiv, 14, 26–7, 79, 98
protectorate, xiv, 87, 126, 134, 136, 143, 148
Puebla, xvi, 65–6, 73–4, 95, 102
Puerto Rico, 23

Quiberon, 52–3
Quintana Roo (state), 78, 84
  Andrés, xxxiv–xxxvi, 27

Raleigh, 5
Rangers (Texas), 73–4
Realejo, 140, 144
republican, xxxi, 68, 89, 93, 113, 115, 154
Resaca de la Palma (Battle of), xi
Revolutionary War (American), 51, 154
Ringgold, Samuel, 49
  (*see* Rio Grande)
Rio Grande, xviii, xx, xxv–xxvi, xli, 16, 40, 55, 59, 69–70, 129
Rio Hondo, 120, 134
Roa Bárcena, José María, 3
Robinson, William Davis, xiii
Rosario (ship), xxxix–xl
Rovira, Jose, 58–9, 81
Royal Navy, 19, 54, 116
royal road (Yucatan), xxxiv
Rush, Richard, 115

Index

Sabán, 126
Salas, José Mariano, 22–3, 27
Saltillo, 38, 56
San Antonio (city), xli, 6, 70
San Antonio (ship), xx, xxx
Sanders, Romulus, 122
Sands, Benjamin Franklin, 30, 62, 64–5, 86
Sandy Hook, 24
San Felipe (fortress), 119–20, 134
San Jacinto (Battle of), x, 57
San Jacinto (ship), xx
San Juan Bautista, xxi, xxviii, xxxix, 7, 25–8, 63–5, 67, 91
San Juan de Nicaragua (Greytown), 88, 121, 123, 129–30, 136–8, 142–3
San Juan River, 88, 130, 143
San Juan de Ulúa (fortress), 21, 31, 42, 45–7, 49–50, 52, 151
San Luis Potosi, 27, 31–2, 34, 40, 55–8, 73
San Salvador (*see* El Salvador) 78, 129, 139, 143
Santa Anna, Antonio Lopez, x, xii, xx–xxi, xxvi, xxxi, xxxiii, xxxiv, xxxvi–xxxix, xli–xlii, 2, 7–9, 24, 27, 31–2, 38, 42, 46, 55–8, 66–8, 72, 91, 94, 97, 129, 151
Santa Cruz (Tenerife), 53
Santa Fe Expedition (*see* expeditions)
Santanista, xxxi, 6, 24
Savage, Henry, 130
Scheldt River, 52
Scorpion (ship), 53
Scott, Winfield, xxiii, 13, 19–21, 31–2, 36–46, 49–52, 54–8, 62, 65–7, 69, 71, 73–4, 88, 95, 102, 107, 125, 135
Scourge (ship), 64
Selva, Buenaventura, 137
Sentmanat, Francisco de, xvii, xxi, xxvii–xxviii, xxx, xxxiv, xxxix, 6–8, 23, 94, 131, 153
Senate (US), x, xiv, 2, 4, 6, 16, 60–1, 88–9, 102–3, 108, 110–11, 114, 116–19, 125, 128, 136
Seminole Wars (*see also* Florida Wars), 43–5, 76, 85, 133, 136, 152
Seven Years' War, 83
Seward, William H., 16, 18
Shields, James, 45, 61

Sisal, xxx, xxxv–xxxvi, xxxviii, xl, 27, 71, 87, 90, 101, 119, 131, 133–4
slavery, xix, 1–3, 10, 150, 153
Slidell, John, 16–8,
smugglers, 69, 73
Somers (ship), 28–9, 63
Sonora, xxvii
South America, 60, 102
spies, 69
Spitfire (ship), 24, 34, 46, 64
spy company (Mexican), 73
Squier, Ephraim G., 137–48
Stanton, Henry, 15
steamboats/ships, xx, xl, 8, 19, 21–6, 34, 36, 44–7, 64–5, 72, 105, 140
Stephens, John L. xxix, xxxvi, 75–8, 90–1, 132
Stockton, Robert F., 140
Stromboli (ship), 63–4
Suez (canal), xiii
Sumter (ship), 22
surfboats, 46–8, 64

Tabasco (state), xi–xvii, xix–xxi, xxvi–xxviii, xxx, xxxiv, xxxix, 6–9, 15, 24–9, 31, 34, 42, 58–9, 61–6, 68–9, 73–4, 77, 86, 94–7, 101
  First Battle of, 26–9, 31, 34
  Second Battle of, 42, 58–9, 61–6
  River (*see* Grijalva River)
Tabi, 126
tactics, 44, 76, 131–3
  Mayan, 76, 79, 131–3
Tacubaya, xxxi
Tamaulipas, xli, 32, 34
Tampa Bay, 34–5
Tampico, xxxix, 29, 31–9, 41–2, 45, 54–8, 63, 90
Tattnal, Josiah, 146–7
Taylor, Zachary, xi, 16, 19, 21, 24, 31–2, 38, 40–1, 49, 55, 57, 73, 127, 136, 145, 149
Tehuantepec (*see also* isthmus of), xii, xxx, 24–5, 29, 59, 61–3, 65–8, 122–3, 140, 145, 148
Tejano, xxiv, xxxii, 2, 15, 69–70
Telchac, xxxviii, xl
Temple, William G., 48, 63
Tepich, 78, 82–3, 134

Texas, x, xiv–xxiii, xxv–xxxvi, xxxix, xli–xliii, 1–6, 8–17, 24, 33–4, 40–1, 54, 57, 61, 69–74, 85, 87, 91–2, 94–5, 98, 112, 114, 116, 118, 135, 145–6, 150–3
   Texas-Yucatan alliance, xvi, xxi, xxxv
   Navy, xx–xxi, xxv, xxix, xxxix, 8
   (*see also* annexation of Texas)
   Rangers, 40, 73–4
Thomas, Charles, 15
Thompson, Edward H., 132
Thompson, Richard W., 102
Thompson, Waddy, 4
Tiger (Tigre) Island, 144, 146 –9
Tihosuco, 78–80, 82, 126–7
Tixkokob, xxxix
Tizimín, 105
Tornel, Jose María, xxxi–xxxiii
Toronto, xxii
Totten, Joseph G., 49
Traconis, Juan Bautista, 24, 26–7
traitors, xx, xxxvii–xxxviii
Treat, James, xviii–xxi
Treaty:
   Bidlack (Panama), 60–1, 124, 136–7
   Clayton-Bulwer, xv, 148–9
   Guadalupe Hidalgo, xii, xv, xxxiii, 89, 109, 122, 128
   Honduras, 141–3
   Nicaragua, 137–43
   Paris, 83
   Webster-Ashburton, xxiv
Trist, Nicholas, xii, 23, 59–61, 88, 97, 101–2
True Blue (ship), 105
Trujeque, Antonio, 80
Tyler, John, 5–6, 9

Upshur, Abel, 4, 19
Usumacinta River, 86–7, 97

Valladolid, xviii, 80–1, 83, 85, 90, 96, 99–100, 104–5, 127
Van Brunt, Gershom J., 65
Van Buren, Martin, xix, xxiii–xxiv, 5
Vanderbilt, Cornelius, 138, 143
Vázquez, Juan, 80
Veracruz, xi, xiv, xvi–xviii, xxi, xxvi, xxviii, xxxi, xxxiv, xxxv, xxxvii, xxxix, 8, 10, 13, 23–4, 26, 31–2, 34, 37–8, 41–3, 45, 47–59, 61–4, 66, 71–4, 90, 94–6, 99–100, 103, 105, 107, 116, 126, 151, 154
   expedition/landing at/Siege of, xiv, 19–21, 26, 31–2, 34, 37, 41–3, 45–57, 59, 61–4, 151
   British influence on, 52–54
   O'Reilly's stop in, 94–6
Vermont, xxiii
Vesuvius (ship), 62, 64, 103–4
Viceroy, 34, 71, 90
Vixen (ship), 24, 64
volunteers (US-Mexican War), 17, 34, 37, 40–1, 44, 47, 105
vomito (*see* yellow fever)

Walcheren expedition, 52
Walker, Patrick, 112, 130–1
Walker, Robert J., 59–61, 81, 110
Walker, Samuel H., 74
War of 1812, 19–20, 22–3, 31, 50, 85, 107, 113
warfare (*see* expeditionary warfare)
Washington
   DC, xix, xxi, xxvi, xxxii, 4–5, 7, 11, 39, 44, 50, 57–9, 62–66, 74, 81, 88–9, 92–3, 95–6, 98–9, 101–2, 105, 107, 109–10, 112, 115–18, 120–2, 124–5, 128, 139–41, 143, 145
   George, 60, 112, 154
Webb, James, xxviii–xxix, 70
Webster, Daniel, xxiv, 108
Webster-Ashburton Treaty, xxiv
West Point, xxiv, 41, 49, 74
Wharton (ship), xl
Whig (American), xlii, 4–5, 17, 22, 66–8, 102, 111–14, 119, 122, 142–3
White, George W., 131, 133
Woll, Adrien, 6
Woodbine, George, 86
Woodburne, Potter, 43

Xalapa, xxvi, 57
Xihum, 82

yellow fever, xvii, 32, 45, 69, 72
Young, Thomas, 84

Yucatan, ix, x, xi, xiv–xix, xxi–xxii, xxv–xxxviii, xl, xlii, 2, 7–8, 13–15, 24, 27–8, 43, 58–9, 68–9, 71, 74–7, 77–9, 81, 83, 86, 89–92, 94–120, 122–8, 130–2, 134–6, 141–2, 150–3
   invasion of (by centralists), xxxvi–xxxix
   US Navy assistance of, 105
   US annexation of, xi, 58, 88–9, 110, 113, 116, 119, 154
   (*see also* annexation of Yucatan)

Zapotec, 67
Zárate, Francisco Ortiz de, 67
Zavala (ship), xx
Zavala, Lorenzo de, 3, 91–4, 119, 151, 153

Dear Reader,

We hope you have enjoyed this book, but why not share your views on social media? You can also follow our pages to see more about our other products: facebook.com/penandswordbooks or follow us on X @penswordbooks

You can also view our products at www.pen-and-sword.co.uk (UK and ROW) or www.penandswordbooks.com (North America).

To keep up to date with our latest releases and online catalogues, please sign up to our newsletter at: www.pen-and-sword.co.uk/newsletter

If you would like a printed catalogue with our latest books, then please email: enquiries@pen-and-sword.co.uk or telephone: 01226 734555 (UK and ROW) or email: uspen-and-sword@casematepublishers.com or telephone: (610) 853-9131 (North America).

We respect your privacy and we will only use personal information to send you information about our products.

Thank you!